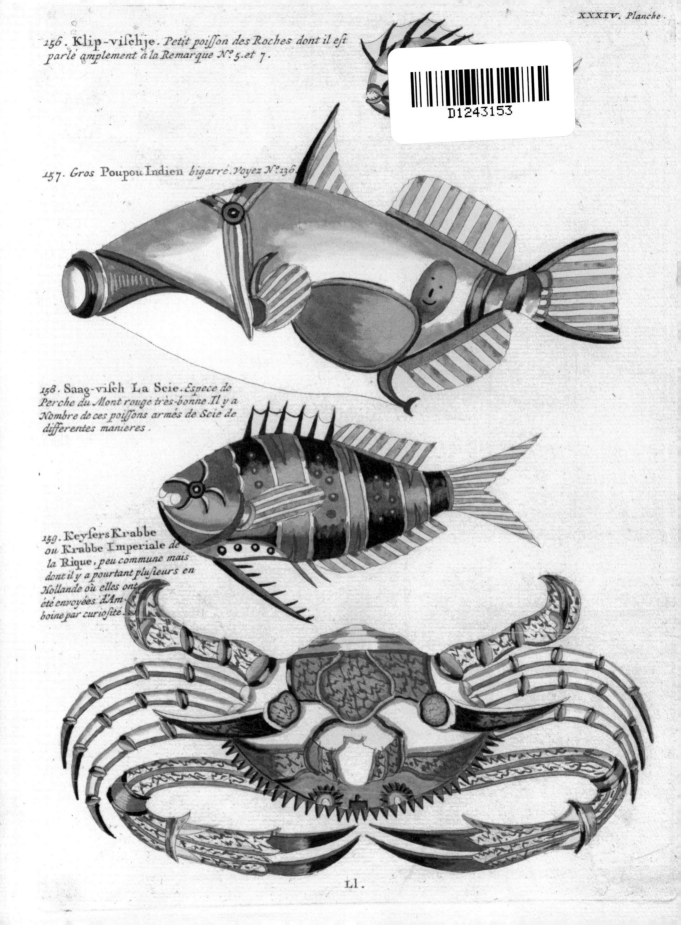

156. Klip-vifchje. *Petit poiſſon des Roches dont il eſt parlé amplement à la Remarque Nᵒ. 5. et 7.*

157. Gros Poupou Indien *bigarré. Voyez Nᵒ. 136.*

158. Saag-vifch La Scie. *Eſpece de Perche du Mont rouge très-bonne. Il y a Nombre de ces poiſſons armés de Scie de differentes manieres.*

159. Keyfers Krabbe ou Krabbe Imperiale de la Rique, *peu commune mais dont il y a pourtant pluſieurs en Hollande où elles ont été envoyées d'Amboine par curioſité.*

THE
MADMAN'S
LIBRARY

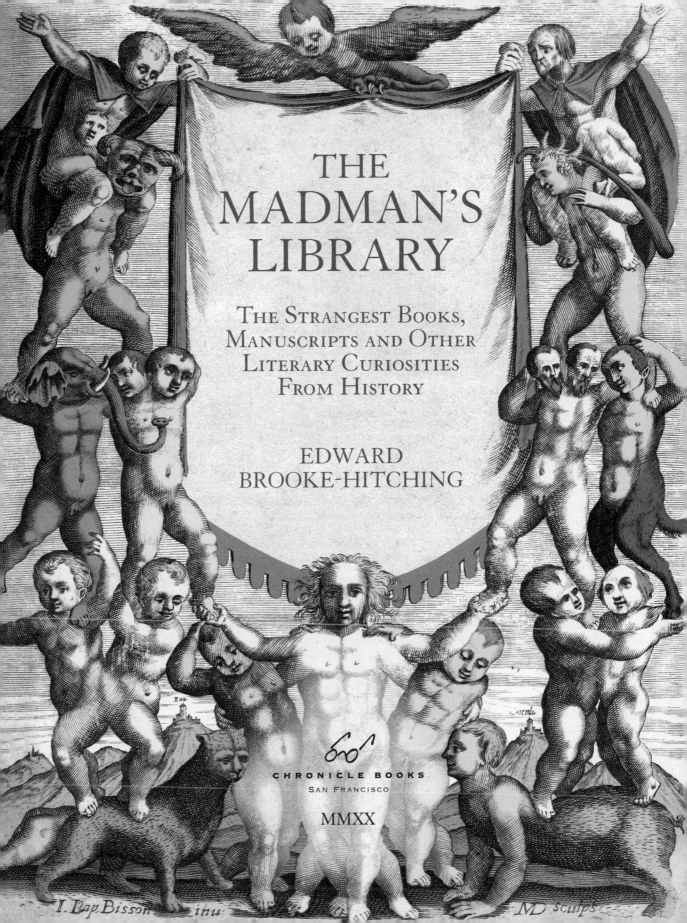

THE MADMAN'S LIBRARY

The Strangest Books,
Manuscripts and Other
Literary Curiosities
From History

EDWARD
BROOKE-HITCHING

CHRONICLE BOOKS
San Francisco

MMXX

To Franklin and Emma
A finely bound pair of 'God's copies'

CONTENTS

So erscheinet Asmodai.

Seim Rauch ist: Cicuta, Ambra, und Eysen Kl.

Illustration from a mysterious supernatural manuscript of c.1775 in the collection of London's Wellcome Library, known as the Compendium of Demonology and Magic *(see p. 150 for more).*

INTRODUCTION

'Books are lighthouses erected in the great sea of time.'
Edwin Percy Whipple

I had just turned one when my father first used me as a bidder's paddle at auction. With an antiquarian book dealer for a parent, home is a house built from books – figuratively, and structurally. Every square inch of wall space is rigged with shelves groaning with leather bindings of radiant colours: rich red morocco (goatskin), white vellum (fine calfskin), naval blues, jungle greens, solid golds and older, moodier antique browns, all glittering with varied degrees of gilt tooling.

The books *breathe*, too, exhaling a perfume of aged papers and leathers, the smell of centuries, varying just perceptibly by place and era of origin. The romance of this atmosphere is, of course, entirely lost on a child. At least, initially. By the age of ten I couldn't imagine there being anything less interesting in all existence than old books. By eighteen I found myself working at a London auctioneering company, spending every hour in their company; and by twenty-five, now hopelessly in love, I was siphoning funds away from comparative inessentials like food and rent to fill the few shelves of my own. ('I have known men to hazard their fortunes,' wrote the great American rare-book dealer A. S. W. Rosenbach in 1927, 'go long journeys halfway about the world, forget friendships, even lie, cheat, and steal, all for the gain of a book.')

At around the same time, across the Atlantic a team at Google were completing a calculation that no one had ever dared attempt. The Google Books initiative, codenamed Project Ocean, had been secretly launched eight years earlier, in 2002, with the remit to source and digitize a copy of every printed book in existence. In order to do this,

the team members determined that they'd need some idea of just how many books this would involve. And so they amassed every record they could find from the Library of the United States Congress, WorldCat and various other global cataloguing systems, until they reached a billion-plus figure. Algorithms then whittled this number down, removing duplicate editions, microfiches, maps, videos and one meat thermometer added to a library card as an April Fools' Day joke long before. Finally, they reached an approximate total of every book available. There were, they announced, 129,864,880 existing titles – and they intended to scan them all.

This number, of course, expands exponentially when considering all the lost works of history, worn away by use, swallowed up by natural disasters (Shakespeare's Third Folio is actually rarer than the First, because the bulk were destroyed with the rest of booksellers' stock in the Great Fire of London in 1666), and, of course, deliberate destruction – whether from burning in great pyres (sometimes accompanied by their authors), or even, in the case of 2.5 million Mills & Boon novels in 2003, shredded and mixed into the foundations of a 16-mile stretch of England's M6 toll road to help bind the asphalt. The British politician Augustine Birrell (1850–1933) found Hannah More's works so boring that he buried the complete nineteen-volume set in his garden. Sometimes, in acts of 'bibliophagia', literature has been literally devoured: the engraved oracle bones (see p. 22) of the ancient Chinese, for example, were often mistaken for dragon bones and ground up for medicinal elixirs. In Italy in 1370 a furious Bernabò Visconti, Lord of Milan, forced two Papal delegates to eat the bull of excommunication they had delivered to him, silk cord, lead seal and all, while the seventeenth-century German lawyer Philipp Andreas Oldenburger was sentenced to not only eat his controversial writings, but to be flogged while doing so, until he had consumed every last page. One of the most spectacular losses was that of the luxury London bookbinders Alberto and Francis Sangorski, who had spent two years completing 'The Great Omar', a magnificent binding featuring over a thousand precious jewels for a manuscript of the *Rubaiyat* for the wealthy American bibliophile Harry Elkins Widener. He excitedly boarded a ship to take the treasure home with him in 1912. The name of that vessel? *Titanic*.[1]

Within that figure of 129,864,880 books are all the great classics of literature that survive today – continually studied, reprinted and retold, and the focus of past literary histories. But as the Google choice of codename – Project Ocean – illustrates, these famous works are, of course, mere droplets in an ancient, endless literary sea. The books I have always been interested in finding are the sunken gems twinkling in the gloom of this giant remainder, the oddities abandoned to obscurity, too strange for categorization yet proving to be even more intriguing than their celebrated kin. Which books, I wondered, would inhabit the shelves of the greatest library of literary curiosities, put together by a collector unhindered by space, time and budget? And what if these books have more to teach us about the men and women who wrote them, and their periods of provenance, than might be expected?

The first problem one faces is the question of what exactly constitutes a curiosity. To an extent the idea is, of course, subjective: strangeness is in the eye of the book-holder. But after nearly a decade of searching through catalogues of libraries, auction houses and antiquarian book dealers around the world, following leads and half-remembered anecdotes, works of undeniable peculiarity leapt out. Each has a great story not just inside it but behind it, and as the books gathered, themes gradually emerged and the uncategorizable began to fall into the bespoke genres that form the chapters herein. 'Books Made of Flesh and Blood', for example, examines the history of anthropodermic bibliopegy (books bound in human skin) and other bizarre bodily means of book production. These practices are not as antiquated as one might think. Take a modern case like the Blood Qur'an of Saddam Hussein (p. 63), a 605-page copy of the holy book commissioned by the Iraqi dictator in 2000, written over a period of two years using 50 pints of his own blood.

---

1 If only the Sangorskis had possessed the prescience to follow the example of the Italian poet Gabriele D'Annunzio (1868–1938), who ordered his books be printed on rubber, so that he could read them while lazing in the enormous sunken tile bath that he shared with his goldfish.

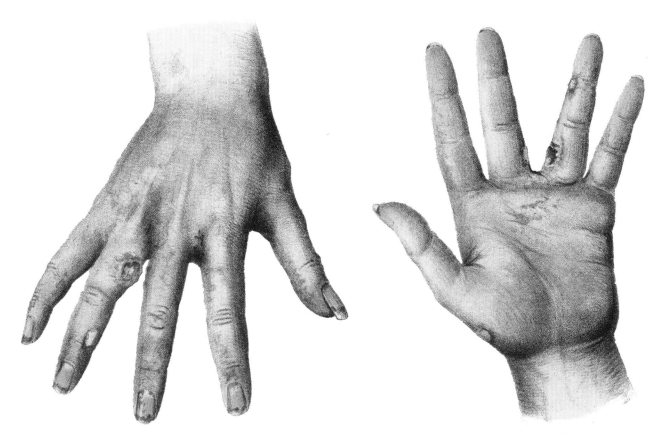

ABOVE: *The dangers of handling arsenic-covered items including book bindings, from the periodical* Annales d'hygiène publique et de médecine légale *(1859). Artists who applied the paint would often poison themselves by licking the tip of their brush to get a fine tip.*

RIGHT: *A lethal seventeenth-century binding. The green paint is rich in arsenic, added by binders to hide their cost-cutting use of old manuscript vellum for the boards (and later, as pest control). It's thought that many such deadly bindings lie unidentified in collections around the world.*

He-Gassen *(literally: 'Fart competitions') is a Japanese scroll of the Edo period (1603–1868) by an unknown artist, depicting characters exercising flatulence against each other, likely as satire.*

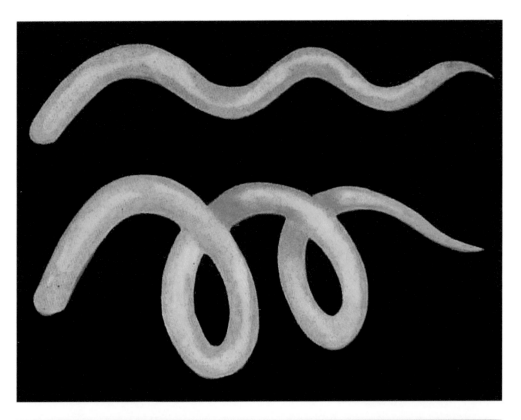

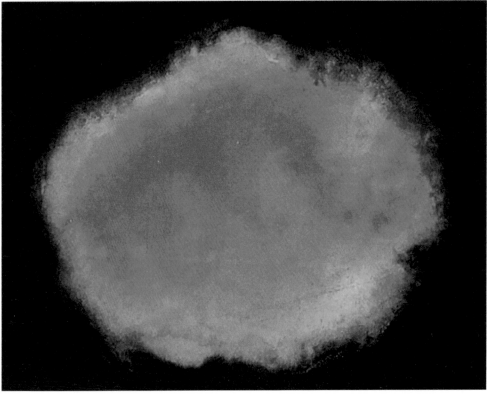

OPPOSITE: Thought-Forms: A Record of Clairvoyant Investigation *(1901), compiled by two clairvoyant London Theosophical Society members, Annie Besant and Charles Leadbeater, who claimed they could observe and illustrate the 'substance of thought' and other intangible things. In the upper image we can see 'the intention to know', otherwise known as curiosity; below it is 'vague pure affection'.*

RIGHT: *We can see the music of the French composer Charles Gounod.*

The chapter 'Curious Collections', meanwhile, features similar projects of obsessive dedication, from medieval manuscripts of fantastic beasts, and guides to criminal slang of Georgian London (with plenty of lascivious highlights provided), to Captain Cook's secret 'atlas of cloth' and the unexpectedly homicidal story of the origin of the *Oxford English Dictionary*. Elsewhere, 'Literary Hoaxes' presents the best of the ancient tradition of deceptive writing – lies in book form – whether it be for satire, self-promotion or as an instrument of revenge. The latter is best exemplified by Jonathan Swift's series of pamphlets written under the pseudonym Isaac Bickerstaff in 1708 (p. 91), a successful campaign by the author to convince all of London of the premature death of a charlatan prophet he despised. 'Cryptic Books', on the other hand, offers highlights in the history of encoded writing. Some of the texts have at one point been cracked to reveal surprising contents, like the seventeenth-century letter from the Devil and the manuscript detailing the eyebrow-tweezing rituals of a German secret society of eccentric ophthalmologists. Other puzzles remain unbroken, presented here for you to attempt your own decryption and collect the reward on offer by more than one of the enduring enigmas.

'Works of the Supernatural', meanwhile, collects scarce examples of sorcerers' grimoires (spell books) and other magical literary arcana, with some truly astounding illustrated material. Included is the automatic writing of spiritual mediums, through which long-dead authors managed to produce works post mortem. Believers included the poet W. B. Yeats, whose wife George 'relayed' 4000 pages of spiritual dictation in the first three years of their marriage. (A compilation of George's automatic writing was published as *A Vision* in 1925, but through seven editions it was only Yeats' name that was credited on the title page.)

On and on stretch the shelves of this eccentric library, around the world and back through millennia. Invisible books, books that kill, books so tall that motors are needed to turn their pages and books so long they could destroy the universe. Edible books. Wearable books. Books made of skin, bones, feathers and hair. Spell books, shaman manuals, alchemist scrolls, sin books and the ancient work known as the 'Cannibal Hymn'. Books to communicate with angels, and books to summon treasure-hunting demons. The lawsuit filed by the Devil, and a contract bearing his signature. Books worn into battle, books that tell the future, books found inside fish or wrapped around mummified Egyptians. Leechbooks, psychic books, treasure-finding texts and the code-writing hidden in the Bible. Japanese rat-mathematics manuals, thumb bibles, the smallest book ever made and the shortest play ever staged. Books of made-up fish, books of impossible shape, books of visions and writings of the insane, a war diary written on a violin

A life-saving book. This copy of the 1913 French pocket edition of Rudyard Kipling's Kim *was carried by the legionnaire Maurice Hamonneau in his breast pocket during an attack near Verdun during World War I. When he regained consciousness he found that the book had stopped a bullet, saving his life by only twenty pages.*

and another on toilet paper. A few others are even stranger.

More than most, these are books with real stories to tell. Each redefines, in its own way, the concept of just what a book can be; each brings a skip to the heartbeat of the bibliophile, rewriting and expanding our sense of what it is we love about books. And yet for one reason or another these volumes were banished to the silted depths of obscurity. But these books breathe. They hold thoughts, knowledge and humour otherwise long gone. Their stories – and to a degree, their authors – are alive upon opening them, undiminished by the violence of time. It seems only right to reach out and recover them, to bring them all together in the pages of this book, a dedicated library all their own. The oddballs, the deviants, the long-lost misfits – the forgotten recollected.

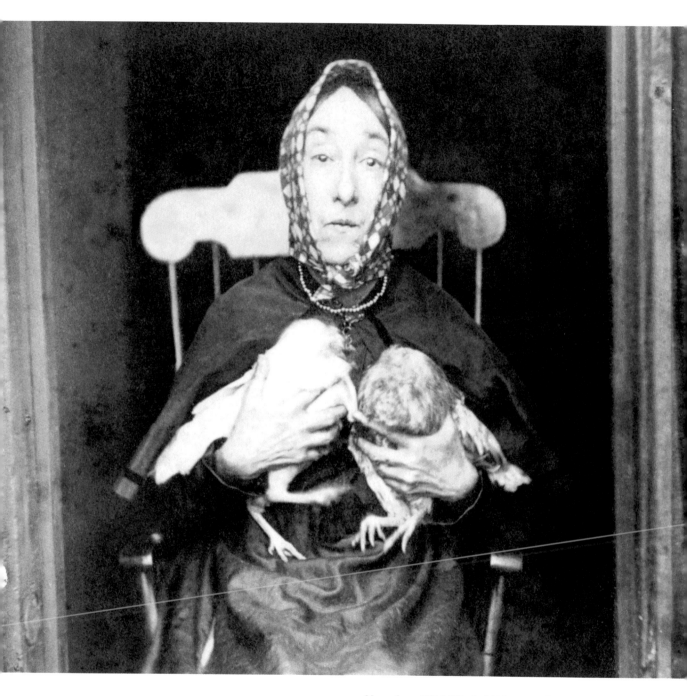

Nancy Luce (1814–90), the 'chicken poet of Massachusetts', posing with her beloved feathered companions Ada Queetie and Beauty Linna. Luce sold the photograph to tourists, along with copies of Poor Little Hearts (1866) *and other books of her poetry, all devoted to her love of chickens. Today the grave of the 'Madonna of the Hens' is decorated with plastic chickens and serves as a tourist attraction.*

ABOVE: *Revolving book reader to allow the reading of multiple large, heavy books with ease. From* Recueil d'Ouvrages Curieux de Mathematique et de Mecanique *by Gaspard Grollier de Serviere, 1719.*

Left: Parole in Libertà Futuriste ('Futurist Words in Freedom') of 1932, a radical experiment in book design of the early twentieth-century Italian Futurist movement which celebrated technology. The book is made entirely of tin, printed with texts by Filippo Tommaso Marinetti.

Below: Aurora Australis, the first book ever written, printed, illustrated and bound in the Antarctic, produced by Ernest Shackleton and the other members of the British Nimrod Expedition (1908–09). Bound with the wooden boards from their supply crates, fewer than seventy copies are accounted for.

BOOKS THAT AREN'T BOOKS

Writing in *The Histories* (4.131.2) Herodotus tells how the Persian King Darius invaded Scythia (now mostly Kazakhstan and southern Ukraine) in *c*.513 BC, and sent a message to demand the surrender of its ruler, Idanthyrsus. In response, a Scythian herald delivered a bird, a mouse, a frog and five arrows. When the Persians asked what this meant, the messenger replied that they had to figure it out for themselves and left. The Persians scratched their heads. Darius decided it signified the Scythians were meekly 'surrendering themselves and their earth and their water to him'. Or, wondered his advisors, if Darius was not going to fly away like a bird, hide like a mouse and flee to water like a frog, were the arrows threatening war?

As it turned out the Scythians were indeed making a declaration of defiance, but it is the unusual form of the message itself that is most interesting here.[1] When we use the word 'book' we refer specifically to the codex form, i.e. quires (folded sheets) of paper bound together and sandwiched between some form of protective outer binding. The idea of this chapter is to look back farther and wider, to find curious literary forms beyond the simple codex definition, from the extremity

1 So as not to leave you hanging, Herodotus reports that the Scythian warriors met Darius's forces on the battlefield shortly afterward, but as they lined up, 'a rabbit ran out between the armies; and every Scythian that saw it gave chase'. Darius asked what all the commotion was about, and was told it was the enemy ignoring the fight to chase a rabbit around. He found the behaviour so worryingly crazy that he told his advisors 'These men hold us in deep contempt ... We need to consider carefully how we shall return safely.'

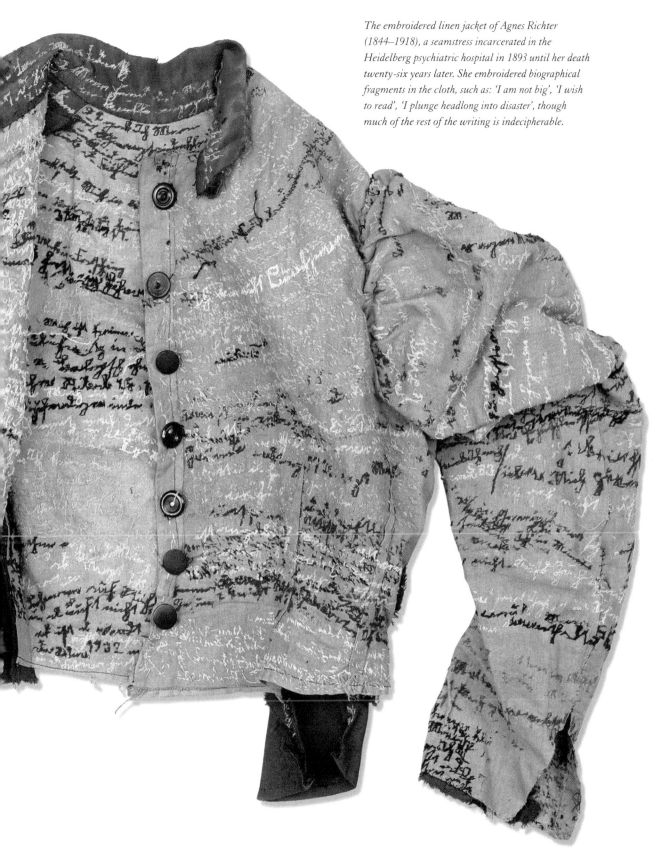

The embroidered linen jacket of Agnes Richter (1844–1918), a seamstress incarcerated in the Heidelberg psychiatric hospital in 1893 until her death twenty-six years later. She embroidered biographical fragments in the cloth, such as: 'I am not big', 'I wish to read', 'I plunge headlong into disaster', though much of the rest of the writing is indecipherable.

of Idanthyrsus's example of transmitted meaning, to other works that, thanks to some fit of inspiration, challenge our preconceptions of the limits of literary form.

Far before the arrival of the codex, we find the book's origins in the ancient use of clay and wax tablets, which evolved to the use of papyrus scrolls, in turn replaced with parchment and vellum (animal skin). Then came the codices, and onwards to paper, the printing press and beyond. But to set the scene, for an early form of curious literature we turn to China. While so many written works of ancient civilizations around the world are lost to us, there are certain ancient Chinese texts that have, remarkably, survived the millennia intact. This is due to the material on which they were written. 'Oracle bones' are animal bones and shells, often from oxen and turtles, upon which questions were written and anointed with blood by fortune-tellers. A heated poker was then pressed against the bone until it cracked, and in these patterns of splits and marks the client's future was divined.

Oracle bones are of such interest to historians because they were often carved with records and predictions of everything from weather forecasts to the outcomes of military campaigns. Surviving examples are, of course, fantastically rare, in part because when discovered in the past they often were mistaken for dragon bones, and were ground up and eaten for their supposed medicinal benefit. The oracle bone shown here, the oldest object in the collection of the British Library, was etched sometime between 1600 BC and 1050 BC. The writing predicts an absence of bad luck for the coming ten-day period, and on its reverse side carries a record of a lunar eclipse.

The ancient Mesopotamians also recorded celestial events and superstitions, in the rather less edible form of clay tablets. Cuneiform, the oldest known system of writing, was developed by the Sumerians from c.3500 to 3000 BC and used by other cultures of Mesopotamia; it is named for the wedge- (in Latin, *cuneus*) shaped style of the letters that were pressed into soft clay before being fired into robust tablets. While these relics have provided countless insights and discoveries, a particularly interesting kind of cuneiform-inscribed object served a practical purpose with magical means. In ancient Sumer, construction workers would insert thousands of prayer-inscribed clay cones resembling giant nails into the foundations of new buildings, seeking the gods' protection. One might, from their age and peculiarity, assume these artefacts to be as rare as oracle bones, but in fact they were produced in huge numbers for each construction project, and so great quantities have frequently been unearthed in archaeological sites in modern Iraq, eastern parts of Syria and south-eastern Turkey.

Filling one's foundations with divine charms solved one problem, but what was the Mesopotamian everyman to do about the evil devils and sprites that routinely sprang from below the ground to cause mischief? Again, inscribed material provided a solution. Often found in excavations of the regions of Upper Mesopotamia and Syria, incantation bowls, also known as 'demon bowls' or 'devil-trap bowls', were a form of protective magic used in the sixth to eighth centuries. A spiral of dense Jewish Babylonian Aramaic text of magical words would start at the rim of the bowl and corkscrew inwards, often with illustrations of bound devils at the centre. Essentially, the items acted like spiritual mouse-traps. One buried the bowl face-down in the corners of rooms (where devils could sneak through the cracks between wall and

LEFT: *Chinese oracle bone carved between 1600 BC and 1050 BC.*

RIGHT: *An Australian Aborigine message stick is a form of proto-writing traditionally used to transmit messages between different clans, often invitations to corroborees (dances), set-fights and ball games.*

BELOW: *An antique Tibetan Buddhist prayer wheel. Thousands of written prayers are rolled around a central spindle in a case of silver and ivory. Tibetan Buddhists believe that turning the wheel while reciting a positive mantra unlocks the power of the prayers and counters negativity.*

ABOVE: *A Sumerian foundation cone, 14cm (5½in) high, inscribed with columns of cuneiform text commemorating the building of a temple. Found in Lagash, Iraq, and dating to c.2100–2000 BC.*

floor), doorways, courtyards and cemeteries, and any evil spirit emerging from the ground was snared in its writing.

Though the majority of recovered incantation bowls were written in Jewish Aramaic, others have been found in Mandaic and Syriac, Arabic and Persian. An estimated 10 per cent, however, were written in total gibberish. These, it's thought, are cheap knock-offs, done by scribe-impersonators to con money from illiterate customers.

While the Mesopotamians filled their walls with cones and sprang devil traps in their living rooms, the makings of a literary mystery involving the longest surviving text of the ancient Etruscan civilization (roughly located in what is now known as Tuscany from *c*.900 BC) was under way. Following Napoleon's campaign in Egypt and Syria between 1798 and 1801, Europeans were gripped with 'Egyptomania' and many were inspired to see the treasures of the country for themselves. One such happy wanderer was a junior Croatian bureaucrat named Mihajlo Barić, who was so overcome with wanderlust that in 1848 he quit his position in the Hungarian Royal Chancellery for Egypt. On arrival in Alexandria, he found a bustling tourist trade in authentic archaeological treasures, and purchased for himself a souvenir in the form of a mummified female corpse housed in a large sarcophagus.

On his return to Vienna, Barić put the mummy on display in the corner of his living room and removed its linen wrappings for display in a separate cabinet. There

the mummy stood until 1859 when Barić died, and his brother, a priest, donated it to the State Institute of Croatia, Slavonia and Dalmatia in Zagreb (the present-day Archaeological Museum in Zagreb). A museum employee spotted strange markings on the linen and made a note, but it wasn't until 1891 that this was correctly identified as Etruscan text by an expert named Jacob Krall, who also realized that the strips of bandage could be reassembled to form a semi-complete manuscript.

Dated to *c*.250 BC, the work, now known as the *Liber Linteus Zagrabiensis*, had started out as a canvas about 3.4 metres (11ft 2½in) wide, which was then folded into twelve pages and used as writing material with black and red ink.

Incantation bowl with an Aramaic inscription around a demon: sixth–seventh century.

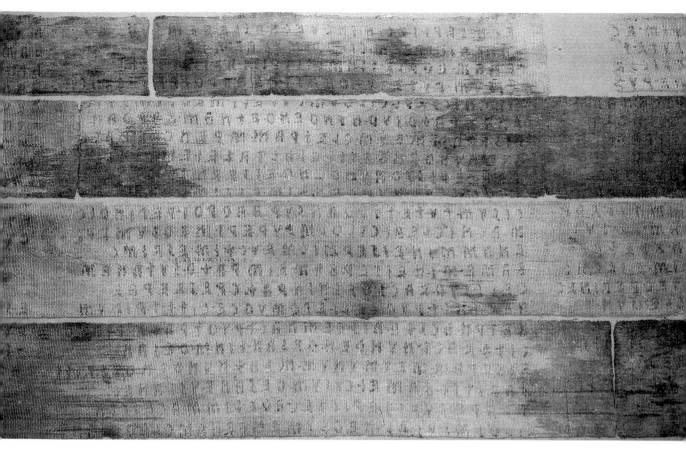

The Etruscan language has not yet been fully deciphered, but among the 1200 legible words of the manuscript are recognizable dates and names of gods that suggest the text is a religious calendar, which from Roman examples we know were used to record religious ceremonies and rituals. But what, it was wondered, could the explanation be for an Egyptian mummy with Etruscan wrappings, considering their disparate geographic origins? From a scrap of papyrus that accompanied the corpse, her provenance was deciphered: she was an Egyptian named Nesi-hensu, wife of Paher-hensu, a tailor from Thebes. She had died at

The Liber Linteus Zagrabiensis, *strips of manuscript found wrapped around a mummified Egyptian corpse.*

a time when mummification of the deceased was just becoming a popular technique, and linen for it was in such high demand that there was a severe shortage. Egyptians turned to whatever they could get their hands on, shredding clothes, sails – and even manuscripts imported by foreign traders.[2]

In comparison, the kind of literary material sometimes found with the deceased of ancient Rome and Greece is of a decidedly more vindictive and personal nature. *Defixiones*, or curse tablets, usually take the

2 Egyptians had long shown ingenuity in book experimentation. When Rameses II compiled his great library in around 1200 BC, the works were made not just of papyrus and linen but also of clay, stone, palm leaves, bark, ivory and bone.

form of lead sheets scratched with messages calling for god-inflicted revenge on thieves of both property and loved ones, written in fairly angry language. The translation of one curse tablet in the British Museum reads: 'I curse Tretia Maria and her life and mind and memory and liver and lungs mixed up together, and her words, thoughts and memory; thus may she be unable to speak what things are concealed, nor be able.' All but one of the 130 curse tablets found in the English city of Bath beg the goddess Sulis Minerva for the return of stolen goods, and for curses to be placed on the thieves. Other examples are inscribed with love spells, wrapped around locks of hair of the intended. Some have blank spaces instead of the names of targets, suggesting that one could buy curses in bulk for revenge against multiple enemies. Not all can be translated, however – some bear language of *voces mysticae*, 'mystical voices', enigmatic nonsense (similar to 'abracadabra') made

A gold Orphic tablet, or totenpass, *second half of the fourth century* BC.

up by the scribe to seem like the language of demons.

Curse tablets have also been found at the grave sites of the young and unjustly killed, apparently to help soothe the deceased's soul after an untimely death. In this way they share a purpose with *totenpässe*, or 'death passports'. When rolled into a capsule tied around the neck of the departed, a golden *totenpass* acted as a kind of Baedeker for the dead, aiding the journey of the deceased, with instructions on how to best navigate the afterlife, and carrying pre-prepared answers for the interview with the judges of the underworld. *Totenpässe* have been found in a variety of tombs, from the burials of presumed followers of the mythical ancient Greek figures Orpheus and Dionysus, to ancient Egyptian and Semitic graves, and in Palestinian graves dating to the second century BC.

It is astonishing that such items could survive so many centuries, especially given the widespread destruction and repurposing of manuscripts evinced by the *Liber Linteus*, which later finds a recurrence on a mass scale across Europe in the Middle Ages. The arrival of printing established the supremacy of the codex book, and in doing so catalysed the obsolescence of parchment. Manuscripts were destroyed *en masse* in Europe, their materials repurposed for a range of uses, from strengthening book bindings to even, as shown overleaf, use in clothing. The accompanying image of a parchment text lining for an Icelandic bishop's mitre is one of the more curious modern discoveries of these wearable books. The object, in the collection of the Arnamagnæan Institute,

ABOVE: *The ancient Moche people, who flourished in what is now north Peru from about AD 100 to 700, used painted Lima beans as a recording system. Evidence of this is found in decorated objects, like this jug, from the third to the fifth century. The Lima bean 'writing' remains a puzzle. Was it for accountancy? Funerary rites? Or perhaps gambling?*

BELOW: *The* totenpass *or 'death passport' rolled up and held in a locket placed around the neck of the deceased, as shown in this gorgeous late-second-century Fayum or 'mummy portrait' of an aristocratic Egyptian boy.*

University of Copenhagen, conjures quite a picture – a bishop soberly conducting a service, completely unaware of the profane Old French love poetry hidden within his headpiece. In 2011, another wearable book curiosity was found by textile conservators when medieval manuscripts were discovered lining the hems of dresses at the Cistercian convent of Wienhausen in northern Germany. The dresses were made by the nuns in the late fifteenth century – not for themselves, but for placing over and thus preserving the

Fragments of a medieval love text from c.1270, repurposed to form a stiff support for an Icelandic bishop's mitre.

modesty of the convent's statues. Though the idea of this brutal reprocessing of manuscripts is horrifying, as the manuscript historian Erik Kwakkel argues, there is at least some benefit to be found in it. There are numerous medieval works we never would have known about were it not for the discoveries of their remnants lining book bindings and mitres, and occasionally the clothing of bashful sculptures.[3]

The German blacksmith Johannes Gutenberg introduced his famed printing press *c.*1454; but it might be surprising for many in the West to learn that in China movable metal-type printing (which allowed the changing of letter blocks) of the kind pioneered in Europe by Gutenberg had existed at least 200 years earlier. The oldest surviving printed work by this process, a Buddhist document known as *Jikji*, was printed in Korea in 1377. (There is no evidence to suggest that Gutenberg knew about these machines, however, and it's believed that the ideas were independently invented.) Before that, in around 1040, the first known movable type system was created in China by the artisan Bì Shēng out of ceramic, which had a tendency to shatter. The use of woodblock printing dates back remarkably further: the earliest known examples are fragments of silk printed with flowers in three colours from the Han Dynasty (before AD 220).

A major driving force in the popularity of early eastern woodblock printing was the explosion in demand for Buddhist works on paper, kicked off during the Sui Dynasty (AD 581–618) by Emperor Wen's encouragement of the religion as the glue to hold together a reunifying empire. In Japan, there was a shared enthusiasm for printed Buddhist prayers, and this led to an extraordinary project of mass printing ordered by the Empress Shōtoku (AD 718–70). The Hyakumantō Darani, or 'One Million Pagoda Dharani' (invocations, or charms) are the oldest extant examples of Japanese printing and among the earliest in the world, printed by woodblock between AD 764 and 770. They were made so perfectly that for the longest time scholars assumed a metal press was used, until recent analysis found small impressions of woodgrain in the text. Each document was enclosed inside a small carved

---

3 As a young man, the Cambridge Librarian Tim Munby repaired his 1925 type 40 Bugatti roadster using pieces of vellum cut from a damaged manuscript. When people asked him about the age of the car, he enjoyed replying that 'parts of it date back to the fifteenth century'.

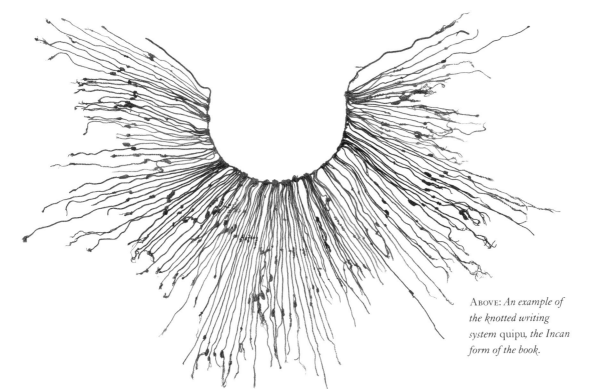

Above: *An example of the knotted writing system* quipu, *the Incan form of the book.*

wooden pagoda for protection, shown here. For Empress Shōtoku, the print run was an act of atonement and reconciliation for bloodily suppressing the *coup d'état* known as the Emi Rebellion in AD 764. In contrition, she had the prayer-filled pagodas painted pure white, and distributed to the ten major Buddhist temples of western Japan.

Worlds away, from the early thirteenth century the Incan Empire grew to be the largest of pre-Columbian America until 1572, when the capture by the Spanish of its last stronghold in Vilcabamba signalled the end of the Incan state. The conquistadors investigating the entirely new culture were struck by the dissimilarity of the Incas to Old World civilizations. The Incas hadn't developed the use of wheeled vehicles, for they had no draft animals to pull them, nor indeed to ride. They knew nothing of iron and steel, and most unusually had no written form of language; to this day our principal sources for Incan life are the chronicles written by Spanish authors. But then the colonists discovered the *quipu*.

Below: *One of the Hyakumantō Darani, 'One Million Pagoda Dharani', the earliest recorded use of woodblock printing in Japan, created on the orders of Empress Shōtoku, seven centuries before Gutenberg. Many still survive at Hōryūji temple, Nara.*

The Incan chief accountant and treasurer holding the quipu *of the kingdom. From the Peruvian chronicle* El primer nueva corónica y buen gobierno *(1615).*

The *quipu* is a complex writing system using knots in broad arrays of strings. Sometimes referred to as 'talking knots', it's a form of record-keeping used in several early civilizations, including several other South American cultures, plus the ancient Chinese, Tibetans, Siberians and the Polynesians. As far as we can tell, the primary function of these knotted strings, which could consist of anything from four cords to more than 2000, was storing and communicating numerical

information in a decimal system used for documenting census and calendrical data, tax obligations, and managing accounts and trades. In fact, in the early period of the Conquest, the Spanish reportedly relied on the *quipu* to resolve arguments about payments of goods in tribute. The men in charge of creating and reading the strings and performing the accountancy duties were known as *Quipucamayocs*, and they, according to Guamán Poma, a seventeenth-century nobleman of the Quechua people, were able to read the *quipu* with their eyes closed. This reading technique was lost, however, in the Spanish destruction of the empire, and several features of the strings, like the presumably significant variations in colour, have not yet been decoded. It's entirely possible that the *quipu* was used for much more than just accountancy, but at the time of writing these mysteries are yet to be deciphered.

On our world tour of 'books that aren't' we should now return to Europe to include another type of book or manuscript that qualifies, the kind that has been transformed into something else entirely through the ingenious addition of practical function to operate as measurement devices, calculating machines and astronomical computers. A simple example can be found in Oxford's Bodleian Library: MS Broxbourne 46.10 is a rare late-seventeenth-century French volume of scientific tracts that can be used to tell the time. The vellum sheet over the sheepskin binding is printed with markings that allow the book to function as a sundial. Similar tools that occur within a work on its pages are known as 'paper instruments', a term coined by the German engineer Georg Hartmann in 1544. The makers of traditional brass and ivory instruments were so panicked by the rise in popularity of paper instruments that they lobbied against the 'paper fraud', as they

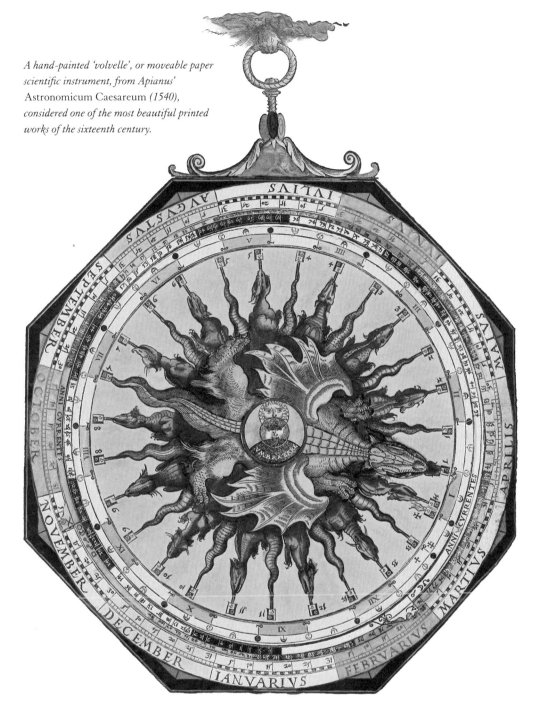

A hand-painted 'volvelle', or moveable paper scientific instrument, from Apianus' Astronomicum Caesareum *(1540)*, considered one of the most beautiful printed works of the sixteenth century.

called it, forcing a ban of the paper-based instrument – 'which does not endure … and is a mere deception through which the buyer is cheated' – to be included in the Nuremberg Statute Thirteen of 1608.

The best known of these paper devices is the 'volvelle', a set of rotating disks mounted on the page to serve as a calculation tool, an idea copied from earlier scholarly Arabic works. The art of the volvelle was most majestically demonstrated in 1540 by a contemporary of Hartmann, Petrus Apianus (1495–1552), with his *Astronomicum Caesareum* or 'Emperor's Astronomy', the greatest masterpiece of the printing art in the sixteenth century.

ABOVE: *A Portrait of 'Miss Campion' carrying her hornbook, 1661.*

ABOVE: *An eighteenth-century English 'hornbook', with the alphabet inscribed on ivory. Made from wood, bone or ivory, these robust learning tools originated in the mid-fifteenth century for young students to handle.*

BELOW: *An Italian prayer-book pistol, custom-made for Francesco Morosini, Duke of Venice (1619–94). The gun, likely for personal protection, can only fire when the book is closed. The trigger is a pin concealed in silk thread to look like a bookmark.*

ABOVE: *An example of a Chinese Jade Book of Heaven, from 1743. In Daoism, Jade Books and their five ancient chapters are described as existing in the various divine Heavens, and are said to have been instruments in the creation of the divine structure of the universe.*

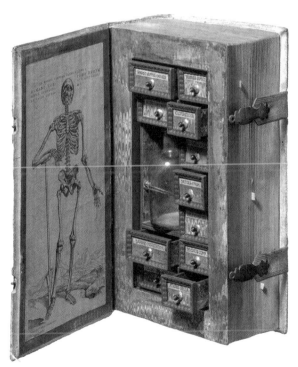

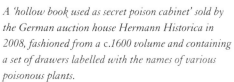

A 'hollow book used as secret poison cabinet' sold by the German auction house Hermann Historica in 2008, fashioned from a c.1600 volume and containing a set of drawers labelled with the names of various poisonous plants.

A literal loo book for the travelling booklover. This portable, disguised oak commode stool unfolds from a large gilt calf bookbinding with the title Histoire des Pays Bas – *'A History of the Low Countries'. Made in France, c.1750.*

ABOVE: *An astrological text of the Chinese Ersu Shaba people. The choice of colour affects the meaning: for example, the 'stars and moon' glyph written in black means 'dim', but in white it means 'shining'.*

(A fine, complete first edition could today set you back about £950,000.) Exquisite in artistic and scientific detail, the *Astronomicum …* is more a portable laboratory of astronomical instruments than a book, allowing its reader to calculate planetary alignments, lunar eclipses and stellar positioning using the ingenious moveable paper volvelles: take folio E4, for example, which carries an instrument of nine printed components, as well as a hidden mechanism to spin around four different axes, to calculate the longitude of Mercury. Apianus spent eight years creating the book for his patrons, the Habsburg rulers Emperor Charles V and his brother Ferdinand, printing and hand-colouring every page in his printing shop in Ingolstadt, Germany. His patrons were delighted with the intricate work and its sumptuous fifty-five hand-coloured leaves (of which twenty-one contain moving parts). Apianus was

rewarded with 3000 guilders and all manner of honours, including appointment as court mathematician and Reichsritter (a Knight of the Empire), and the powers to appoint poets laureate and legitimize children born out of wedlock.

From the seventeenth-century popularity of collectors' curiosity cabinets emerged the peculiarity known as a xylothek (sometimes xylarium), or wooden library. The scientific aim behind the xylothek was to record arboreal biodiversity by forming a library from the trees themselves. Each volume is made of the wood of a different tree, their spines composed of the bark (sometimes even with moss still attached), their contents being specimens of the tree's leaves, seeds, branches and roots, and usually accompanied by a detailed description of its biology and common uses.

Xylothek collections of native flora can be found around the world, at Padova University in San Vito di Cadore, Italy, for example, as well as the Australian National University, and the Holzbibliothek (Wood Library) at Hohenheim University, Germany.

ABOVE: *The 'Lone Dog winter count' of the Native American Yanktonais Nakota community. The pictographs on tanned buffalo hide mark the notable events of the years 1801–76 in South Dakota, including the Leonid meteor shower of 1833.*

BELOW: *Examples of an eighteenth-century xylothek, or wooden library, at Lilienfeld Abbey, Austria. Each volume is made from a different type of tree, containing samples of its bark, leaves, seeds etc.*

Purchased at Nashville Tenn.,
May 1st 1863. Has been with
Co. B, 87th Ind. Vols., at the
following named places:
Triune, Salem, But-Buckle Gap,
Hoover's Gap, Fairfield, Manchester,
Wartrace, Elk River, Deckard,
Winchester, Cumberland Mountain,
Fort McCook, Raccoon Mountain
Sand Mountain ... Gap,
... Mountain, Chickamauga,
Chattanooga, Tenn,
...onary Ridge, Rossville
...ville, Ringgold
Tunnel Hill, Buzzard...
...ton, Resaca, Calhoun
Kingston, ...ville
...worth
...Jack Jack Hills,
Marietta,
Kenesaw Moun...
Chattahoochie, Jonesboro,
...pt Point
Rough and Rea... Decature, Oxford
Atlanta, Rome, Kingston
...esville,
Milledgeville, Sandersville, ...
Sandtown, Thomas Station
Winnsboro, Louisville
... Jacksonburg

Opposite: *The battle diary of Union soldier Solomon Conn, etched into his violin.*

Right: *A page from a herbarium book of 1811. Herbariums are collections of plant samples pressed to the pages. Antiquarian examples like these can sometimes be found to contain extinct species.*

The first wooden library is thought to be the Schildbach in the Ottoneum in Kassel, Germany, which was built between 1771 and 1799 by Carl Schildbach and houses 530 wooden volumes; but the largest is the Samuel James Record Collection in the United States, which holds a staggering 98,000 examples. While all libraries possess a distinctly musty scent, the smell that greets the nostrils upon entering the climate-controlled environment of a xylothek really is one to experience (albeit briefly, as the overwhelming odour of stale moss soon makes itself known).

Outside of the arboreal ranks of the xylothek, a sensational example of a wooden book in contrasting form is the journal of Solomon Conn, found in the vast collection of the Smithsonian Museum. After the outbreak of the American Civil War in 1861, Conn, the son of an innkeeper in Minamac, Indiana, enlisted at the age of twenty-four as a private in the Union-supporting 87th Indiana Infantry. In 1863, he bought a violin in Nashville, Tennessee, and carried it everywhere with him while serving. He never learned to play it. Instead, he carved every inch of its surface with the records of the soldiers of the 87th and the thirty battles they fought, including the Battle of Chickamauga in September 1863, and Kennesaw Mountain in June 1864. By the end of the war, the 87th had lost 283 men, but Conn and his violin survived, with it now acclaimed as a unique memento of the common soldier during the Civil War.

The journal of the Norwegian resistance fighter Petter Moen is another unusual record of war. Moen was an actuary for a large insurance company when the Germans occupied Norway during World War II. He joined the local resistance, and edited the underground newspaper *London Nytt*. When he was caught by the Germans in February 1944, he was brutally interrogated and thrown into solitary confinement in an Oslo jail. In his dark cell, with no pen or paper, Moen began his unique diary by taking a pin from the blackout curtain and pricking his words into squares of toilet paper. He was often caught and his work confiscated, but he

OPPOSITE: *Folia from David Livingstone's 1871 field diary. The Scottish explorer used pages of* The Standard *newspaper of 24 November 1869. The ink of his dense overwriting had long since faded until it was recently revealed by the cutting-edge work of the David Livingstone Spectral Imaging Project.*

ABOVE: *The ventilation grille through which the prisoner-of-war Petter Moen pushed his toilet paper diary.*

would simply begin again. After completing each chapter Moen would roll it up and press it through a ventilation shaft, never thinking the diary would ever be found, let alone published. The following September, when Moen was transported on the German prison ship *Westphalen*, he mentioned the diary to a couple of his fellow prisoners. The ship struck a mine off the coast of Sweden

and sank. Moen was killed, but one of the five Norwegian survivors returned to Oslo after its liberation, prised open the shaft and found the toilet paper. The diary was published in 1949. 'It is a devastating self-analysis of one man – and all men,' reads the jacket text, 'written with the honesty that only fear, loneliness and impending death can produce.' The book was a bestseller in Scandinavia, and was issued in English in the United States in 1951.[4]

A book capable of causing actual physical damage is Uwe Wandrey's *Kampfreime*

---

4 To this genre of the literal loo book we can also add the work of Yugoslav politician Milovan Đilas (1911), who was imprisoned for ten years for his anti-communist criticism of Josip Broz Tito's presidency. While behind bars he translated John Milton's *Paradise Lost* into the Serbo-Croat language, writing out the entire work on toilet paper.

Kampfreime *('Battle Rhymes')* of 1968, both a book and a weapon.

('Battle Rhymes') of 1968, apparently the first book specifically designed to be used as a weapon. The pocket-sized 'handy combat edition' (62 × 117mm / 2½ × 4½in) of rhyming resistance chants and poster slogans was created for use in the violent 1968 student uprisings in West Germany. The front board is made of a sharp-edged metal, with the marking inside *Notwehrtauglich* ('Suitable for self-defence'). 'I've often been told that the pen (and by extension, the book) is mightier than the sword,' wrote Wandrey. 'But what if the book is the sword?' While the metal sheath certainly makes for a fearsome weapon, its other purpose was to scrape away propaganda posters and advertisements. (This destructive intent puts *Kampfreime* on the same shelf as an earlier example by the artists Guy Debord, Asger Jorn and V. O. Permild titled *Mémoires* (1959), which has a dust jacket made of heavy-grade sandpaper, designed to destroy any book it was shelved beside. 'By

looking at people,' explained the authors, 'you should be able to tell whether or not they had had the book in their hands.')

A book designed to *be* destroyed was published in 2012, when Land Rover printed for its Dubai customers a guide to surviving the desert in the event of a mechanical breakdown. The pamphlet gives illustrated instructions on how to build shelters, signal for help, light a fire and hunt local wildlife, and how to get your orientation by using the north star. The metal binding can be removed for use as a cooking skewer, and the reflective packaging can help signal for help. As a last resort, the book urges you, eat it: the pages of the *Land Rover Edible Survival Guide* are made out of consumable paper and ink – the book claims to offer the same nutritional value as a cheeseburger.

Which brings to mind the announcement, made in 2018 by the University of Michigan, of their purchase of one of only ten copies of *20 Slices of American Cheese* by the New York publisher Ben Denzer. The book's bright yellow clothboard binding holds twenty individually wrapped American single cheese slices. A box

of twenty-four slices of Kraft American cheese slices costs $3.50 roughly – *20 Slices* sold for $200. 'This cheese book begs many questions,' wrote librarian Jamie Lausch Vander Broek, herself lactose intolerant, 'including: is someone the author of the cheese book? What is its subject? Is it about cheese if it *is* cheese?'

'How is the book's condition?' I asked Emily Ann Buckler at the University of Michigan Library about their copy. 'It's apparently "shelf stable", she assured me, 'but … we'll see how long it lasts.' Denzer's other works, by the way, include *200 Fortunes*, a small volume of Chinese restaurant fortunes; *$200 in Order*, a book of 200 one-dollar bills; the self-explanatory *30 Napkins from the Plaza Hotel*; and *20 Sweeteners*, an elegantly bound collection of twenty artificial sweetener packets.

20 Slices *by Ben Denzer, a book made of cheese.*

BELOW: 20 Sweeteners *by Ben Denzer.*

BOOKS MADE OF FLESH AND BLOOD

If a creature has run, hopped, slithered or swum on this planet, at some point its skin has been used to bind a book. Stingray, monkey, ostrich and shark – the latter known as shagreen, although 'Oriental shagreen' is usually ass's skin – have all clothed literature. The 'sympathetic' form of bibliopegy (bookbinding) matches the written material with appropriate outer material: the British Museum holds the only copy of Governor Phillip's *Voyage to Botany Bay* (1789) bound in the skin of a kangaroo.[1] Copies of Charles James Fox's *A History of the Early Part of the Reign of James II* (1808) were sold in fox skin. In auction records of the last 100 years can be found copies of *Mein Kampf* bound in skunk, *Das Kapital* in boa constrictor hide, *Moby-Dick* in whale and *Gone with the Wind* in Confederate battle flag. Snakeskin books have been around since the 1800s, when vainglorious big-game hunters looked for ways to show off their conquests. At least one first edition of Oliver Wendell Holmes's *Elsie Venner: A Romance of Destiny* (1861), the story of a snake/human hybrid seeking social acceptance, was bound in python. The American explorer Osa Johnson had a copy of her sparky autobiography *I Married Adventure* (1940) bound in elephant hide. And snapped up at the 1812 sale of the library of John Ker, 3rd Duke of Roxburghe, were rabbit-skin pamphlets of the famous eighteenth-century case of Mary Toft, the Englishwoman who claimed to have given birth to a litter of the creatures (see p. 206).

The Ruige blauwe *register (The 'Hairy Blue Register') of the Court of Holland for recording who is to be assigned which government function, 1518–40. The unusual binding is a cow hide of thick hair, making it easily locatable on the shelf.*

---

1 Clean, unmarked kangaroo skin was always notoriously difficult to source due to the long claws of the males – binders frequently had to deal with scratches and scrapes in the leather, known as 'mating marks'.

LEFT: *A fifteenth-century Holy Qur'an in an unusual round shape with Maghrebi script calligraphy. Its West African creators made use of the coastal materials available to them: the pages of the manuscript are fish skin.*

BELOW: *A Hebrew lexicon printed in Europe in 1645, bound in America using otter skin painted by a Native American of the eastern woodlands. The book once bounced along in the saddlebag of the Rev. David Brainerd (1718–47), a legendary Christian evangelist.*

It isn't just the binders of books that have cut swathes through the animal kingdom. Before the development of paper,[2] parchment was sourced from sheep, calves and goats. Its finest form, vellum, is made from the softer skin of young calves and lambs. On average, between fifty and seventy sheep were needed to produce enough parchment for a medieval manuscript Bible, which then took nearly a year to copy out. One of the most spectacular works in British history, the Lindisfarne Gospels – written and decorated at the end of the seventh century by the monk Eadfrith – required the skins of 128 calves, although an estimated 400 skins would have been prepared before the pages were painted, using a brush made of squirrel hair. All of which resulted in a hefty weight of 8.7kg

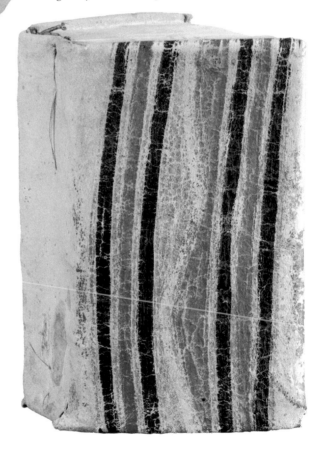

2 While cotton and linen paper dominated until the arrival of wood pulp paper in 1860, there had been the occasional challenge. By 1825, 50 per cent of England's paper was being made by machine at great speed and volume, and stocks of rags ran short. Out of this panic, paper alternatives were created from sources as diverse as manure, grass, marsh mallow, thistles, silk, asparagus and even hornets' nests.

ABOVE AND LEFT: *A traditional eighteenth-century Nepalese* jhānkri *(shaman) manual, containing protective charms and spells for exorcizing spirits. The exterior of the book is covered in blood, skin and flesh fragments taken from the Five Beasts – buffalo, chicken, dog, goat and cow – representing the five senses and the five passions.*

(19.1lb, or as the leaflet advertising its 2013 exhibition at Durham University noted, 'as much as an adult badger'). Isaac Disraeli mentions in his *Curiosities of Literature* of 1791 that the volumes written by the ancient Iranian spiritual leader Zoroaster, collectively titled *The Similitude*, were 'said to have taken up no more space than 1260 hides of cattle'.

None of these materials nor processes, however, quite compares to a singularly gruesome practice with a murderous history, the art of 'anthropodermic bibliopegy' – otherwise known as bookbinding with human skin.

OPPOSITE: *An exquisite 1760 set of John Milton's* Paradise Lost *and* Paradise Regained *appropriately bound in snakeskin by the London artisans Sangorski and Sutcliffe.*

OROCHO

Short-eared owl?

ABOVE: *A decorated page of calfskin parchment from the seventh-century Lindisfarne Gospels.*

RIGHT: *Sometimes flaws in the parchment page would require repair; or if you were as bored as the twelfth-century scribe who transcribed this copy of Saint Bernard of Clairvaux's commentary on the Song of Solomon, you could turn them into a doodle.*

OPPOSITE: *The Feather Book (1618) of Dionisio Minaggio, chief gardener of the Duchy of Milan, features 156 illustrations – 113 of which are of birds indigenous to the Lombardy region of Italy – made entirely out of feathers. 'We have no idea why he made it,' writes the McGill University Library cataloguer.*

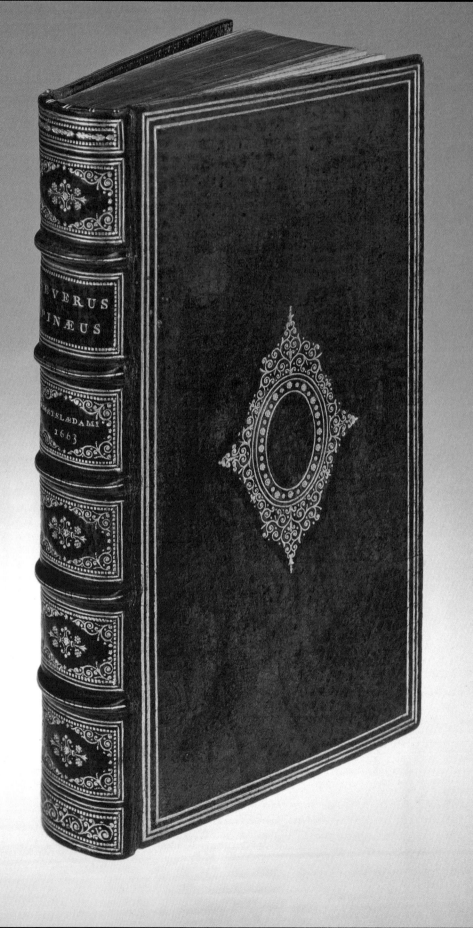

BOOKS BOUND IN HUMAN SKIN

As common as it is to hear of readers devouring a good book, the strange fact is that in the past some books have devoured readers. Surviving examples of anthropodermic bibliopegy are not just rare, but rarely discussed. Some libraries and institutions have embraced reluctantly the infamy of such holdings, but others are silent, fearing a ghoulish reputation. The result of this tradition of secrecy is that, in order to ascertain just how many confirmed examples of human-skin bindings exist, it's necessary to explore an underworld thick with historical rumour, false boasts and bloody surprises.

The most obvious question to ask first is *why*? Why bind a book in human skin? As unthinkably weird as it is to modern sensibilities, in Europe and America in mostly the eighteenth and nineteenth centuries it became an acceptable decorative extra when publishing accounts of murderers' crimes and medical studies. Towards the end of the nineteenth century it morphed into more of a romantic metaphor, to encapsulate great writing in flesh just as the mortal body encloses the soul. A human-skin book was also, frankly, a great thing to show off at parties. The method of preparation is no more difficult than treating any other animal leather, it being cured in one of two ways.

OPPOSITE: *A book bound in human skin.* De integritatis et corruptionis virginum, *a treaty on virginity, pregnancy and childbirth by Séverin Pineau, printed in Amsterdam in 1663. The book's owner, Dr Ludovic Bouland, explains with a note: 'This curious little book ... has been re-dressed in a piece of the skin of a woman tanned for myself.'*

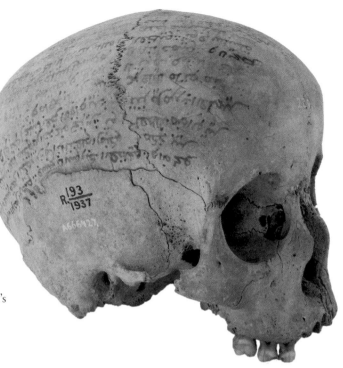

ABOVE: *A human skull covered in prayers for the deceased. Collected by Robert Baden Powell's Asante (Ghana) expedition in 1895.*

The traditional method was to soak the skin in lime water, then remove any flesh, fat or hair by hand and leave it to soak for a few more days before moving it to increasingly strong baths of tannin. The alternative was simply to soak it in urine, a method thousands of years old. The ammonia dissolves the flesh, fat, and hair, leaving the skin to be stretched and dried. (From the second-half of the eighteenth century, tanneries around Europe would also add to their noxious odour by incorporating into the process a solution of water mixed with the faeces of dogs and pigeons, to give the leather a healthy shine.)

Bookbinding with human leather dates back to at least the thirteenth century, with the record of a Latin Bible bound in an unknown woman's skin, and a Decretals found in a Sorbonne library during the reign

A tanner preparing leather with his bare feet in a tub, a stretched skin drying behind him. From the house book of Konrad Mendel, 1425.

of Napoleon III, which was then moved to Tuileries. (Both books can today be found in the Bibliothèque Nationale). The bulk of known human-skin examples, though, were produced from the late 1600s through to the late 1800s. In England, there is the story of Henry Garnet (July 1555–3 May 1606), an English Jesuit priest who had met several times with Robert Catesby, a conspirator in the Gunpowder Plot of 1605. Garnet learned of the plan to kill King James I and destroy the Houses of Parliament, but felt he

could not pass on the information as he had received it under the seal of the confessional. Regardless, for his complicity he was hanged on 3 May 1606 and his skin used to bind *A True and Perfect Relation of the Whole Proceedings Against the Late Most Barbarous Traitors, Garnet a Jesuit and His Confederates*, published by the king's printer, Robert Baker, in London 1606. One of the first Britons on record to make such a binding was the physician and bibliophile Anthony Askew (1722–73) who, according to the bibliographer Thomas Frognall Dibdin, had a *Traité d'anatomie* bound in the material.

In the eighteenth century, across the Channel, French physicians happily dabbled with the potential uses of human leather. Valmont de Bomare reports that 'M. Sue' – whom I assume to be the distinguished Paris surgeon Jean-Joseph Sue – gave to the King's Cabinet a pair of slippers made of human skin. Further north, the Dutch naturalist Hermann Boerhaave (1668–1738) was piecing together his collection of medical curiosities that included three full human skins, a shirt made of internal organs and a pair of ladies' high-heeled shoes made of leather from the skin of an executed criminal, whose nipples were used to decorate the front of the instep.

Revolutionary France, already a period with a bloody reputation, bubbled with rumours of anthropodermic experimentation. The story goes that the Jacobin leader Louis Antoine Léon de Saint-Just had a pair of breeches made for him from a servant girl executed for theft. He reportedly never tired of telling the story, always ending it by cheerfully slapping his buttocks and roaring: 'But here she is, the rogue: here she is!'[3] This

---

3 Another version of the story has it that the girl spurned his romantic advances and it was a waistcoat he had made out of her. As with the history of anthropodermic bibliopegy the truth is hard to pin down in the murk of legend. Either way, Saint-Just was clearly *deux sandwiches* short of a *picnique*.

was during the especially violent episode of the French Revolution known as the Reign of Terror, when an estimated 40,000 people were executed and the country was overwhelmed by corpses. It was rumoured that, in response, the Committee of Public Safety gave permission for Castle Meudon, outside of Paris, to be used as a secret tannery to exclusively process the 'valuable resource'. (For this grant, the committee members were allegedly gifted human-leather boots.) Human-skin accessories became all the rage. Duke Louis Philippe Joseph d'Orléans was reported to have worn a pair of human-leather breeches to a Palais-Royal ball; as was the Republican General Jean-Michel Beysser into battle, inspiring other army officers to follow suit.

As for book bindings, several volumes of the French Constitution were famously bound at this time in human leather. The English bookbinder Cyril Davenport in *The Book* (1907) records his wonder at seeing one such copy of 1793, bound in the skin of a revolutionary, exhibited in the Bastille Room of the Carnavalet Museum, Paris. Its light green leather resembled calfskin, although Davenport notes that it was apparently 'difficult to get entirely rid of the hair'.

Where we find the richest cache of anthropodermic examples, however, is with the surgical dissections of the cadavers of executed criminals. As vital as this was for the progress in scientific learning, these examinations also carried a sense of post-mortem punishment of the condemned, a grisly form of revenge palatable to a bloodthirsty public. There was a poetic justice to using the skin of the lawbreaker to make a book, the emblem of civilization. (As criminal deterrents go, it takes some beating.)

In Britain, the Anatomy Act of 1832 allowed anyone with lawful possession of a

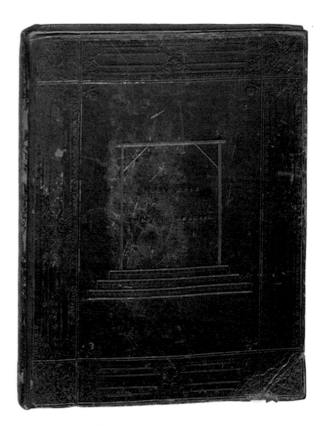

The volume bound in the skin of the executed murderer John Horwood.

dead body to submit it for medical dissection; but before this, it was only the cadavers of murderers that could legally go under the anatomist's blade. In fact, this was mandated by the Murder Act of 1751 'for better preventing the horrid crime of murder ... that some further terror and peculiar mark of infamy be added to the punishment'. Thus we have stories like that of John Horwood of Bristol, who was convicted in 1821 of the wilful murder of Eliza Balsom with whom he had been obsessed. Enraged at seeing her walking with another man, he'd thrown a pebble at her, which struck her temple and caused her to fall into a brook. At the British Royal Infirmary, the chief surgeon Richard Smith declared her wound infected and performed a trepanation, an ancient practice that involves drilling a hole into the skull to relieve pressure. She died four days later, likely as a result of the operation, but Horwood, 'the pebble-thrower', was arrested and with the testimony of Smith was found guilty of murder and hanged. Smith dissected his body, and in June 1828 had a book of papers relating to the case bound in the man's skin, at a cost of £1.10.0 (approximately £130 today). The cover of the book is inscribed with the words 'Cutis Vera Johannis Horwood' – 'The True Skin of John Horwood'. The volume is owned by the Bristol Record Office, on display beside Smith's dissection table, donated by Smith's son, who for years had used it as a sideboard.

The popularity of such medical study increased dramatically at the turn of the nineteenth century with the developments of surgical science. The throngs of young medical students keen to take apart corpses soon outnumbered the available cadavers. As a result, grave-digging and body-snatching (by so-called 'resurrection men') became rife to feed demand, to the point that relatives kept a careful watch over their deceased before burial and continued their vigil over the grave, lest their beloved be

A night watchman disturbs a body-snatcher dropping a stolen corpse into a hamper, while the anatomist runs away (1773).

THE ANATOMIST OVERTAKEN by the WATCH in CARRYING OFF MISS W— in a HAMPER

spirited away for a knife-happy surgeon in the dead of night. The most famous pair of characters in this episode of history are William Burke and William Hare, who met (and greatly profited from) the demands of the Edinburgh surgeon Robert Knox for fresh subjects by committing a spate of sixteen killings in 1828.

Though the story of Burke and Hare continues to be celebrated in popular culture, less well known is the fate of Burke's skin following his hanging in 1829 (Hare was offered immunity for turning king's evidence and fled to an obscure fate). Burke's body was publicly dissected at Edinburgh University's Old College, during which Professor Alexander Monro dipped his pen into Burke's blood and wrote, 'This was written with the blood of WM Burke, who was hanged at Edinburgh. This blood was taken from his head'. Burke's body was flayed, and a segment of his skin was used to make a wallet for 'the doorkeeper of an anatomical classroom in Edinburgh'. A larger piece was used to make the pocketbook shown here, which came up for sale at auction shortly after the dissection and is now held in the collection at Surgeon's Hall, the head office of the Royal College of Surgeons of Edinburgh. On the front it reads 'BURKE'S SKIN POCKET BOOK', with an inscription on the back that reads 'Executed 28 Jan 1829'. It even comes with a handy pencil.

This was a custom that continued throughout the century. The skin of a hanged man named James Johnson was used to bind a copy of Samuel Johnson's *Dictionary of the English Language*. The skin of William Corder, convicted of killing Maria Marten in a case known as the Red Barn Murder in Suffolk in 1827, was tanned by the surgeon George Creed and used to bind an account of

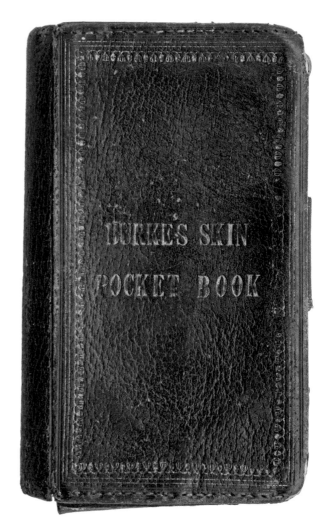

The pocket book made from the skin of William Burke, after his corpse had been publicly dissected by Professor Alexander Monro at the University of Edinburgh. On the back an inscription reads 'Executed 28 Jan 1829'.

his crimes. (His skeleton was also reassembled and used as a teaching aid at West Suffolk Hospital.) A fine dressed-white copy of Tegg's 1852 edition of Milton's *Poetical Works* was made from the corpse of the Devon hunchback, rat-catcher and murderer George Cudmore, who was hanged for poisoning his wife.

In the United States, libraries including those of Brown University, Harvard, the College of Physicians of Philadelphia and the Cleveland Public Library contain books bound with human skin. The Boston Athenaeum, the United States' oldest private membership library, holds a particularly curious example, titled *Narrative of the life of James Allen, alias George Walton ... the highwayman: being his death-bed confession, to the warden of the Massachusetts State Prison* (1837), which is stamped in gold and bound in the author's own skin, treated to look like grey deer skin. James Allen (1809–37) was a notorious Massachusetts highwayman in the early nineteenth century who ironically once declared himself 'master of my own skin'. While writing his memoir in Massachusetts State Prison, he expressed admiration for the one victim that had fought back and ultimately helped bring him to justice. In 1833, he'd held up John Fenno Jr of Springfield on the Salem Turnpike – Fenno resisted and Allen shot him, but the bullet ricocheted off his suspender buckle and he survived. Allen died in 1837, with the request that two copies of his memoirs be bound in his own skin – one to be given to the prison doctor, and one to Fenno with his compliments. (It seems the idea came to him not from the history of such bindings but from his previous work as a shoemaker.) After his death, his wishes were honoured. A binder dyed the leather grey, added some gilding and sent the 40-page volume to a startled Fenno, whose daughter later donated the book to the Athenaeum.

The Mütter Museum of the College of Physicians of Philadelphia has five anthropodermic books, making it the world's largest collection. Three of these books were bound by the same man – the surgeon and bibliophile Dr John Stockton Hough – who used a piece of thigh skin he had taken post mortem from a 28-year-old patient named Mary Lynch, with whom

ABOVE: *A copy of Arsène Houssaye's* Des destinées de l'ame, *bound in the skin of an unclaimed body.*

he had made the first diagnosed case of the parasitic illness trichinosis, at Philadelphia General Hospital in 1868. The doctor found the material to be 'relatively cheap, durable, and waterproof', almost indistinguishable from pigskin, and he used it to bind three medical texts on female health.

Anthropodermic bibliopegy continued to flourish into the late Victorian era. A peculiar record is that of the anatomist and gigantism expert Dr Charles Humberd binding a seventeenth-century book on the pituitary

OPPOSITE: Life and Death Contrasted; or, An Essay on Man. *(c.1770.)*

The WAGES of ___ SIN is DEATH. Rom VI.23.

Man ___ that is born of a Woman, is of
few ___ days, ___ and full of trouble.
He ___ cometh forth like a flower, and is
cut down ___ he fleeth also as a shadow, and
continueth ___ not. Job XIV. 1.2.
    All flesh is as grafs, and all the glory
of Man, as the ___ flower of grafs. 1 Peter I. 24.
    They spend ___ their days in wealth, and
in a moment go ___ down to the grave. Job XXI. 13.
    This their way ___ is their folly ___
When he dieth, he ___ shall carry nothing away,
his glory shall not de ___ scend after him. Psa.XLIX.
    Verily every Man ___ at his best state   13.17.
is altogether vanity. Psalm XXXIX. 5.
The lofty looks of Man ___ shall be humbled. Isa. II.
It is appointed unto Men ___ once to die, but   11.
after this the Judgment. Heb. IX. 27.

Here in the rich, the honour'd ___ fam'd and great,
See the false scale of happi ___ nefs complete.
                                                    Pope.
HERE LIES THE GREAT. Fal ___ se Marble! Where?
Nothing but poor and sordid ___ Duft lies Here.
                                                    Cowley.
        REMEMBER DEATH ___

PEDIGREE

PANTHEON
Masquerade

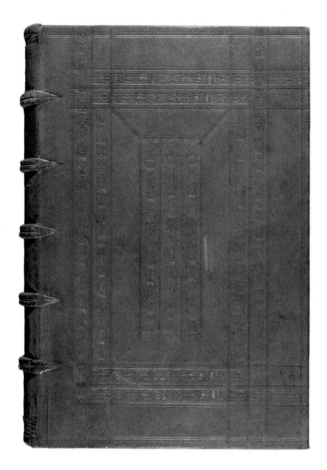

HIC LIBER FEMINEO

CORIO CONVESTITUS EST

LEFT AND ABOVE: *An 1863 binding of a 1544 copy of* Chirurgia è Graeco in Latinum conuersa *with a small gilt-lettered panel mounted on the front paste-down endpaper, stamped in Latin:* Hic liber femineo corio convestitus est – *'This book is bound in a woman's skin'.*

gland, *Exercitatio anatomica de glandula pituitaria*, in the skin of a 2.6-metre (8ft-6in) Ringling Brothers' circus giant named Perky. But for most other examples of this period, there is a noticeable shift to a more romantic theme of literary content bound in human skin. A copy of the French poet Arsène Houssaye's *Des destinées de l'ame*, a collection of essays from the 1880s meditating on the human spirit, is one of the more notorious items in Harvard's Houghton Collection. A memorandum in the book, now missing, stated the book to be bound in the skin from the 'back of the unclaimed body of a woman patient in a French mental hospital who died suddenly of apoplexy'. The volume is a presentation copy from Houssaye to his friend, the medical doctor and book collector Ludovic Bouland of Strasbourg (1839–1932).

It was Bouland who took the skin of the dead woman, her body having lain unclaimed. 'This book is bound in human skin parchment,' Bouland inscribed in the book, 'on which no ornament has been stamped to preserve its elegance.'

In 2014, the book underwent an analytical process called 'peptide mass fingerprinting', which identifies the proteins in the material, and a form of liquid chromatography, to determine the order of amino acids which vary with species. The use of human skin was confirmed. This was one of a number of tests organized by an American team of scientists and librarians known as the Anthropodermic Book Project, who also tested two other books in Harvard's collection, long thought to be of human origin, and found them to be made of sheepskin. 'Almost every book tested has some sort of surprise involved,' said Megan Rosenbloom, project member and author of *Dark Archives* (2020), an account of their investigations, when I asked about the progress of the project. 'Something like, oh that book is far too large, and then it turns out to be real. That's what is so exciting about having the peptide mass fingerprinting test results, because now we can really know for

LEFT: *A notebook bound in it what its accompanying label alleges is human skin, from the time of the American Revolutionary War (1775–83), held at the Wellcome Collection, London.*

had flayed the 'marvellously attractive young woman', whose name he was forbidden from revealing, just 'a few minutes after she passed on'. Flammarion obligingly had a copy of his 1877 novel *Les terres du ciel* ('The Worlds of the Sky') bound in her leather. The following inscription is on the front cover of the book: '*Execution pieuse d'un voeu anonyme. Reliure en peau humaine (Femme) 1882.*' ('Pious Fulfilment of an Anonymous Wish, Binding in Human Skin (Woman) 1882.')

When the newspapers picked up on the story Flammarion confirmed it in a letter to the editor of *La chronique medicale*: 'The binding was successfully executed by Engel, and from then on the skin was inalterable … this fragment of a beautiful body is all that survives of it today, and it can endure for centuries in a perfect state of respectful preservation.' Today the book can be found in the library of the Juvisy Observatory in France.

Anthropodermic bibliopegy finally died out in the first quarter of the twentieth century, by now too gruesome for public taste, and records dwindle from contemporary accounts to binders' reminiscences. In Dard Hunter's autobiography *My Life with Paper* (1958), for example, the American book designer recalls being commissioned by a young widow to bind a volume of letters dedicated to her late husband, using his own skin. The widow later remarried, and Hunter couldn't help but wonder whether her new husband was concerned he would become Volume Two. 'Let us hope,' Hunter concluded, 'that this was strictly a limited edition.'

sure.' At the time of writing, the project has tested thirty-one suspected human-skin books in public collections around the world and have found eighteen to be authentic.

Another famous example involves the French astronomical writer Camille Flammarion, who once complimented a handsome young countess on the charm of her skin. She was an infatuated fan of his and, suffering from tuberculosis as she was, she left instructions that on her death the skin that Flammarion had so admired be removed and sent to him as a gift, with the request that he use it to bind his latest work. The woman died in 1882 and, in accordance with her wishes, her skin was taken by the celebrated Paris physician Dr Ravaud, who delivered the roll of skin to Flammarion's residence himself. He told Flammarion he

BOOKS WRITTEN IN BLOOD

'Of all writings I love only that which is written with blood,' wrote Friedrich Nietzsche in *Thus Spoke Zarathustra* (1883–91). 'Write with blood: and you will discover that blood is spirit.' T. S. Eliot shared the passionate sentiment: 'The purpose of literature,' he wrote, 'is to turn blood into ink.' The metaphor is clear – but how many have taken the idea literally?

Through the history of ink, blood runs deep. In Egypt, for example, in the fourth century BC spells and charms were written on papyrus with their magical power enhanced by special ink. As well as the blending of myrrh, for some charms the blood of a baboon, a sacred animal, was sometimes mixed in the ink for dream spells that called on the power of Thoth-Hermes, with whom the animal was associated.

In Chinese Buddhism, the earliest recorded instance in the long history of scribes writing out holy texts in their own blood took place in AD 579, when a prince known as Shuling used his own blood to write out a copy of the *Nirvana Sūtra*. Blood was drawn by ritually slicing the fingertips, the base of the tongue or the chest above the heart, and was thought to represent the soul: the lighter the shade of blood, the greater the purity of the author. Known as *xieshu*, the practice was considered an ascetic form of sacrifice to prove one's piety and earn merit to be transferred to one's relatives after death. 'This is called paying reverence to the Correct Dharma; it is also called using the Dharma to make offering to Buddha,' wrote the Chinese Buddhist monk Ouyi Zhixu (1599–1655) in the preface of a layman's blood scripture. 'I, a follower of the bodhisattva precepts, Zhixu, vow to prick my tongue to copy Mahāyāna scriptures and *vinaya* in my blood.' Ouyi Zhixu is also known to have written a letter to his mother in his own blood. In 1578, the wandering monk Hanshan Deqing (1546–1623) copied out the sūtra known as *The Flower of Adornment* using ink made from his own blood as penance. 'Above, this would tie me to the karma of *prajna* [wisdom],' he explained, 'and below it would repay my parents for their benevolence.'

The earliest surviving blood scriptures are from the collection of 40,000 Buddhist scrolls discovered in 1900, hidden in a sealed cave near Dunhuang, western China, dating from the late fourth century to the early eleventh century. Perfectly preserved by the dry desert air, several have a colophon (a statement at the end of a book, usually with a printer's emblem, to give information on authorship) proclaiming the text to have been written in blood. The grandest of these is the 'Diamond Sūtra', today found in the collection of the British Library; it was created in AD 868, making it the earliest known complete survival of a dated, printed book. Dr Lionel Giles, who first catalogued the Dunhuang scrolls for the British Museum, noted that in a booklet containing a copy of the Diamond Sutra was a colophon that revealed the work to have been 'copied by an old man of 83, who pricked his own hand to draw blood [to write with], on the 2nd day of the 2nd moon of bingyan, the 3rd year of Tianyu'.

While most blood-writing isn't immediately identifiable thanks to dilution with ink, there are striking examples, like the one shown overleaf, another of the Dunhuang

OPPOSITE: *An English devotional text c.1480–c.1490 in the collection of the British Library features a startling ten consecutive pages painted with representations of the bleeding wounds suffered by Christ. Some pages are faded from the repeated kissing by worshipful readers.*

collection. This is a Tibetan manuscript copy of the Sūtra of Aparimitayus, a work of devotion to Amitābha, the celestial Buddha of Infinite Light. The ink of this document has been found to have a remarkably high iron content, and appears to have dried quickly with visible clotting in places, indicating blood. Iron gall ink was popular at this time too (used by, among others, Leonardo da Vinci), but that tends to blacken over time, whereas this 'ink' retains a telltale reddish hue.

While practitioners of blood-writing were admired by some, others viewed it as blasphemous and were horrified at the extremes to which its practitioners went. Guanxiu (AD 832–912) writes of a fellow monk with 'ten fingers drained [of blood] to complete seven scrolls'. Another monk, Dinglan (d. AD 852), was said to have 'punctured himself in order to copy out scriptures in his own blood, made burns on his arms, and eventually went so far as to cut

A Tibetan manuscript copy of the Sūtra of Aparimitayus, thought to have been written in blood in the ninth century or earlier.

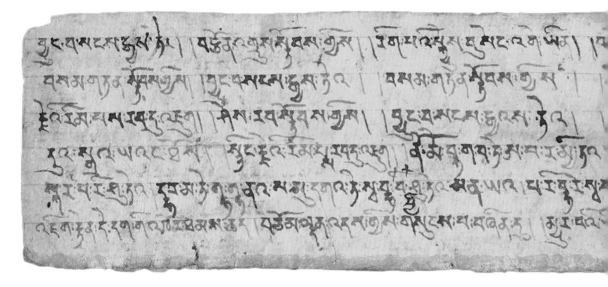

off his ears and gouge out his eyes in order to feed them to wild birds and beasts'. In part they were driven by the exhortations of the sūtras themselves. *The Flower of Adornment*, the text copied out by Deqing, related how the Buddha Vairocana 'peeled off his skin for paper, broke off a bone for a pen, and drew his own blood for ink'.

Like anthropodermic bibliopegy in Europe, traditional blood-writing in China survived, just as surprisingly, into the twentieth century. And while there was no such ancient tradition of blood-writing in the West, a truly extraordinary European blood curiosity was created in dramatic circumstances in the nineteenth century. On 22 July 1821, the *Blenden Hall*, a 450-ton vessel chartered to the East India Company, struck rocks in South Atlantic waters 20 miles south of the Tristan da Cunha islands. As the ship keeled over onto its starboard side the captain started shaking the passengers' hands goodbye, but as the weather cleared they saw that they were close to shore. A crude raft was fashioned and several men made it to land, including Mr Gormby, the quartermaster, who had

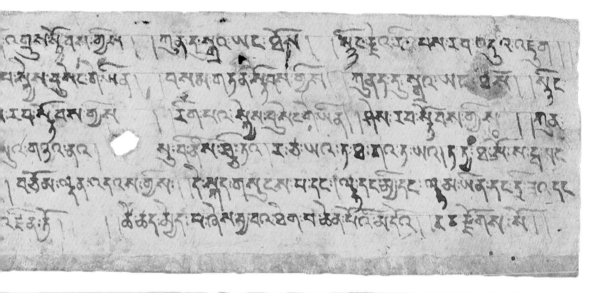

pushed past his wife and child to leap aboard the raft and save himself. The passengers and all but two of the crew eventually made it to shore, including the captain, Alexander Greig. The uninhabited landmass that had accorded them such a hostile welcome was the aptly named Inaccessible Island.

These details, and those of the ensuing ordeal endured by the survivors, come to us from the journal kept by Greig, which he wrote entirely in penguin blood. A bundle of the London *Times*, as well as a writing desk and pens, had washed ashore intact – but no ink. So Greig improvised. 'From a Journal kept on the Islands, and written with the Blood of the Penguin' reads the subtitle to the 1847 publication of his account, *Fate of the Blenden Hall*, which features a frontispiece illustration of 'The foraging party, attacking the Sea Elephant'; the livers and brains of those animals made up the daily cuisine of the eighty-two shipwrecked souls until their rescue by natives of Tristan da Cunha four months later.

Easier to find is *Marvel Comics Super Special #1* (1977), a 40-page comic book featuring the rock band Kiss in a fictional adventure. As witnessed by a notary public, the musicians had vials of their blood withdrawn and mixed into the reservoir of red ink used to print the issue. 'Printed in real KISS blood,' cries the cover.

The strangest of all blood books, though, is a more recent creation. On his sixtieth birthday in 1997, the Iraqi dictator Saddam Hussein commissioned the master calligrapher Abbas Shakir Joudi al-Baghdadi to produce a Qur'an written entirely in Hussein's blood. 'My life has been full of dangers in which I should have lost a lot of blood,' he wrote in a letter published by Iraqi state media in September 2000 upon the book's

The frontispiece illustration of Fate of the Blenden Hall *(1847), a journal originally written entirely in penguin blood.*

completion, 'but since I have bled only a little, I asked somebody to write God's words with my blood in gratitude.'

According to Joudi, Hussein summoned him to Ibn Sīnā hospital, where his son Uday was recuperating from an attempted assassination, and informed him of his participation in the project. Over a period of two years, somewhere between 24 and 27 litres (some 50–57 pints) was allegedly drained from Hussein and mixed with other chemicals to produce enough 'ink' to write out the 336,000 words in 6000 verses. 'It's an incredible amount, if that [figure] is correct,' Celso Bianco, an executive at America's Blood Centers, told reporters at the time. 'That certainly would have made him anaemic.'

Exquisitely beautiful, the Blood Qur'an was eventually displayed in another of Hussein's enterprises, the Umm al-Ma'arik (Mother of All Battles) mosque in Baghdad, which was designed with minarets shaped like Scud missiles to memorialize the First Gulf War. The Australian journalist Paul McGeough caught a glimpse of a page of the Blood Qur'an, and wrote that 'the blood lettering is about two centimetres tall and the broad decorative borders are dazzling – blues, light and dark; spots of red and pink; and swirling highlights in black'. After the fall of Baghdad, remnants of the old regime, like the numerous bronzes of Hussein's likeness, were destroyed in acts of *damnatio memoriae*. The Blood Qur'an was hastily stored away by curators until they could decide how to deal with it, as it presented a dilemma.

Saddam Hussein's 'Blood Qur'an' when it was on display at the 'Mother of All Battles' Umm al-Ma'arik, mosque: picture taken 11 March 2003 in Baghdad, Iraq. The mosque was built with minarets styled after Scud missiles.

For while it is *haraam* (forbidden) to reproduce a Qur'an in such a manner, it is equally unthinkable to destroy a Qur'an, regardless of how it was made. At the time of writing the dilemma is unresolved. In 2010, the Iraqi Prime Minister's spokesman, Ali al-Moussawi, proposed that the Blood Qur'an should be kept 'as a document for the brutality of Saddam', but it remains out of sight, hidden in a vault to which there are three keys, each held by a separate public official, none with any idea of what to do with the extraordinary book.[4]

---

4 In 2018, a French 16-year-old named Adrien Locatelli went arguably a step further and became the first human being to inject himself with verses of the Bible and Qur'an. The texts were transcoded into artificial DNA macromolecules and injected into each leg – the Bible verse went into his left thigh; the Qur'an verse the right. The Bible verse caused mild inflammation. Locatelli called his effort a 'symbol of peace between religions and science'. UCLA biochemist Sri Kosuri called the experiment 'unfortunate', adding '2018 can't end soon enough'.

CRYPTIC BOOKS

By the sixteenth century, the practice of using lemon juice as invisible ink and heating it to become visible had long been known, as was the Arab substitute of tree sap. A polymathic Italian scholar named Giambattista della Porta (1535–1615), nicknamed 'professor of secrets', sat down to invent a new technique for passing secret messages to his friends imprisoned by the Spanish Inquisition. The guards, he noticed, took apart and searched just about every item brought into the prison, except eggs. So della Porta devised a way to write on an egg beneath its shell without cracking it. He concocted an ink from one ounce of alum (a colourless compound used in dying and tanning) and a pint of vinegar. Written directly onto the shell, the chemical mixture soaked through the porous shell to the egg albumen beneath. Boiling the egg caused the chemical to react, and when the shell was peeled away the message was revealed on the hardened egg white.

This particular form of secret communication, in which one actively disguises the very existence of a message, is known as steganography, and goes back centuries earlier than della Porta's eggs. Pliny the Elder wrote in the first century AD of how the 'milk' of the tithymalus plant

could be used as invisible ink. As with many organic solutions, heating turns it visible by causing the carbon in the ink to char. (This is why, in a pinch, writing in urine can also achieve the same effect.) In 1641, Bishop John Wilkins recommended onion juice, alum and ammonia salts, though one should be sure

mimi numinum niuium minimi munium nimium uini muniminum imminui uiui minimum uolunt

ABOVE: *As a joke to show just how impenetrable Gothic script could be, fourteenth-century scribes used this invented Latin sentence,* Mimi numinum niuium minimi munium nimium uini muniminum imminui uiui minimum uolunt, *which translates as 'The shortest mimes of the snow gods do not wish at all, in their lifetimes, for the great burden of [distributing] the wine of the walls to be lightened'.*

to add the 'distilled Juice of Glowworms' to make it luminescent. In ancient China, messages too long or complicated to be memorized were written on silk then screwed up into a tight ball and covered in wax. This could then be hidden on, or more commonly *in*, the messenger, either by swallowing it, or secreting it via what we shall call an alternative route.

From Herodotus we learn of two examples of hidden writing in antiquity. The first is the story of Histiaeus, a Greek tyrant who in 499 BC passed the message to Aristagoras of Miletus to launch a rebellion against the Persian king Darius I. Histiaeus shaved the head of his most trusted slave, tattooed the message on his scalp, and when the hair had grown back sent the human communiqué on his way.

OPPOSITE LEFT: *Giambattista della Porta, in a portrait from his work* De humana physiognomonia *(1586).*

OPPOSITE RIGHT: *A cryptographic volvelle (paper wheel) table from della Porta's* De Furtivis Literarum notis *('On Secret Writing'), 1563. As well as his invisible egg-writing trick, in the book della Porta also explains how to hide a message on the edge of a pack of playing cards.*

Herodotus also claims in *The Histories* that it was this covert art that thwarted an attempted Persian conquest of Greece. As Xerxes began mustering forces, an exiled Greek named Demaratus living in the Persian city of Susa caught wind of the invasion plan and wondered how he could smuggle a warning to his homeland. This he managed by 'scraping the wax off a pair of wooden folding tablets, writing on the wood underneath what Xerxes intended to do, and then covering the message over with wax again. In this way the tablets, being

BELOW: *Wooden writing tablets from* AD *500–700 Byzantine Egypt of the kind that carried Demaratus' warning to the Greeks of the Persian invasion plan. The recessed areas of these tablets were filled with wax, into which writing was scratched with a wooden stylus.*

REX·REGUM·DOMINUS·MUNDUM·DICIONE·GUBERNANS
IMPERITASCEPTRUM·REGNANS·QIURE·PERENNI
INMORTALCTENES·CUM·CRIMINAMULTAPARENTUM
LAXASTINCVCETIUSTITIAECUMFRENALOCARAS
OMNIBUS·EGOTUIS·SERVISUPERASTRA·BEATAM
SPERARE·HINCVITAMCVIOCHRISTEDEDISTI
DONIQUEESTMODO·CRISTEECSPATRISQETUIQE
NUNC·NOMENORITEIAMCUNCTA·STUPEBANT
SAECULADVDVMENCRTHCEQODGESTATURAMICA
SUMMIXPIOLÆDLCNATRITECERENDUMHOC
PERIUSTAMXPIHRONVMAVIDOQODTOLLERELEGEM
ATQDECETTOTUMAUGVSVONUTUEXCOLATORBEM
NAMHOCPACHVSTANTCIRANDOCARDINEPRODIT
ORBS·CIAINTCCVSULTUCAESARISORET
AVGVSTOPVRE·PERRALMHINCLAVDECORONAM
NAMOPTIMIDEXTRAORTVDIVINAPARETARTE
STIPS·TESVVADETATRINVMPOSCIMVSOMNES
IAMALMVMIVTOTVTITIAEQQUODREGNETUBIQE
HAEC·SILIRAATVELIGATVGIRET·AMICO
DVMAFFERTLOVCACCVAXITVSIC·IPSAPARATVM
OPTEMVS·NOSSENPERAMICVMNEMPIECHRISTVS
RETVTATVRPQRLLVSIAEVLOPREMITAST·FVR
RASVELINILLPROTERATHOSTIS·CRIMINEDIRO
DEFENSORARTISEDVRMONSTRATAMANDVM
IVSORNATVLANCCARARIBTINETHAVSTVM
OMENSITQRAIVORVMPEIVMMANET·ORBE
ENREGNACRAINTMONNEPERAMVNERADONANT
ET·PERSADATSICVVECIVSROLLISLATVSAMBIT
CENS·PLEBSLETAPROPGOVINNVMPIEDONAT
MVSAMVIVATENTESVNENTSCVTVET·AMARE
SPEMECSVLSCEPTRATENENDOVFIDEISDAT·VBIQ
REMHAVSTVDONECSNECLASVDEPELLITABARTE
QAEFORMOSEIVRATENEBVSTELANEPASSINT
ET·SEDAREQSEVRASOIDANDAPROTERVIAM
QVAMEST·SOLISVPIRMANTEGITAVGVSTOVILE
TRANSFORMATMARDICIISTICVMCLARATRIBVTA
IVRECOLENDMODVREQTROFAETRANS·DAT
QVAEHOC·INTNOMEDIOMEANSTOMEANTABORE
NEMPETONSTVRGETQVEPROBETVSDIVAMARI
SIT·TREMOREST·QVEBONAEDVMFRETVNTLITAQ
PROFICIINDEORBAMODVMFRETVNLITAQ
SICABICIRPORTVCRVCEDAT·LAEVVMSEQITVRQ
HVNCTIBIENIMINTODATVMOSEMPERCASTEPIQ
CAESARLANGEMODOVISVTVCASTRANIMICIAST
TERRES·SPEMQETIMORVINIMICAFVGANS·DAT
TU·PIVS·ET·GRATMIVMPRONVMROGATHAECGENS
ADVENIAMIREANVSNOBIS·ADIVSSAPARENTIS
CONSCRIPSIDVDVMNAMCRISTILAVDELIBELLVM
VERSIBVS·ET·PROSATIBIQEMNVNC·INDVPERATOR
OFFEROSANCTELIBENS·CVIVS·PRAECEDIT·IMAGO
STANSARMATAFIDEVICTOREMMONSTRAT·VBIQVE

ABOVE: *One of the figural 'pattern poems' of the Frankish Benedictine monk Rabanus Maurus (c.780–856), written in a grid, from his* De laudibus sanctae crucis *('In Praise of the Holy Cross').*

OPPOSITE: *A Latinized reproduction of a scytale, a Spartan encryption/decryption tool using lettered leather strips. The Ancient Greeks, particularly the Trojans, used the scytale to relay messages safely during military campaigns.*

apparently blank, would cause no trouble with the guards along the road.' The Greeks found Demaratus' message beneath the wax, and were able to prepare an enormous navy that successfully repelled the Persian fleet at the Bay of Salamis near Athens on 23 September 480 BC.

Before looking at specific cryptic works, perhaps the difference between codes and ciphers should be clarified. A code is a word or phrase that is swapped out with another word, number or symbol. By contrast, a cipher substitutes each letter, not just each word, with a new letter or symbol, to create documents that can resemble pages of an alien language. These two methods of creating 'cryptograms' (encrypted messages) for conveying both political and personal secrets go back, like steganography, over 2000 years.

One of the earliest references to using substitution ciphers can be found, somewhat unexpectedly, in the *Kama-sūtra,* written in the fourth century AD but drawing on manuscripts made as early as the fourth century BC. Along with advice for women on domestic arts like cookery, other pursuits like bookbinding, carpentry, chess and conjuring are also encouraged. The forty-fifth listed art is *mlecchita-vikalpa*, 'the art of understanding writing in cypher, and the writing of words in a peculiar way', which is recommended for helping to keep romantic affairs secret.

Julius Caesar was a great fan of substitution ciphers. 'If he had anything confidential to say,' wrote Suetonius, 'he wrote it in cipher, that is, by so changing the order of the letters of the alphabet, that not a word could be made out.' In Julius Caesar's *Gallic Wars*, his commentary on his military campaigns against the Gallic tribes in 58 BC to 50 BC, he gives one dramatic example of sending a communiqué to a besieged Cicero, whose situation was so dire that he was mulling surrender. The encrypted message was fastened to the thong of a spear and hurled deep into Cicero's surrounded camp. Unfortunately, it struck a tower high up and stayed embedded there for two days before it was noticed and delivered to Cicero, inspiring him to keep fighting.

This kind of surreptitious personal cryptography is a technique that runs through the centuries to modern day, particularly in diary-keeping. In Britain, the best-known use is that of Samuel Pepys (1633–1703), who for his diaries of 1660–69 used the cryptic shorthand system devised by the stenographer Thomas Shelton in 1626. The first published edition of the Pepys diary only appeared in 1825, and was barely half of the original manuscript – this was partly because the man tasked with

16 ⁵⁹/60.

... Axe-yard h₃ ... — ℰ Jane —

... 63.

... Lamb. ...

... Lawson ... — River — Monke ... Scott ...

... Lamb: ... 7 ... 2 ...

... Monke ...

... 22 ...

... h₃ ...

... Mr Downing ...

OPPOSITE: *The first page of Samuel Pepys's diary, written in cryptic shorthand.*

its decryption, who had spent three years labouring on the project, was unaware until he'd nearly finished that the key to the shorthand sat just a few shelves above the diaries in Pepys's library. The other reason for so much omission was that Pepys littered his diaries with lascivious details of his sexual activities, considered so depraved by scholars that it wasn't until 1970 that the publication of the full unexpurgated diary was finally begun. (Extracts could be provided here, but honestly, they're exactly what you think they are.) On the excision of the 'passages which cannot possibly be printed', the editor of the 1893–99 edition, Henry B. Wheatley, wrote in the preface that 'readers are asked to have faith in the judgement of the editor'.[1]

The first in medieval Europe to rediscover and develop the cryptographic arts from classical and Islamic works were not in royal or military service, but were the scholars and manuscript-makers of the monasteries. Spurred on by the popularity of riddles for which Anglo-Saxon scribes are known, monks placed their own codes in the colophon at the end of a manuscript as a way of documenting how, and by whom, the manuscript was created. The monastic interest in code was whetted in part by the fact that the Bible contains instances of intentional cryptography.

The Atbash cipher system is a substitution cipher that was originally used to encrypt the Hebrew alphabet by replacing a letter with its reverse: the first letter is swapped with the last one, the second is swapped for the second-last, etc. (This is where it derives its name from: Aleph, Taw, Bet and Shin are the first, last, second and second-last letters of the Hebrew alphabet.) In Jeremiah 25:26, for example, we find 'The king of Sheshach shall drink after them'. Decrypted with the Atbash system, Sheshach translates to Babylon. Though these Biblical ciphers were likely devised to create an air of spiritual mystery, monks of the medieval era nevertheless developed their fascination with cryptography by recovering old systems and developing their own, giving rise to its eventual Western popularity.

And so, unsurprisingly, the first European work on the subject was written by a monk: 'A man is crazy who writes a secret in any other way than one which will conceal it from the vulgar,' wrote the Franciscan friar Roger Bacon (*c.*1219/20–*c.*1292), in *Letter on the Secret Works of Art and the Vanity of Magic*, a letter to a 'William of Paris' in which he outlines seven methods for disguising messages, while also dismissing necromancy and providing alchemical formulae. By the fourteenth century, cryptography's facility for mystery had become popular with magicians, alchemists and writers including Geoffrey Chaucer (1343–1400), whose scientific manual *The Equatorie of Planetis* (only discovered in 1952, with its attribution disputed) features several paragraphs encrypted by a simple substitution cipher using symbols not letters.

So far we have looked at shared and established systems of encryption; but the most famous cryptic manuscript of the

---

1 In 2016, Anne Frank's diary was found to have two secret pages, not encrypted but hidden behind pasted brown paper. Using digital image-processing, Dutch researchers were able to read them. 'I'll use this spoiled page to write down "dirty" jokes,' she wrote. 'A man had a very ugly wife and he didn't want to have relations with her. One evening he came home and then he saw his friend in bed with his wife, and the man said: "He gets to, and I have to!!!" ' She then writes about prostitution: 'Women like that accost [men] on the street and then they go together. In Paris they have big houses for that,' she writes, adding, 'Papa has been there.'

ABOVE: *An elaborate fold-out diagram from the undeciphered work known as the Voynich Manuscript.*

OPPOSITE AND FOLLOWING SPREAD: *Pages from the Voynich Manuscript.*

medieval period is – as far as we know – written in a unique language that to this day remains understood only by its author. It was found in 1912 by a Polish rare book dealer named Wilfrid Voynich, hidden among a pile of manuscripts in the Villa Mondragone, Italy. Voynich was immediately captivated by its unknown language and the strange illustrations of mostly non-existent plants and groups of nude bathers, and purchased it along with twenty-nine other items. (During more than thirty years Voynich sold the British Museum more than 3800 books, many of which were so unusual that they were given their own 'Voynich' shelf mark.)

The cryptic text now known as the Voynich Manuscript has since been the obsessive focus of study around the world, and as yet none of the professional and

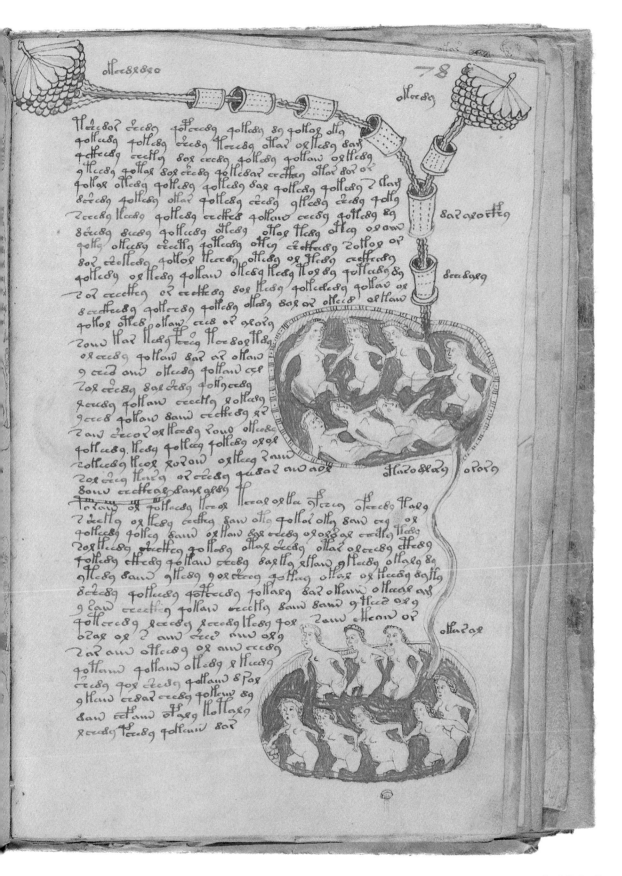

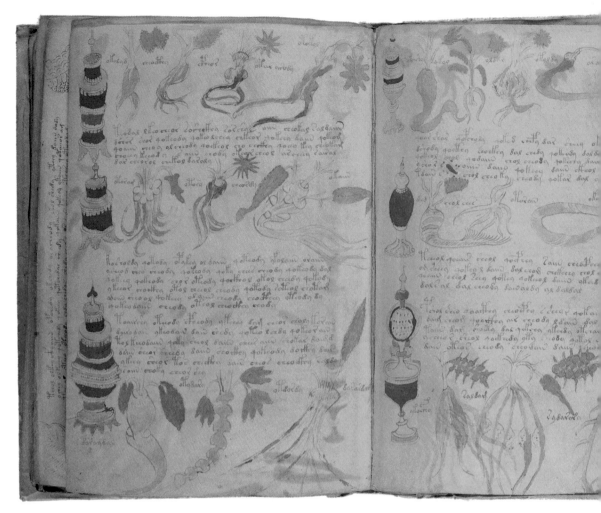

amateur cryptographers – including American and British codebreakers of both World War I and World War II – has been able to crack it. Perhaps this is because it exhibits characteristics of both a complete, natural language and a complicated designed cipher, with letter-shapes tantalisingly similar to known shorthand symbols. It doesn't follow the structural rules of the contemporary Renaissance polyalphabetic ciphers, yet it *does* show clear signs of having its own internal structure. And this, really, is its eternal attraction, the sense that the key to unlocking its secrets is within reach; that with enough patience and the right approach anyone, linguist or layman, can break it.

Of course, this is assuming it's not a sophisticated hoax, which is an entirely possible explanation. Over the years, the language of the Voynich Manuscript has been claimed confidently to be seventh-century Welsh/Old Cornish; an early German language; the Manchu language of the Qing dynasty (1636–1911) of China; and Hebrew enciphered by Roger Bacon, describing alien technology of the future for generating DNA with sound. Perhaps it's the Nahuatl language of the Aztec written by Francisco Hernández de Toledo (1514–87), naturalist and court physician to the King of Spain; or it could be the language of the angels, linked to John Dee's *Book of Enoch*, with the illustrations of

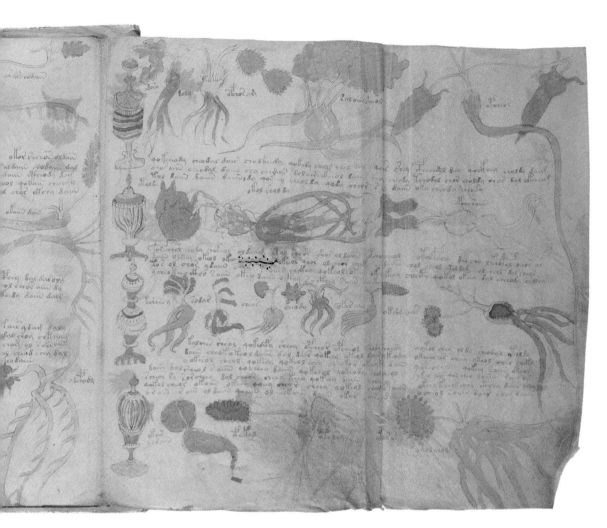

unknown plants perhaps being the original species found in the Garden of Eden. It's a recipe book; a diary; a guide to viewing galaxies using telescopes (by Roger Bacon again); a nonsense stage prop made by Francis Bacon; an early work by Leonardo da Vinci; a record of speaking in tongues; outsider art; and so on. Wilfrid Voynich, incidentally, referred to it with true dealer's aplomb as 'The Roger Bacon Manuscript', and held the unfounded belief that John Dee had sold it to Rudolf II, Holy Roman Emperor (1552–1612).

So what exactly *do* we know about the possibly celestial, possibly nonsensical manuscript? In 2009, its vellum pages were radiocarbon-dated to between 1404 and 1438

with 95 per cent certainty, although there is no way yet to prove that its writing was added at this time. The smooth unhesitating handwriting of its right-handed author has been described as reminiscent of the Italian Quattrocento style of *c*.1400–1500. The spelling of some marginalia in the zodiac section suggests that the manuscript was at one time in south-west France, and the handwriting of two other owners/readers suggest it was likely already written before 1500. To add to the challenge, the evidence suggests that the pages were originally arranged in a different order, and that the written numbers of both the folios and quires were added later.

ABOVE: *A detail of a letter written in invisible or 'sympathetic' ink from Colonel Charles McMahon in Paris to British Foreign Secretary George Canning, 19 September 1807, just two months before the French invasion of Portugal. Marked 'Most Secret'. Sympathetic ink was used for sending secret intelligence into the late nineteenth century.*

BELOW: *A c.1550 French cypher machine in book form with the arms of Henri II, measuring 25 × 11cm (10 × 4.5in), in the collection of the Musée National de la Renaissance, France. The alpha-numerical system employed by this machine, in which letters were translated into numbers based on a pre-agreed key, was quickly abandoned as it was vulnerable to pattern recognition.*

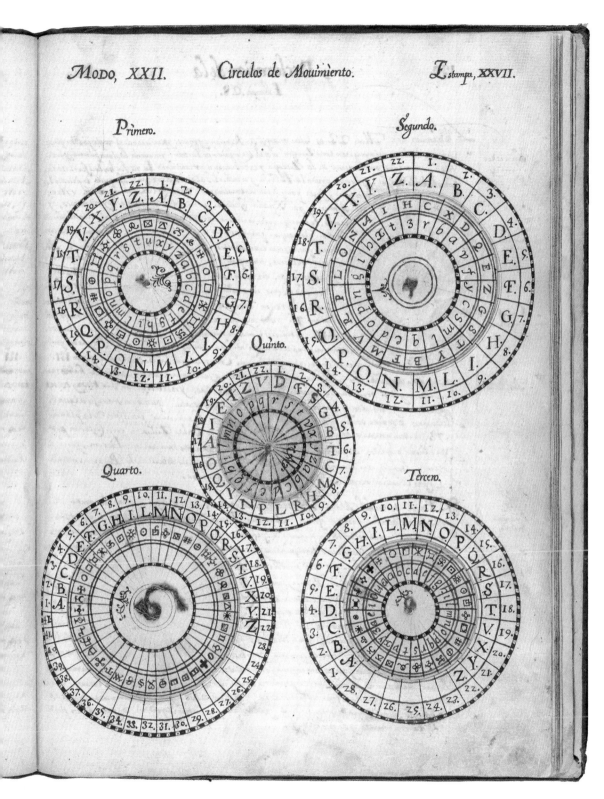

A page from a c.1600 Spanish manuscript guide to cipher writing, by a cryptographer in the service of Martin de Cordova, Viceroy of Navarre.

A ✉ 🐌 Sir L___e Dund 🐂

W🐦👁 consider w🌳🌲 have ready done for my 🐀hoof, and t🎩

it may never again hap🕯 🐝 in 🌲r way 🐴ist my emissarys as

🛏erly 👁🍵 not forb🐑enting 🌲r late mis🏰tune, 🍞re🎩itulate

🌲r ser🔩s would 🐝 endless — In the🐍 🪣⁷⁶🌲 grasped🐟t 🎩 oppor

tunity 🍞 get 🫘 by the 💀 of thou🦴s of 🔫ilys — In Ger🚶y w🐦

Commis🪚ry🦴 the 🦊y🌲 sent thou🦴s 🦴 the 🪺 for w🐌 of

since com🚶cing Baro▬🌲 have🐝n no less assiduous in 👑ing

my 🦎dom by Ncouraging 🐱ner of wickedness, by gaming 🐒 false

swea⭕🕯 serve 🌲r & my ends, for 🐟 which ser🔩s 🌲 may asure

🌲rself of 🐝ing made a 🍒 of my 💃dom and my priv👁 coun-

sellor for ever

👁 am 🌲rs &c

The

OPPOSITE: *Hieroglyphic letter to Sir L - e Dund--*
from the Devil. Copperplate engraving by John Kay
from A Series of Original Portraits and Caricature
Etchings*, 1837–38.*

By 1969, the manuscript was in the
possession of the dealer Hans P. Kraus, who
donated it to Yale University's Beinecke
Rare Book and Manuscript Library. Today,
with endless patience, the librarians
politely accommodate an unending flood
of examination requests from enthusiasts
around the world. Every year there is a
new claim to having successfully unlocked
its secret that ultimately proves unfounded.
If indeed the Voynich Manuscript does have
a story to tell, its secrets – alien, angelic or
otherwise – remain its own for now.

Cryptic writing using a confusing medley
of language and symbols, usually more
distinguishable than that of the Voynich
Manuscript, remained a popular feature
of occult works for centuries, a literary
equivalent of speaking in tongues. An
interesting seventeenth-century religious
example of this was written, unusually, not
by a monk but by a nun. At the convent of
Palma di Montechiaro, Sister Maria Crocifissa
della Concezione (born Isabella Tommasi)
was said to have screamed and fainted while
writing cryptic letters that she claimed were
dictated to her by a swarm of demonic spirits
sent by Beelzebub, in an attempt to sway her
to the service of evil. She was allegedly passed
two further messages but successfully resisted
having to write them, despite the devils
smearing her face with ink and threatening
to beat her with the inkwell. 'Do not ask
me about them, for pity's sake,' she told her
sisters, 'I cannot in any way speak of them.'

After centuries of translation attempts, it
was only in 2017 that the one surviving letter,
written on 11 August 1676, was successfully
decrypted by researchers at the Ludum Science
Centre in Sicily, with the assistance of a
code-cracking computer algorithm discovered
in the lawless murk of the Dark Web. Using
software primed with ancient Greek, Arabic,
Runic and Latin, a computer was tasked with
decrypting the sequences of archaic alphabets.
The contents certainly honoured its diabolic
promise. The author labels God, Jesus and the
Holy Spirit as 'deadweights' and sarcastically
sneers: 'God thinks he can free mortals' with
a system that 'works for no one'. This is
followed with the revelation that God and
Zoroaster were invented by man.

A work rivalling this eccentricity is the
Copiale cipher. When it was cracked in 2011,
it gave up a secret odder than any imagined,
revealing the existence of a secret society of
German doctors who ritualistically plucked
each other's eyebrows. The work is a 105-
page manuscript containing some 75,000
cryptic characters that held its secrets for over
260 years until 2011, when the American
scholar Kevin Knight and Swedish scholars
Beáta Megyesi and Christiane Schaefer
used computers to successfully decode the
first 10,000 words of the manuscript. The
homophonic cipher uses a complicated
substitution code using both Roman and
Greek letters, symbols and accents for its
text and spaces. In the 1970s, scientists at
the German Academy of Sciences in Berlin
had dated the manuscript to between 1760
and 1780, but the 2011 team learned that
the document had been created earlier,
in the 1730s, by a secret society, the 'High
Enlightened (*Hocherleuchtete*) Oculist Order'
of Wolfenbüttel, or 'Oculists', a group of
ophthalmologists for whom sight was not just
their trade but a metaphor for knowledge.

The first sixteen pages of the manuscript
are initiation rites for inducting '*Der
Candidat*'. This includes a ritual in which

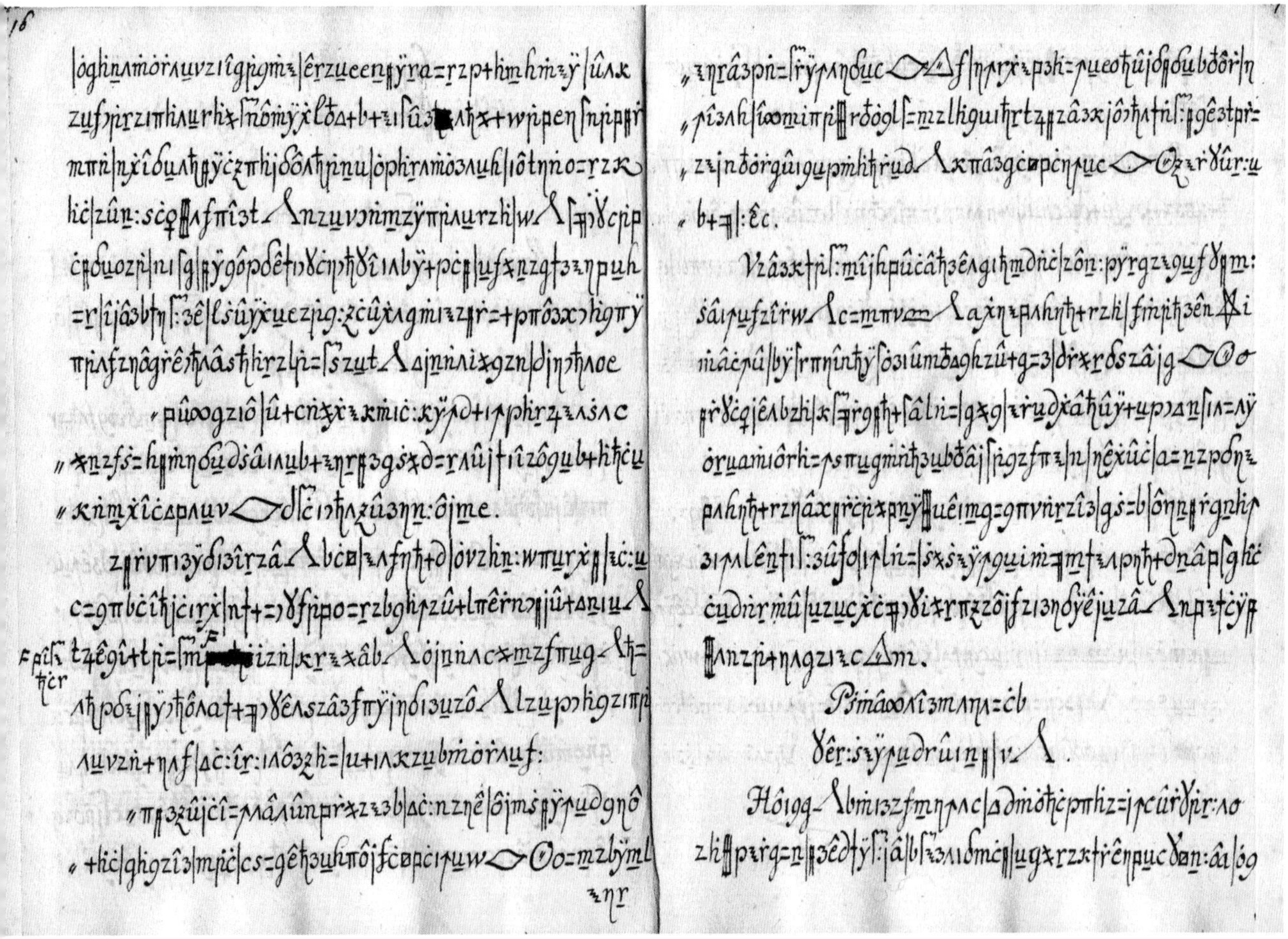

ABOVE: *Pages 16 and 17 of the Copiale cipher*

the candidate is challenged to read a blank piece of paper. When he admits to finding this impossible, his new brothers present him with eyeglasses and demand he try again. When he fails a second time his eyes are washed with a cloth, after which he is subjected to an 'operation' in which a single hair is plucked from his eyebrow. It is also from the Copiale cipher that we learn that the Oculist order, led by Count Friedrich August von Veltheim,

were not just ophthalmologists but also Freemasons, whose secret society was apparently founded to keep alive Masonic traditions in defiance of the 1738 Papal ban of Freemasonry.[2]

Outside of military communication and occult gimmickry, cryptic curiosities also crop up in the field of treasure-hunting.

---

2 In the British Library is an eighty-page encrypted rulebook and sole source for an equally mysterious female secret society called 'The Association of Maiden Unity and Attachment'. Published in London in 1835, the book, titled *Ebpob es byo Utlub, Umgjoml Nýflobjof*, 'is a mystery for which it is difficult to account,' wrote a journalist at the *Pall Mall Gazette* in April 1869. 'Its printing must have cost more money than a mere hoaxer would care throw away. Is it possible that the association of which it speaks is flourishing among us? Or is the whole book the mere embodiment of the ravings of some lunatic, whose prevailing delusion is the idea that a number of women could keep a secret?'

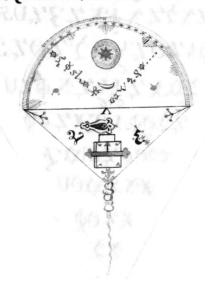

The Triangular Book of Count St Germain (c.1750), an encoded French occult work which boasts the secret to extending life. The mysterious and eccentric Count St Germain was an adventurer and alchemist who thrilled eighteenth-century Europe's high society with his claim to have uncovered the secret to longevity. He was so old, he said, that he had attended the wedding at Cana where Jesus turned water to wine. Horace Walpole wrote of the Count: 'He sings, plays on the violin wonderfully, composes, is mad.'

ABOVE: *The Cipher Wheel, a 300-metre (1000-ft)-long strip of canvas pasted with the pages of Shakespeare's works, rotated between two giant wheels for careful inspection. Its crackpot inventor, the American physician Dr Orville Ward Owen (1854–1924), claimed to have used the device to decipher hidden messages proving Francis Bacon to be the true author of the texts.*

OPPOSITE: *This sample cigarette paper with a code legend was found under the floorboards of the Horns Inn, Kennington, in 1792. Stare at it long enough and you'll see that the apparently meaningless jumble actually reads 'I am puzzled how to live while kingcraft may abuse my rights and tax the joys of day'.*

Should you be able to crack the Beale cipher texts, for example, an alleged $43 million reward awaits you. In 1885, a pamphlet was published that told of how a treasure of gold and silver was buried by a man named Thomas J. Beale at an unknown site somewhere in Bedford County, Virginia, in the 1820s. Beale had accumulated the treasure in the early 1800s while leading a group of thirty Virginian fortune-seekers hunting buffalo through the western plains. The group arrived in Santa Fe before heading north when, according to Beale's note: 'The party, encamped in a small ravine, were preparing their evening meal, when

one of the men discovered in a cleft of the rocks something that had the appearance of gold. Upon showing it to the others it was pronounced to be gold, and much excitement was the natural consequence.'

The men mined the spot for eighteen months, harvesting about three tons of precious metals that Beale ferried back to Virginia and buried for safety. He encrypted three messages giving the treasure's location, describing the treasure and listing the names of its owners and their relatives. This location is thought to be Montvale in Bedford County, Virginia. The story goes that Beale entrusted a box holding these coded messages to a local innkeeper named Robert Morriss. Beale then disappeared, and was never heard from again. Morriss eventually broke a promise to Beale and opened the box twenty-three years later, giving the texts to a friend who after twenty years of work managed to decrypt Paper #2, using the United States Declaration of Independence as a key. It reads:

I have deposited in the county of Bedford, about four miles from Buford's, in an excavation or vault, six feet below the surface of the ground, the following articles, belonging jointly to the parties whose names are given in number three, herewith:

The first deposit consisted of ten hundred and fourteen pounds of gold, and thirty-eight hundred and twelve pounds of silver, deposited Nov. eighteen nineteen. The second was made Dec. eighteen twenty-one, and consisted of nineteen hundred and seven pounds of gold, and twelve hundred and eighty-eight of silver; also jewels, obtained in St. Louis in exchange to save transportation, and valued at thirteen thousand dollars.

The above is securely packed in iron pots, with iron covers. The vault is roughly lined with stone, and the vessels rest on solid stone, and are covered with others. Paper number one describes the exact locality of the vault, so that no difficulty will be had in finding it.

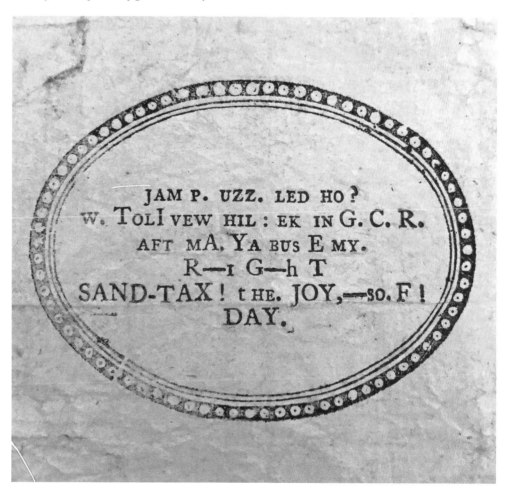

The unnamed friend then published all three cipher texts in a pamphlet which was advertised for sale in the 1880s.

No one has managed to crack the other texts (see opposite page) so far, leading to the claim that the texts are a 'secret vault' hoax perpetrated by James B. Ward, a Mason, who authored the 1885 pamphlet, the sole source of the story. In support of this idea the American sceptic Joe Nickell points to apparently anachronistic terms used in the text like 'stampeding', which originated later.

(Also, the third cipher does appear to be too short to list thirty individuals' next of kin.) Of course, this hasn't prevented treasure-hunters continually flocking to Bedford County in the hopes of discovering a clue that might have been overlooked in over a century of searching.

Across the Atlantic, a British artist named Kit Williams sparked his own national treasure hunt with the publication of his picture-book *Masquerade* in 1979. The book was advertised with the claim that Williams had fashioned an 18-carat golden hare set with ruby, mother-of-pearl and moonstones, with a value of £5000 (£25,000 today), and buried it at a secret location with the television host Bamber Gascoigne as a witness. 'The clues to its whereabouts are hidden in the riddles and puzzles and pictures,' claimed the publisher's promotional material. 'A child of ten is as well placed to solve the mystery as an Oxford don.' The book was a sensation, selling out its first print run in two days, receiving international press and eventually selling over a million copies. Treasure-hunters dug holes in public and private gardens around the country. 'Haresfield Beacon' in Gloucestershire suffered especially, and Williams agreed to pay for a sign specifically proclaiming the hare to not be buried there.

LEFT: *Bean Tombstone (1860s). The cryptic tombstone was erected by Canadian doctor Samuel Bean in Rushes Cemetery near Crosshill, Wellesley Township, Ontario, in memory of his first two wives, Henrietta and Susanna. Starting on the seventh character from the left in the seventh row down, and progressing in a jagged anticlockwise spiral pattern, the inscription reads: 'In memoriam Henrietta, 1st wife of S. Bean, M.D. who died 27th Sep. 1865, aged 23 years, 2 months and 17 days and Susanna his 2nd wife who died 27th April, 1867, aged 26 years, 10 months and 15 days, 2 better wives 1 man never had, they were gifts from God but are now in Heaven. May God help me, S.B., to meet them there.'*

71, 194, 38, 1701, 89, 76, 11, 83, 1629, 48, 94, 63, 132, 16, 111, 95, 84, 341,
975, 14, 40, 04, 27, 81, 139, 213, 03, 90, 1120, 8, 15, 3, 120, 2018, 40, 74,
758, 485, 604, 230, 436, 664, 582, 150, 251, 284, 308, 231, 124, 211, 486,
225, 401, 370, 11, 101, 305, 139, 189, 17, 33, 88, 208, 193, 145, 1, 94, 73,
416, 918, 263, 28, 500, 538, 356, 117, 136, 219, 27, 176, 130, 10, 460, 25,
485, 18, 436, 65, 84, 200, 283, 118, 320, 138, 36, 416, 280, 15, 71, 224, 961,
44, 16, 401, 39, 88, 61, 304, 12, 21, 24, 283, 134, 92, 63, 246, 486, 682, 7,
219, 184, 360, 780, 18, 64, 463, 474, 131, 160, 79, 73, 440, 95, 18, 64, 581,
34, 69, 128, 367, 460, 17, 81, 12, 103, 820, 62, 116, 97, 103, 862, 70, 60,
1317, 471, 540, 208, 121, 890, 346, 36, 150, 59, 568, 614, 13, 120, 63, 219,
812, 2160, 1780, 99, 35, 18, 21, 136, 872, 15, 28, 170, 88, 4, 30, 44, 112, 18,
147, 436, 195, 320, 37, 122, 113, 6, 140, 8, 120, 305, 42, 58, 461, 44, 106,
301, 13, 408, 680, 93, 86, 116, 530, 82, 568, 9, 102, 38, 416, 89, 71, 216,
728, 965, 818, 2, 38, 121, 195, 14, 326, 148, 234, 18, 55, 131, 234, 361, 824,
5, 81, 623, 48, 961, 19, 26, 33, 10, 1101, 365, 92, 88, 181, 275, 346, 201,
206, 86, 36, 219, 324, 829, 840, 64, 326, 19, 48, 122, 85, 216, 284, 919, 861,
326, 985, 233, 64, 68, 232, 431, 960, 50, 29, 81, 216, 321, 603, 14, 612, 81,
360, 36, 51, 62, 194, 78, 60, 200, 314, 676, 112, 4, 28, 18, 61, 136, 247, 819,
921, 1060, 464, 895, 10, 6, 66, 119, 38, 41, 49, 602, 423, 962, 302, 294, 875,
78, 14, 23, 111, 109, 62, 31, 501, 823, 216, 280, 34, 24, 150, 1000, 162, 286,
19, 21, 17, 340, 19, 242, 31, 86, 52, 88, 16, 80, 121, 67, 95, 122, 216, 548, 96,
11, 201, 77, 364, 218, 65, 667, 890, 236, 154, 211, 10, 98, 34, 119, 56, 216,
119, 71, 218, 1164, 1496, 1817, 51, 39, 210, 36, 3, 19, 540, 232, 22, 141, 617,
84, 290, 80, 46, 207, 411, 150, 29, 38, 46, 172, 85, 194, 39, 261, 543, 897,
624, 18, 212, 416, 127, 931, 19, 4, 63, 96, 12, 101, 418, 16, 140, 230, 460,
538, 19, 27, 88, 612, 1431, 90, 716, 275, 74, 83, 11, 426, 89, 72, 84, 1300,
1706, 814, 221, 132, 40, 102, 34, 868, 975, 1101, 84, 16, 79, 23, 16, 81, 122,
324, 403, 912, 227, 936, 447, 55, 86, 34, 43, 212, 107, 96, 314, 264, 1065,
323, 428, 601, 203, 124, 95, 216, 814, 2906, 654, 820, 2, 301, 112, 176,
213, 71, 87, 96, 202, 35, 10, 2, 41, 17, 84, 221, 736, 820, 214, 11, 60, 760

ABOVE AND RIGHT: *Thomas J. Beale's three ciphers, supposedly hiding the location to an immense treasure buried somewhere in Bedford County, Virginia, USA. The second was deciphered using the United States Declaration of Independence as a key.*

115, 73, 24, 807, 37, 52, 49, 17, 31, 62, 647, 22, 7, 15, 140, 47, 29, 107, 79,
84, 56, 239, 10, 26, 811, 5, 196, 308, 85, 52, 160, 136, 59, 211, 36, 9, 46,
316, 554, 122, 106, 95, 53, 58, 2, 42, 7, 35, 122, 53, 31, 82, 77, 250, 196, 56,
96, 118, 71, 140, 287, 28, 353, 37, 1005, 65, 147, 807, 24, 3, 8, 12, 47, 43,
59, 807, 45, 316, 101, 41, 78, 154, 1005, 122, 138, 191, 16, 77, 49, 102, 57,
72, 34, 73, 85, 35, 371, 59, 196, 81, 92, 191, 106, 273, 60, 394, 620, 270,
220, 106, 388, 287, 63, 3, 6, 191, 122, 43, 234, 400, 106, 290, 314, 47, 48,
81, 96, 26, 115, 92, 158, 191, 110, 77, 85, 197, 46, 10, 113, 140, 353, 48,
120, 106, 2, 607, 61, 420, 811, 29, 125, 14, 20, 37, 105, 28, 248, 16, 159,
7, 35, 19, 301, 125, 110, 486, 287, 98, 117, 511, 62, 51, 220, 37, 113, 140,
807, 138, 540, 8, 44, 287, 388, 117, 18, 79, 344, 34, 20, 59, 511, 548, 107,
603, 220, 7, 66, 154, 41, 20, 50, 6, 575, 122, 154, 248, 110, 61, 52, 33, 30,
5, 38, 8, 14, 84, 57, 540, 217, 115, 71, 29, 84, 63, 43, 131, 29, 138, 47, 73,
239, 540, 52, 53, 79, 118, 51, 44, 63, 196, 12, 239, 112, 3, 49, 79, 353, 105,
56, 371, 557, 211, 505, 125, 360, 133, 143, 101, 15, 284, 540, 252, 14, 205,
140, 344, 26, 811, 138, 115, 48, 73, 34, 205, 316, 607, 63, 220, 7, 52, 150,
44, 52, 16, 40, 37, 158, 807, 37, 121, 12, 95, 10, 15, 35, 12, 131, 62, 115,
102, 807, 49, 53, 135, 138, 30, 31, 62, 67, 41, 85, 63, 10, 106, 807, 138, 8,
113, 20, 32, 33, 37, 353, 287, 140, 47, 85, 50, 37, 49, 47, 64, 6, 7, 71, 33, 4,
43, 47, 63, 1, 27, 600, 208, 230, 15, 191, 246, 85, 94, 511, 2, 270, 20, 39, 7,
33, 44, 22, 40, 7, 10, 3, 811, 106, 44, 486, 230, 353, 211, 200, 31, 10, 38,
140, 297, 61, 603, 320, 302, 666, 287, 2, 44, 33, 32, 511, 548, 10, 6, 250,
557, 246, 53, 37, 52, 83, 47, 320, 38, 33, 807, 7, 44, 30, 31, 250, 10, 15, 35,
106, 160, 113, 31, 102, 406, 230, 540, 320, 29, 66, 33, 101, 807, 138, 301,
316, 353, 320, 220, 37, 52, 28, 540, 320, 33, 8, 48, 107, 50, 811, 7, 2, 113,
73, 16, 125, 11, 110, 67, 102, 807, 33, 59, 81, 158, 38, 43, 581, 138, 19, 85,
400, 38, 43, 77, 14, 27, 8, 47, 138, 63, 140, 44, 35, 22, 177, 106, 250, 314,
217, 2, 10, 7, 1005, 4, 20, 25, 44, 48, 7, 26, 46, 110, 230, 807, 191, 34, 112,
147, 44, 110, 121, 125, 96, 41, 51, 50, 140, 56, 47, 152, 540, 63, 807, 28, 42,
250, 138, 582, 98, 643, 32, 107, 140, 112, 26, 85, 138, 145, 53, 20, 125, 371,
38, 36, 10, 52, 118, 136, 102, 420, 150, 112, 71, 14, 20, 7, 24, 18, 12, 807,
37, 67, 110, 62, 33, 21, 95, 220, 511, 102, 811, 30, 83, 84, 305, 620, 15, 2,
10, 8, 220, 106, 353, 105, 106, 60, 275, 72, 8, 50, 205, 185, 112, 125, 540,
65, 106, 807, 138, 96, 110, 16, 73, 33, 807, 150, 409, 400, 50, 154, 285, 96,
106, 316, 270, 205, 101, 811, 400, 8, 44, 37, 52, 40, 241, 34, 205, 38, 16, 46,
47, 85, 24, 44, 15, 64, 73, 138, 807, 85, 78, 110, 33, 420, 505, 53, 37, 38, 22,
31, 10, 110, 106, 101, 140, 15, 38, 3, 5, 44, 7, 98, 287, 135, 150, 96, 33, 84,
125, 807, 191, 96, 511, 118, 40, 370, 643, 466, 106, 41, 107, 603, 220, 275,
30, 150, 105, 49, 53, 287, 250, 208, 134, 7, 53, 12, 47, 85, 63, 138, 110, 21,
112, 140, 485, 486, 505, 14, 73, 84, 575, 1005, 150, 200, 16, 42, 5, 4, 25,
42, 8, 16, 811, 125, 160, 32, 205, 603, 807, 81, 96, 405, 41, 600, 136, 14, 20,
28, 26, 353, 302, 246, 8, 131, 160, 140, 84, 440, 42, 16, 811, 40, 67, 101,
102, 194, 138, 205, 51, 63, 241, 540, 122, 8, 10, 63, 140, 47, 48, 140, 288

For three years, Williams and Gascoigne were the only two people to know the location of the hare, until in 1982 Williams was sent an answer that he immediately recognized as being correct. To find the solution, one had to draw a line from the eye or paw of animals in the paintings to a letter in the border. This eventually revealed the phrase: closebyampthill ('close by Ampthill'). Curiously, the winner, a Ken Thomas, didn't seem to have solved the puzzle in that way but had stumbled across the answer out of dumb luck, and claimed the prize.

Then came a twist to the story. On 11 December 1988, the *Sunday Times* ran a story accusing the winner of having conducted his own masquerade. Ken Thomas was revealed to be the pseudonym of Dugald Thompson, whose business partner was the boyfriend of Veronica Robertson, a former live-in girlfriend

317, 8, 92, 73, 112, 89, 67, 318, 28, 96, 107, 41, 631, 78, 146, 397, 118, 98,
114, 246, 348, 116, 74, 88, 12, 65, 32, 14, 81, 19, 76, 121, 216, 85, 33, 66,
15, 108, 68, 77, 43, 24, 122, 96, 117, 36, 211, 301, 15, 44, 11, 46, 89, 18,
136, 68, 317, 28, 90, 82, 304, 71, 43, 221, 198, 176, 310, 319, 81, 99, 264,
380, 56, 37, 319, 2, 44, 53, 28, 44, 75, 98, 102, 37, 85, 107, 117, 64, 88, 136,
48, 151, 99, 175, 89, 315, 326, 78, 96, 214, 218, 311, 43, 89, 51, 90, 75,
128, 96, 33, 28, 103, 84, 65, 26, 41, 246, 84, 270, 98, 116, 32, 59, 74, 66,
69, 240, 15, 8, 121, 20, 77, 89, 31, 11, 106, 81, 191, 224, 328, 18, 75, 52,
82, 117, 201, 39, 23, 217, 27, 21, 84, 35, 54, 109, 128, 49, 77, 88, 1, 81, 217,
64, 55, 83, 116, 251, 269, 311, 96, 54, 32, 120, 18, 132, 102, 219, 211, 84,
150, 219, 275, 312, 64, 10, 106, 87, 75, 47, 21, 29, 37, 81, 44, 18, 126, 115,
132, 160, 181, 203, 76, 81, 299, 314, 337, 351, 96, 11, 28, 97, 318, 238, 106,
24, 93, 3, 19, 17, 26, 60, 73, 88, 14, 126, 138, 234, 286, 297, 321, 365, 264,
19, 22, 84, 56, 107, 98, 123, 111, 214, 136, 7, 33, 45, 40, 13, 28, 46, 42, 107,
196, 227, 344, 198, 203, 247, 116, 19, 8, 212, 230, 31, 6, 328, 65, 48, 52, 59,
41, 122, 33, 117, 11, 18, 25, 71, 36, 45, 83, 76, 89, 92, 31, 65, 70, 83, 96,
27, 33, 44, 50, 61, 24, 112, 136, 149, 176, 180, 194, 143, 171, 205, 296, 87,
12, 44, 51, 89, 98, 34, 41, 208, 173, 66, 9, 35, 16, 95, 8, 113, 175, 90, 56,
203, 19, 177, 183, 206, 157, 200, 218, 260, 291, 305, 618, 951, 320, 18, 124,
78, 65, 19, 32, 124, 48, 53, 57, 84, 96, 207, 244, 66, 82, 119, 71, 11, 86, 77,
213, 54, 82, 316, 245, 303, 86, 97, 106, 212, 18, 37, 15, 81, 89, 16, 7, 81, 39,
96, 14, 43, 216, 118, 29, 55, 109, 136, 172, 213, 64, 8, 227, 304, 611, 221,
364, 819, 375, 128, 296, 1, 18, 53, 76, 10, 15, 23, 19, 71, 84, 120, 134, 66,
73, 89, 96, 230, 48, 77, 26, 101, 127, 936, 218, 439, 178, 171, 61, 226, 313,
215, 102, 18, 167, 262, 114, 218, 66, 59, 48, 27, 19, 13, 82, 48, 162, 119,
34, 127, 139, 34, 128, 129, 74, 63, 120, 11, 54, 61, 73, 92, 180, 66, 75, 101,
124, 265, 89, 96, 126, 274, 896, 917, 434, 461, 235, 890, 312, 413, 328, 381,
96, 105, 217, 66, 118, 22, 77, 64, 42, 12, 7, 55, 24, 83, 67, 97, 109, 121, 135,
181, 203, 219, 228, 256, 21, 34, 77, 319, 374, 382, 675, 684, 717, 864, 203,
4, 18, 92, 16, 63, 82, 22, 46, 55, 69, 74, 112, 134, 186, 175, 119, 213, 416,
312, 343, 264, 119, 186, 218, 343, 417, 845, 951, 124, 209, 49, 617, 856, 924,
936, 72, 19, 28, 11, 35, 42, 40, 66, 85, 82, 115, 119, 236, 244,
186, 172, 112, 85, 6, 56, 38, 44, 85, 72, 32, 47, 63, 96, 124, 217, 314, 319,
221, 644, 817, 821, 934, 922, 416, 975, 10, 22, 18, 46, 137, 181, 101, 39, 86,
103, 116, 138, 164, 212, 218, 296, 815, 380, 412, 460, 495, 675, 820, 952

Kit Williams (left) with his cryptic treasure-hunt book Masquerade *in 1980.*

of Kit Williams, who had gleaned from the artist the rough location. Despite this revelation, the hare was auctioned by Ken Thomas/Dugald Thompson at Sotheby's for £31,900 (£84,830 today) to a collector in the Middle East.

Despite the bombardment of public attention turning Kit Williams into a virtual recluse, this hasn't dissuaded others from deploying cryptic clues to buried treasure for the same promotional reasons, sometimes with lethal results. In 2010, an art dealer and former United States Air Force pilot named Forrest Fenn published *The Thrill of the Chase: A Memoir*, which he claims holds clues to a treasure chest worth around $2 million. The valuables include a bracelet embedded with 200 rubies and sapphires, gold jaguar claws, a 200-year-old necklace made of quartz crystal and antique Chinese jade carvings that he claimed would make you 'just want to cry when you see them'. Hidden somewhere 'in

the mountains somewhere north of Santa Fe', the prize sparked off a treasure hunt throughout the American Rocky Mountains, in the states of New Mexico, Colorado, Wyoming and Montana. Four people, including a Colorado pastor, have died searching for Fenn's treasure, and more have been injured. Despite urging from authorities, the millionaire dealer has refused to call off the hunt. 'Of course it's very tragic,' he told reporters. 'But every time you get in a car you put yourself at risk.' He emphasizes that the treasure trove is not in a dangerous or hard-to-reach place, and takes pride in the fact that his hunt has got people exploring the outdoors. 'We sit on our couch and watch the TV, or play with our little machines. We're too comfortable because we know what to expect.'

Examples of the art of 'fore-edge painting'. These secret decorations were applied to the edges of a book's pages. Invisible when the book is closed, when the pages are slightly fanned out, the picture is revealed. The technique was practised in the second half of the seventeenth century in London and Edinburgh, and popularized in the eighteenth century.

A selection of cryptic postcards kindly provided for this book by the German hacker and IT security expert Tobias Schrödel, from his lifetime's collection of 235 such items. Cryptic postcards were a fashion of young lovers in the nineteenth and early twentieth centuries wanting to conduct their romance in secret, usually by using basic substitution cyphers. The writings range from the innocent to the intimate: 'I feel the heat coming up ...' begins the dirty-talking author of card number 3 (bottom-left), sent in 1881.

LITERARY HOAXES

There is something thrilling about holding in your hand a book that was designed to deceive. Whether it was written out of satire, revenge or self-promotion and profit (the most common motives, as we'll see), a literary hoax is a lie with an extraordinary quality: a physical form. You can touch it, smell it, riffle through its perfidious pages and savour every carefully crafted misleading detail with the satisfaction of knowing its inauthenticity. You are in on the joke with the author, winking back at them.

The literary hoax is very far from being a modern invention. One of the great examples from antiquity is that of the Stoic philosopher Dionysius the Renegade (*c*.330 BC–*c*.250 BC), or as some referred to him, 'the Spark'. As a joke on his former teacher, Heraclides Ponticus, a corpulent fellow who had the nickname Pompicus among Athenians, Dionysius wrote a fake Sophocles tragedy titled *Parthenopaeus*. When Heraclides fell for the hoax and referenced passages of the play in his own writing about Sophocles, Dionysius took delight in confessing what he had done.

Heraclides refused to believe him, so Dionysius pointed out an acrostic he had hidden in the text: 'Pancalus', the name of a close friend. Heraclides remained unconvinced, claiming coincidence. So Dionysius showed him other snares he'd laid, including the lines: 'An aged monkey is not easily caught; he's caught indeed, but only after a time'; and the rather more conclusive: 'Heraclides knows nothing of letters and has no shame.'

Over 2000 years later and the same trick is still employed by writers with grudges to settle. In 2005, the literary critic A. N. Wilson published an acclaimed biography of John Betjeman, which triumphantly featured a previously unpublished love letter written by the poet that Wilson had been sent by a woman named Eve de Harben. After Wilson's *Betjeman* was published, the true provenance of the letter came to light.

RIGHT: *The cover of* Nat Tate: An American Artist 1928–1960*, a hoax biography of a fictional artist, written by William Boyd to fool the art world. The book was launched at a party in 1998 organized by his accomplice David Bowie.*

ABOVE: *Grey Owl feeding Jelly Roll, his pet beaver. The renowned Native American conservationist wrote several books about his life in the Canadian wilderness. After his death it was discovered his real name was Archibald Stansfeld Belaney (1888–1938), a white Englishman who had run away at the age of sixteen in search of adventure in Canada.*

Years before, Wilson had written a scathing review of Bevis Hillier's own 1988 biography of John Betjeman. In revenge, Hillier had concocted the letter and sent it on to Wilson. The name Eve de Harben is an anagram for 'Ever been had?', and the first letter of each line spells out 'A. N. Wilson is a shit'.

Three centuries after Dionysius, there is the curious story of Alexander of Abonoteichos (AD c.105–c.170), a Greek mystic who used hoax literature and a hand puppet to found his own prophetic snake cult. It's the Syrian writer Lucian (AD c.125 – after 180) who passes down the story of how Alexander created and buried in the temple of Asclepius a set of fake tablets that prophesied the appearance of the healing god in Alexander's hometown, Abonoteichos. When the 'relics' were discovered, every mystic and follower travelled to the town to build a new temple to the god. Then Alexander arrived. Dressed in prophet's robes, he pointed to a snake on the ground (a tame one that he had brought with him), and announced that Asclepius had returned in serpent form and wished to be known as Glycon. Alexander's snake cult grew swiftly in popularity, mainly because he

secretly read his followers' sealed messages to Glycon before making uncannily accurate predictions for their lives; and because he fearlessly commanded a live snake in his bare hand – sort of. According to Lucian, his courage was entirely sourced from the fact that the snake was a hand-puppet made from linen that 'would open and close its mouth by means of horsehairs; and a forked black tongue … also controlled by horsehairs, would dart out'. From archaeological evidence, it appears Alexander's Glycon snake cult lasted for over 100 years after his death in AD 170.

In such successful imposture Alexander had a spiritual descendant in the mysterious George Psalmanazar, author of the wonderful and utterly fabricated book *An Historical and Geographical Description of Formosa* (1704). Though full of 'autobiographical' detail, we still have no idea as to the true identity of the

blond-haired, blue-eyed pale-skinned man who appeared in London at the beginning of the eighteenth century claiming to be the first Formosan (Taiwanese) to have set foot on the European continent. The spurious tales of his life and travels became a publishing sensation and quickly made him a celebrity in England, thanks to endless salacious details (and crucially, illustrations) of human sacrifice, cannibalism, polygamy, infanticide and other gruesome tales of daily Formosan life. In Psalmanazar's Formosa, people went about their business in the nude, save for a gold or silver plate covering their genitals. Polygamy was standard, although in the event of infidelity, the husband reserved the right to eat his cheating wife – a break from the usual daily diet of serpent-meat. Murderers were hung upside down and shot full of arrows, while an annual sacrifice was made of the hearts of 18,000 young boys, roasted on a grill, their bodies eaten by the Formosan priests.

Psalmanazar toured with his lectures and delighted dinner guests by guzzling his meat raw at table. He was a man of brilliant wit, dancing circles around sceptics. His pale skin? Why, that was because Formosans lived underground without light. Surely the overhead Sun shines directly down the chimneys of his country, pointed out Edmund Halley during a grilling at the Royal Society, for it lies in the tropics. An excellent point, agreed the fake Formosan, were it not for the fact that chimneys there are corkscrew-shaped – the sunlight never makes it to the bottom.

Top Left: *A late second-century AD statue of Glycon, the ancient snake deity that was actually a hand puppet. The marble statue was discovered during excavation beneath the former Pallas railway station in Constanța, Romania. The Romanians celebrated the find by depicting the Glycon on a banknote of 10,000 lei in 1994. (See image below the statue.)*

The book is wholly fictitious, and borrows liberally from contemporary accounts of travels to Aztec and Incan sites in the New World, as well as Bernhardus Varenius's *Descriptio regni Japoniae et Siam* (1649). But of course it was a runaway bestseller. In the following year came an expanded edition, in which the author counters criticisms levelled by sceptics. It was only when Psalmanazar's genuine autobiography *Memoirs of ****, Commonly Known by the Name of George Psalmanazar* was published posthumously in 1764 that the full extent of his masquerade was realized. Dr Johnson, a close friend, was once asked if he had ever confronted him over the deception. 'I should as soon have thought,' said Johnson, 'of contradicting a bishop.'[1]

While Psalmanazar toured Britain promoting his fake *Description ...*, we find Jonathan Swift (whose infamous child-eating satire *A Modest Proposal* was reportedly inspired by the cannibalistic stories of the fake Formosan) revelling in a literary spat with a London astrologer-quack named John Partridge. The *Dictionary of National Biography* describes Partridge's almanac of predictions, *Merlinus Liberatus*, as carrying 'the phraseology of equivocation ... to a pitch of rare perfection'; but less ambiguous is the heavy slant Partridge gave his writings to serve the interests of the Whig party, and it was this that aggravated Swift into action.

In 1708, an almanac to rival that of Partridge appeared on the market, written by an 'Isaac Bickerstaff' and titled *Predictions for the Year 1708* – today a highly sought-after collector's item. Among the vague divinations was a forecast that specifically predicted the

'George Psalmanazar' (1679–1763), the fake Formosan, whose real identity was never discovered.

impending death of the charlatan Partridge: 'I have consulted the star of his nativity by my own rule,' writes Bickerstaff/Swift, 'and find he will infallibly die upon 29 March next, about 11 at night, of raging fever.' Swift then published a second pamphlet under the Bickerstaff pseudonym, *The Accomplishment of the first of Mr Bickerstaff's Predictions. Being an account of the Death of Mr Partridge,* which featured an interview with a grovelling Partridge on his deathbed, admitting with his final words that he was a fraud, before perishing.[2]

---

1 For more of these kinds of geographical inventions see *The Phantom Atlas* (Simon & Schuster, 2016).

2 Swift wrote under several pseudonyms, including Countess of Fizzlerumpf, Andrew Tripe and of course Lemuel Gulliver; but in sheer quantity of aliases he is beaten by Daniel Defoe (born Daniel Foe), whose 200 pen-names include Betty Blueskin, Boatswain Trinkolo, Count Kidney Face and Sir Fopling Tittle-Tattle.

Two illustrations from Psalmanazar's Description … : the Formosan idol of the Devil (Above) and the 'Formosan' alphabet that he invented for the book (Opposite).

The Formosan Alphabet

Name	Power		
Am̃	A	a	ăo
Mem̃	M	m̃	m
Nen̄	N	ñ	n
Taph	T	th	t
Lam̃do	L	ll	l
Sam̃do	S	ch	s
Vomera	V	w	u
Bagdo	B	b	b
Hamno	H	kh	h
Pedlo	P	pp	p
Kaphi	K	k	ϰ
Om̃da	O	o	ω
Ilda	I	y	i
Xatara	X	xh	x
Dam	D	th	d
Zamphi	Z	tſ	z
Epſi	E	ε	η
Fandem̃	F	ph	f
Raw	R	rh	r
Gomera	G	g	j

Figure — Name

T. Slater sc.

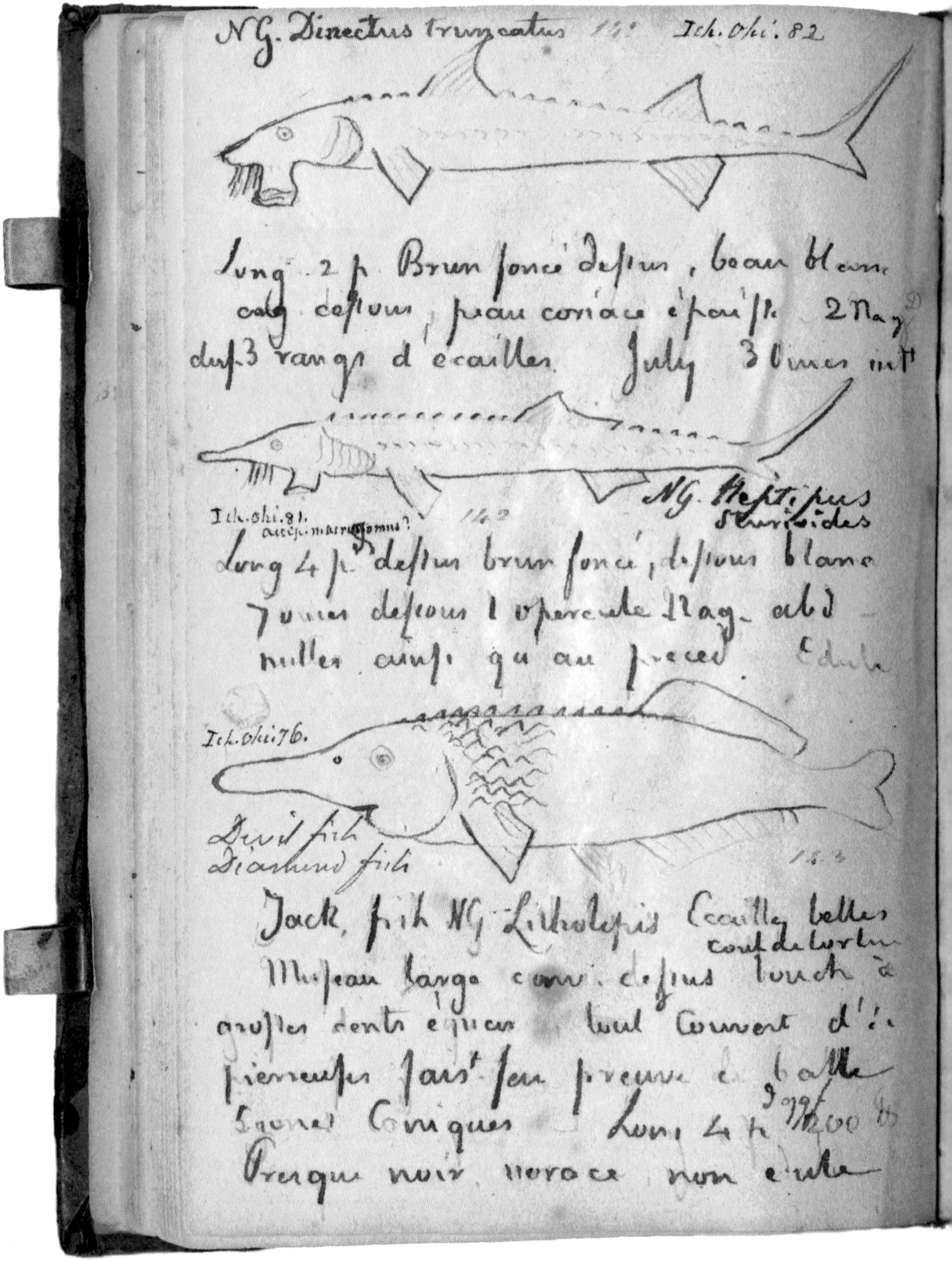

N.G. Dinectrus truncatus 141. Ich. Ohi. 82

Long. 2 p. Brun foncé dessus, beau blanc
cale dessous, peau coriace épaisse. 2 Nag
dur 3 rangs d'écailles. July 3 Oines int

Ich. Ohi. 81. 142 N.G. Heptopus
accip. macrostomus? Sturioides

Long 4 p. dessus brun foncé, dessous blanc
7 oines dessous l'opercule Nag. abd
nulles ainsi qu'au preced. Edule

Ich. Ohi. 76.

Devil fish
Diamond fish 143

Jack, fish N.G. Litholepis Ecailles belles
cou de tortue
Museau large conv. dessus touch à
grosses dents équar tout couvert d'..
pierreuses fait feu preuve à balle
Ecaille Coniques Long 4 p. 1200 lb
Presque noir vorace non edule

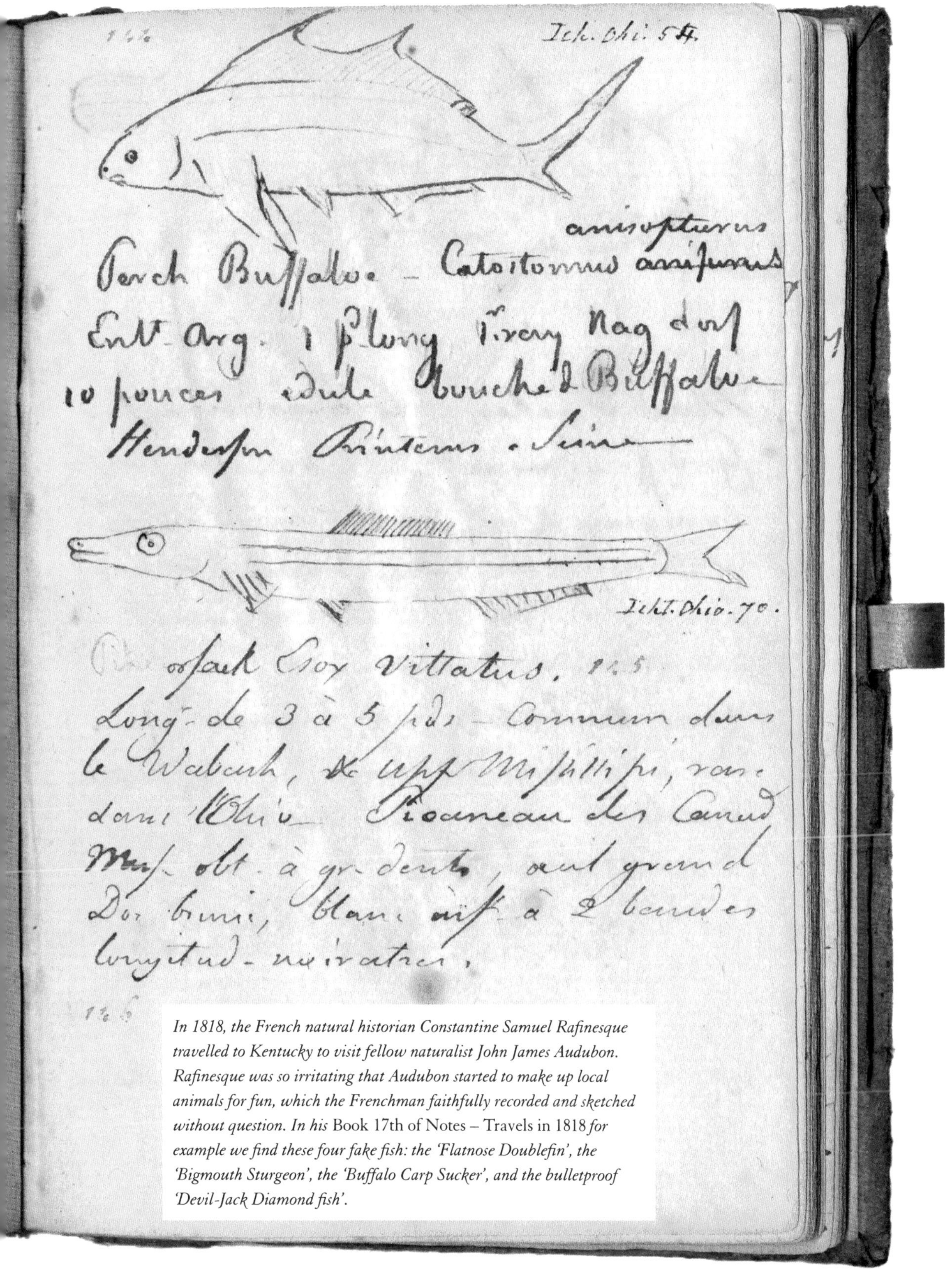

In 1818, the French natural historian Constantine Samuel Rafinesque travelled to Kentucky to visit fellow naturalist John James Audubon. Rafinesque was so irritating that Audubon started to make up local animals for fun, which the Frenchman faithfully recorded and sketched without question. In his Book 17th of Notes – Travels in 1818 *for example we find these four fake fish: the 'Flatnose Doublefin', the 'Bigmouth Sturgeon', the 'Buffalo Carp Sucker', and the bulletproof 'Devil-Jack Diamond fish'.*

The books fooled everyone. Mrs Partridge was offered condolences in the street, and a priest called on her to offer help with the funeral arrangements. The Company of Stationers removed Partridge's name from their register of living authors. (Meanwhile, a rumour circulated that the Spanish Inquisition had ordered the writings of Bickerstaff to be burned on suspicion of witchcraft, due to their uncanny accuracy.) When Partridge learned that work had begun on his gravestone, he frantically issued a pamphlet denying Bickerstaff's claim, with personal anecdotes provided as proof of life. He was dismayed to find this was instantly countered by Swift with *A Vindication of Isaac Bickerstaff, Esq.*, which denounced the new Partridge pamphlet as the work of an impostor. Such was the success of Swift's hoaxing that it was six years before Partridge was able to resume publishing with credibility.

The perfect bibliohoax could be defined, I think, as one in which a small and simple design is inversely proportional to the volume of mayhem it triggers in the world, like dropping a pebble into a pond and watching the ripples grow to tsunamis. In this sense, the Fortsas Affair sets the gold standard. It is hard to imagine there having ever been a literary event as bizarre as that which took place on 10 August 1840, when a swarm of bibliophiles and rare book dealers from all over Europe descended on the small Belgian town of Binche, to attend the auction of the magnificent private library of the recently deceased Jean Nepomucene-Auguste Pichauld, Comte de Fortsas. Each bidder gripped one of the 132 issued copies of the itemized *Catalogue of a Very Rich but Very Select Collection of Books From the Library of M. Comte J.N.-A de Fortsas.* The fervour was due to the fact that the fifty-two books described in the catalogue were all previously

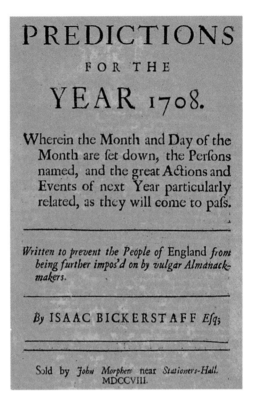

The title page of Jonathan Swift's death-hoaxing of John Partridge.

unknown, and immensely valuable. 'The Comte de Fortsas admitted upon his shelves only works unknown to all bibliographers and cataloguers,' reads the catalogue's introduction. 'He pitilessly expelled from his shelves books for which he had paid their weight in gold … as soon as he learned that a work, up to that time unknown, had been noticed in any catalogue.'

The collection included two unknown works of the seventeenth-century Dutch printer Elzevir; incunabula of Arend de Keyser's prestigious Audenarde press; and tantalisingly indecent works like *Doubtful and Questionable Issues in the Genealogies of the Principal Families of the Netherlands*; and the curious *The Rooms of Pleasure or the Discomforture of the Great King in the Low Country* (1686). The latter, notes the

RIGHT: *A painting from 1810 of the blind third-century Scottish poet Ossian, described as 'the greatest Poet that has ever existed', by the American founding father Thomas Jefferson, and admired by Napoleon, Diderot and Voltaire. It's now believed that Ossian and his epic poems were invented in the eighteenth century by the Scottish poet James Macpherson.*

cataloguer, is 'a libel of disgusting humour' that relates intimate medical details of Louis XIV's troublesome bottom, and features an illustration that 'represents the royal backside under the form of a fan surrounded with rays, with the famous royal motto: *Nec pluribus impar* [not unequal to many]'. Among the interested parties hurtling in carriages towards the small town was the director of the Belgian Royal Library, Baron de Reiffenberg, who sent ahead a demand to reserve several of the lots; and a proxy of the Princess de Ligne, who was under strict instruction to win a book that the Princess feared might contain embarrassing bedroom exploits of her grandfather, the Grand Monarch.

But as the buyers arrived, there was immediate confusion, for no one could find the office of the town notary where the sale was to be held. There wasn't even a 'rue de l'Église', the street on which the office was supposedly located. Strangest of all, no one in Binche seemed to have heard of the count, his library or the auction. While the visitors tried to makes sense of this, word spread that the auction had been cancelled and the books acquired by the town library. This was even more perplexing, for Binche had no town library. When the buyers demanded an explanation, it emerged that the Count, the books and the auction were entirely fictitious. The catalogue was a hoax. The culprit remained unidentified for sixteen years, until the printer of the pamphlet finally gave up the name of Renier-Hubert-Ghislain Chalon, a retired military officer and bibliophile.

ABOVE: *The title page of the original hoax catalogue of the library of the Comte J. N.-A de Fortsas, 1840.*

Le public est informé que la belle bibliothèque de M.ʳ le Comte de FORTSAS ne sera
pas vendue aux enchères. Messieurs les Ama-
teurs l'apprendront sans doute à regret, mais
cette précieuse collection ne sera pas perdue
pour le pays : elle a été acquise par la ville
de Binche pour sa bibliothèque publique.

MONS. TYPOGRAPHIE D'EM. HOYOIS.

A notice circulated the day before the Fortsas sale,
announcing the cancellation of the event as the lots
had all been bought by the city of Binche for its
(non-existent) public library.

It was then that someone recalled seeing
Chalon mingling with the bewildered crowd
at the time of the auction, enjoying himself
immensely. The fourteen-page catalogue
of the Fortsas sale was reprinted numerous
times and has since become a prized
collector's item – in July 2018 a first edition
sold at Christies for just under £12,000.[3]

Perhaps it was the contemporary
fondness for hoax newspaper articles that
partly inspired Chalon to cause his chaos.
Though modern newspapers confine this
tradition to 1 April, bored journalists of the
nineteenth century in particular were fond

of filling column inches by simply inventing
the most colourful news story they could
imagine. In 1874, New York was the setting
for a newspaper-created confusion known
as the 'Wild Animal Hoax' or 'Central
Park Zoo Escape', a bizarre prank played
by the *New York Herald* on 9 November.
'AWFUL CALAMITY' cried the headline,
'The Wild Animals Broken Loose from
Central Park – TERRIBLE SCENES OF
MUTILATION – A Shocking Sabbath
Carnival of Death – SAVAGE BRUTES
AT LARGE – Awful Combats Between the
Beasts and the Citizens.' Eyewitnesses told
of animals escaping Central Park Zoo and
leaving forty-nine people dead and over 200
seriously injured. Twelve of the beasts were
still missing and at large somewhere in the
city, though they reported that Governor Dix
had shot the Bengal tiger in the street himself.

In response to the article, William
Frederick Havemeyer, the mayor of New
York City, instructed the citizenry to stay
inside and lock their doors. There were
reports of armed mobs roaming Fifth Avenue
and Broadway on a hunt for the animals,
bursting into churches, offices and
department stores. Unaware of the joke, the
Herald's own war correspondent, Dr George
W. Hosmer, rushed into the paper's offices
brandishing two large service revolvers and
cried 'Well, here I am!'; while Major George
F. Williams, city editor of the rival *Times*
newspaper, went straight to police
headquarters to furiously complain about
them giving the scoop to the *Herald*. In an
interview with *Harper's Weekly* in 1893, a
former *Herald* editor, Thomas Connery,
admitted to dreaming up the hoax in an effort
to draw attention to the zoo's shoddy conditions,

---

3 Though every aspect about this story is delightful, I was amazed to discover that the Fortsas catalogue was first
translated and printed in English in the 1860s by my ancestor, the printer and bibliographer William Blades (1824–90).

The Great Zoo Hoax illustrated in Harper's Weekly *at the time.*

The cover of the hoax travel book Cruise of the Kawa *(1921).*

Image of the Cruise of the Kawa *author 'Walter E. Traprock' (George Shepard Chappell).*

intending the article to be 'a harmless little hoax, with just enough semblance of reality to give a salutary warning'.

The American writer George Shepard Chappell possessed similar concerns of shoddiness when he launched his own hoax against a literary genre popular in 1921 that he despised: the exotic travel journal. The hilarious screwball adventure *The Cruise of the Kawa: Wanderings in the South Seas* by 'Walter E. Traprock' is presented as a true account of a Pacific voyage of discovery, now held in fond regard by historians of exploration. The book is a completely fictitious tale of the crew of the good ship

Kawa's journey to the 'Filbert islands' written by Traprock, the ship's captain, who is described as having previously authored an alternative musical adaptation of *Les Misérables* titled *Jumping Jean*, as well as the seminal works *Curry-Dishes for Moderate Incomes*, and *Around Russia on Roller Skates*.

Upon arriving at the islands, Traprock immediately begins to document the crew's discoveries of the Filbertine people and their local wildlife. This includes the friendly Ooza snake and its diet of coconut milk; enormous crabs capable of pulling small vessels; and most remarkable of all the native Fatu-liva bird, 'with its unique gift of laying square eggs'. (Chappell provides a photograph of the square eggs (see overleaf), which are clearly dice.) The crew encounter natives with names like Baahaabaa (Durable Drinker), Abuluti (Big Wind Constantly Blowing) and Zambao-Zambino (Young Man Proud of His Waist-Line); and Traprock weds a Filbertine woman, though in the chapter 'Marital Memories' mentions an initial hurdle to their relationship:

> *I had been married over a week and I did not know my wife's name.*
>
> *'Kippiputuonaa,' she murmured musically.*
>
> *'Taro ititi aa moieha ephaa lihaha?' I questioned, which, freely translated, is: 'What?'*

The book sold well, and was taken by many to be genuine despite its tongue-in-cheek tone and farcical elements, which include photographs of the crew and native scenes that are clearly taken against fake backdrops of a cheap set. Walter Traprock was even invited to lecture on his voyages in Washington, DC, by the editorial board of the *National Geographic*.

'The Nest of the Fatu-liva bird', with 'eggs' that seem remarkably similar to dice.

To sit on the shelf beside the account of the *Kawa*, no collection of literary hoaxes would be complete without the slim volume self-published by the Author's Club of New York in 1917 in the interests of 'establishing a literary balance, an amity of the pen between the great peoples of America and Russia'. *Feodor Vladimir Larrovitch: An Appreciation of His Life and Works* celebrates the author lauded as the grandfather of Russian literature. To mark the publication, a party of more than 300 guests was held, the club's largest of the year, and 'an indication of the respect felt to be due the great Russian', claimed Richardson Wright, the organizer. The essays written for the biography by club members were read out – the most heartfelt being that by the eldest member of the club, Titus Munson Coan, MD, titled 'Talks with Larrovitch'.

'Yes, I knew him well,' begins Coan, 'and how vivid, after these fifty years, are my recollections! Not only of his words but of his voice, his smile, the flash of his eye, his gestures, as he spoke.' He goes on to recount fondly how the men would often cross paths in Paris in the late 1860s. Coan, it seems, didn't realize that the group had invented the Russian writer as a joke on the other members. 'He was quite old at the time,' explained Wright. 'His memory of Larrovitch visiting the American Legation in Paris was very touching.'

In 1943, Australia's most celebrated literary hoax followed in a similar vein. At the Victoria Barracks in Melbourne, land headquarters of the Australian army,

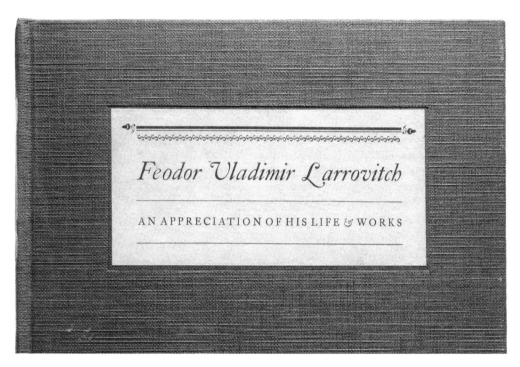

The pasted label of the autobiography of the fake artist
Feodor Vladimir Larrovitch (1917).

Lieutenant James McAuley and Corporal
Harold Stewart shared a love of poetry and
an alarm at 'the gradual decay of meaning
and craftsmanship in poetry', believing
modern avant-garde poetry to be 'insensible
of absurdity and incapable of ordinary
discrimination'. The soldiers decided to
invent a modern poet of their own: 'Ernest
Lalor Malley', a motor mechanic at Palmer's
Garage on Taverner's Hill in Sydney, and
after a single afternoon's work the men
produced a collection of poems, snatching
phrases from whatever works were to hand,
including *Ripman's Rhyming Dictionary*
and an American report on the draining of
mosquito-infested swamps.

When they were satisfied with their
terrible verse they submitted two of the
poems to the Australian literary journal
Angry Penguins, a magazine at the forefront
of the modernist artistic movement. The

journal's founder and editor, Max Harris, was
so captivated that he dedicated the autumn
1944 issue of *Angry Penguins* to Malley,
reprinting his collection of sixteen poems in
full. Expecting a rapturous reception, Harris
was ridiculed and accused of writing the
poems himself. In a panic he hired a private
detective to find Ern Malley, but was told the
poet appeared not to exist. Sydney's *Sunday
Sun* eventually broke the story, and McAuley
and Stewart triumphantly owned up. But the
story took off in a new trajectory when Harris
was charged with obscenity for publishing the
poetry, despite the fact that the state couldn't
pinpoint exactly *how* the poems were obscene.
Detective Vogelsang, for the prosecution,
insisted that the poem *Night Piece* qualified
because: 'Apparently someone is shining a
torch in the dark, visiting through the park
gates. To my mind they were going there for
some disapproved motive ... I have found
that people who go into parks at night go
there for immoral purposes.' In *Perspective
Lovesong* he also found the word 'incestuous'

to be indecent but admitted: 'I don't know what "incestuous" means.' He also objected to 'any description of the female parts in poetry'.

Harris passionately defended the Malley poems, but the magistrate told him he had 'far too great a fondness for sexual references' and he was fined five pounds in lieu of six weeks in prison. Here is *Night Piece*, the poem that so disturbed Detective Vogelsang:

> The swung torch scatters seeds
> In the umbelliferous dark
> And a frog makes guttural comment
> On the naked and trespassing
> Nymph of the lake.
> The symbols were evident,
> Though on park-gates
> The iron birds looked disapproval
> With rusty invidious beaks.
> Among the water-lilies
> A splash — white foam in the dark!
> And you lay sobbing then
> Upon my trembling intuitive arm.

The American journalist Mike McGrady found a considerably larger readership for his hoax that was inspired in 1966 by the success of trashy sex novels like Jacqueline Susann's *The Valley of the Dolls* and Harold Robbin's *The Adventurers*. He recruited twenty-four journalists, including Pulitzer prize-winner Gene Goltz, to collaborate on a deliberately terrible, all-out sex romp to be titled *Naked Came the Stranger*. It would tell the story of a radio talk show host named Gillian Blake, who in revenge against a cheating husband attempts to sleep with every married man in Great Neck, New York. 'There will be unremitting emphasis on sex,' McGrady told his writing team. 'Fine writing will be expurgated … true excellence in writing will be blue-pencilled into oblivion.' It took them two weeks to write it. Dedicated to 'Daddy', the following is a typical passage:

The cover of the Ern Malley issue of Angry Penguins.

'In the darkened room, now thirstier than ever, Gillian was suddenly aware of the presence beside her of Mario Vella. He had allowed his left elbow to brush gently against her. In any other surrounding, in any other circumstances, Gillian Blake would have gracefully withdrawn. She didn't. She held her ground and his elbow became more persistent.'

A publisher was soon found in Lyle Stuart, who recognized it as a hoax but saw potential for success regardless. He allocated an enormous promotional budget of $50,000 and added a risqué dust jacket illustrated with a nude woman. The publishing deal alone was enough to make McGrady's point, but the writers were curious to see the public's reaction. The results were astonishing.

In the first month, 20,000 copies of *Naked Came the Stranger* were sold. Critically it received mixed reviews, but the team were delighted to see a rival paper, the *Long Island Express*, gush: 'This scorching novel makes *Portnoy's Complaint* and *Valley of the Dolls* read like *Rebecca of Sunnybrook Farm*.' When the hoax was revealed, public appetite went into overdrive and 9000 copies were bought in the hour after the news broke. In total, around 100,000 copies of the book were sold, with the publishing company Dell buying the rights for a six-figure sum. To McGrady's horror, a separate publisher offered him $500,000 for a sequel, which he turned down. The book was translated into a dozen languages, and McGrady received over twenty different offers for the film rights. He was mortified by the book's success. 'It was all too easy,' he said. 'It went all too smoothly. America, you sit there, you plump beauty, still buying neckties from sidewalk sharpies, still guessing which walnut shell contains the pea … America, I sometimes worry about you.'

To the novice hoaxer it might seem logical that when writing a fake autobiography selecting a *deceased* subject is key to minimizing the risk of getting caught. Convincing a publisher to pay hundreds of thousands of dollars for a fake autobiography of someone still alive takes a level of *chutzpah* found in only a few people, one of them being Clifford Irving, who convinced the publisher McGraw-Hill that he had the permission of the reclusive billionaire Howard Hughes to ghostwrite his autobiography. Irving forged documents with Hughes's signature (copied from a magazine article) and claimed to have had a series of intimate interviews with his subject.

McGraw-Hill offered $100,000 – Irving talked them up to $650,000 for himself, and $100,000 'for Hughes'. The deal was made, and Irving's Swiss wife Edith deposited

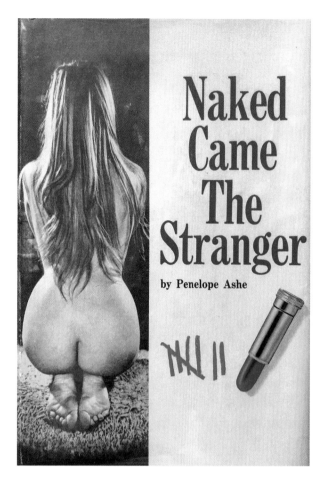

The provocative cover of the hoax book Naked Came the Stranger *(1969).*

the cheques made out to 'H. R. Hughes' in a Zurich bank account she had opened under the name of 'Helga R. Hughes'. By the end of 1971, Irving had delivered the manuscript, complete with notes in 'Hughes's' handwriting, that he'd somehow had authenticated by an expert.

Those who knew Hughes, meanwhile, were assuring McGraw-Hill that *The Autobiography of Howard Hughes*, though convincing, couldn't possibly be genuine, and so Irving was asked to take a polygraph test. He actually managed to pass it, although 'inconsistencies' were noted in his answers. (The title of Irving's earlier book – *Fake!* –

Howard Hughes standing in front of his new Boeing Army Pursuit Plane, c.1940.

must have, in retrospect, felt like a red flag.) The whole con rested on Irving's calculation that Hughes was too reclusive to learn of the book, or too insane or embarrassed to object to it. Unfortunately, Hughes called his bluff, and on 7 January 1972 held a telephoned news conference to state that he had never met nor given any form of authorization to Clifford Irving. Irving initially had the gall to claim that the voice on the telephone was a Hughes impostor, but he was done. Hughes

sued the publisher, the Swiss bank gave up Edith Irving, the money was returned and the couple were jailed for fraud.

The German petty criminal Konrad Kujau had never intended to forge so many volumes of Hitler's diaries – it was just that people kept buying them. In the early 1980s, Gerd Heidemann, a reporter for the German magazine *Stern*, was amazed to come across a volume of the dictator's journal allegedly written during the years 1932–45, at the home of a Nazi memorabilia collector, who had bought it from a Stuttgart antiques dealer. The story was that at the end of World War II, a plane carrying sensitive documents dispatched from Hitler's bunker had crashed in East Germany (this part was true, and was called 'Operation Seraglio'), and the contents had been rescued and squirrelled away by locals who came upon the wreckage. This supposedly included a large case of diaries written in Hitler's own hand.

Heidemann tracked down the 'antiques dealer', Kujau, who was making a living forging items with fake certificates of authenticity to private collectors, and offered him 2 million marks for the rest of the diaries. Kujau agreed, and here the story takes on a multi-level structure of duplicity. Kujau couldn't let on that the other diaries didn't exist (as he hadn't written them yet) and so he told Heidemann it would take time for the volumes to be smuggled out individually from East Germany by his brother (a railway porter whom Kujau promoted to 'army general' for the story). Heidemann, meanwhile, set about convincing his newspaper to buy the books and pay him a huge sum for his work on them. Heidemann told Kujau that *Stern* agreed to a figure of 85,000 marks per volume – in fact, they had settled on 200,000 marks, and Heidemann was pocketing the difference.

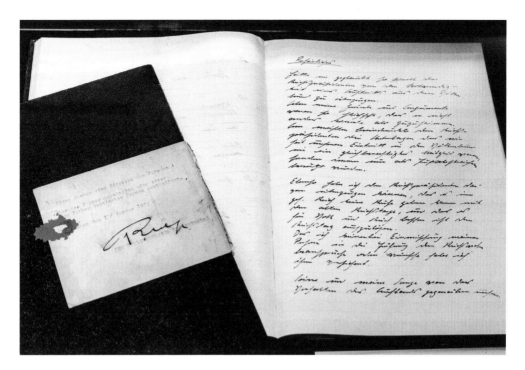

One of the fake Hitler diaries.

Using period paper and inks, Kujau crafted an astonishing output of sixty full volumes, for which *Stern* ultimately paid a total of 9.3 million Deutsche Marks (£2.33 million or $3.7 million). The magazine set about selling the international serial rights, and the *Sunday Times* expressed interest, but having been previously fooled by a hoax set of Mussolini's diaries, sent the expert Hugh Trevor-Roper to examine them. Overwhelmed by the sheer quantity and detail of the writing, he was convinced they were genuine. *Stern* were delighted and held a press conference for Trevor-Roper to say as much before the world's press. Instead, he announced that he'd changed his mind and couldn't vouch for the books' authenticity. The red faces at *Stern* bundled the books off to the German Federal Archives for analysis where they were swiftly denounced as fake. Heidemann and Kujau were jailed for fraud, the latter testifying against the former when he found out the true figure *Stern* had paid for his work.

The diaries are, in the words of graphologist Kenneth W. Rendell, 'bad forgeries but a great hoax'. Kujau was so preoccupied with writing at speed and volume that he wrote whatever he could think of, and so the books are filled with unlikely Hitlerian laments like 'The English are driving me crazy' and 'How on earth does Stalin manage it?' *Der Führer* also grumbles about his horrible flatulence and breath, and in December 1938 writes: 'Now a year is nearly over. Have I achieved my goals for the Reich? Save for a few small details, yes!' He also notes to himself: 'Must get tickets for the Olympic games for Eva.' Kujau also managed to craft an entire opera written by Hitler, and even a third volume of *Mein Kampf*.

'People still want to know, how could this happen?' *Die Zeit's* editor-in-chief, Giovanni di Lorenzo, later told the *New Yorker*. 'Today, if a colleague came into the newsroom and said, "I just bought Friedrich the Second's crutches from Goering's collection," I would advise him to seek psychological help.'

CURIOUS COLLECTIONS

Well over a century had passed since the publication of Dr Johnson's *Dictionary of the English Language* (1755) when in March 1879 the schoolteacher James Murray agreed to head the project to compile a new definitive lexicon of the English language: the *Oxford English Dictionary*. The challenge that lay ahead was gargantuan. Murray began the task in a corrugated iron outbuilding called the 'Scriptorium', working his way through the initial batch of material gathered by the Philological Society. He quickly realized it would take him years to collect just a fraction of the necessary entries, and so decided to crowd-source. Via bookshops and libraries in both Britain and North America, Murray put out an invitation to the public to submit words with their definitions and example quotations. By 1880, he had received 2,500,000 quotation slips, and they kept coming.

One of the most prolific contributors, providing many thousands of quotations, was a man Murray had never heard of before. Dr William Chester Minor of the Broadmoor Asylum for the Criminally Insane devoted all his time to the dictionary project, scouring his large personal library for the requested quotations. Over years of correspondence, Murray and Minor became friends, but whenever Murray suggested meeting, the doctor declined. Finally, after over a decade, Minor relented, and in January 1891 Murray took a train to Crowthorne in the county of Berkshire. Only on his arrival did he discover, to his astonishment, that Dr Minor was not an employee of Broadmoor Asylum – he was an inmate.

Minor had been a surgeon in the American Civil War and was later institutionalized in a lunatic asylum for eighteen months. Then, after moving to London for recuperation, one night in 1871 he shot and killed an innocent passer-by named George Merrett, believing him to be a thief. Minor was confined to Broadmoor Asylum, but was judged by staff not to be dangerous and lived in relatively comfortable quarters, using his US army pension to buy and read books. Remarkably,

Merrett's widow occasionally visited Minor, bringing books for him each time. When Minor came across Murray's appeal for public contributions, he had nothing but time to immerse himself in the challenge. His work filled the dictionary. In 1899, Murray paid tribute to Minor's gigantic contribution, saying, 'We could easily illustrate the last four centuries from his quotations alone.'

Over 100 years earlier, the originators of the *Encyclopædia Britannica* had faced a similar logistical mountain to climb, but without the benefit of an erudite madman with his own library. The first editor was a Scotsman named William Smellie (1740–95), a printer, naturalist and antiquary. He was joined in the project by the 1.37-metre (4ft-6in)-tall Andrew Bell, who dealt with jokes about his enormous nose by bolting from the room and returning wearing an even larger papier-mâché one. The first edition of the *Britannica*, which appeared in 100

OPPOSITE: *Ernst Haeckel's* Kunstformen Der Natur *('Art Forms of Nature', 1904) two volumes of 100 engravings and descriptions by the German zoologist displaying his fascination with the symmetry and level of organization in nature.*

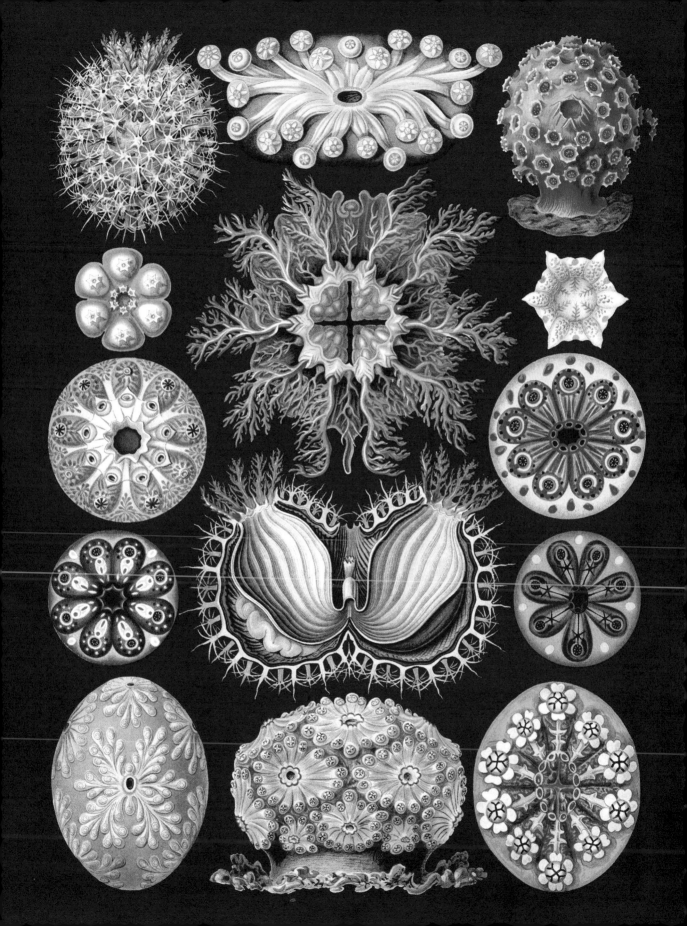

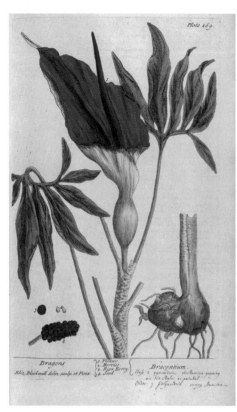

weekly instalments ('numbers') from 1768 to 1771, was notorious for gross errors and wild speculations. It states, for example, that excessive use of tobacco has the effect of 'drying up the brain to a little black lump consisting of mere membranes'; and describes Callifornia [*sic*] as: 'A large country in the West Indies, possibly an island or a peninsula'. The entry for 'woman' reads simply: 'The female of man. See *homo*.'

LEFT: *A collection created out of love: this is Plate 269, the* Draconium, *from the magnificent* A Curious Herbal, *a collection of medicinal plant illustrations that were drawn, engraved and hand-coloured by the artist Elizabeth Blackwell. She published the books in 1737 to raise money for the freedom of her husband, Alexander, from debtors' prison.*

BELOW: *The* Hjertebogen *('Heart Book'), a collection of eighty-three love ballads created in the 1550s in the circle of the Court of King Christian III.*

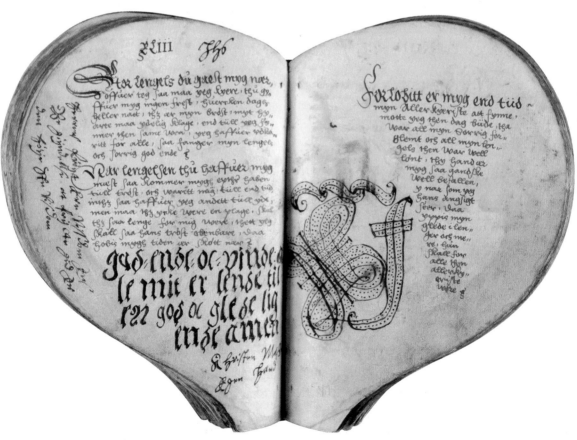

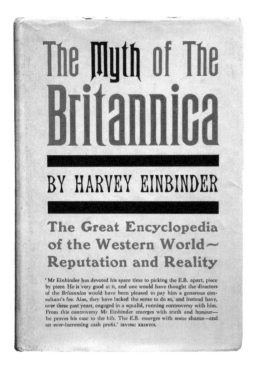

Above: The Myth of The Britannica *(1964),
physicist Harvey Einbinder's 390-page attack on
the* Encyclopædia Britannica.

Right: *Some of the approximately 10 million word
slips in the archive of the* Thesaurus Linguae Latinae,
*a Munich-based project to create a complete dictionary
of the Latin language over a thousand years. Begun in
the 1890s by the classicist Eduard Wölfflin, 125 years
later the modern scholars of the project are currently
tackling the letter R, and hope to complete the final
entry,* zythum, *an Egyptian beer, by 2050.*

Future editions gradually ironed out
inaccuracies but were still far from perfect (and
full of curious nuance – the 1956 edition of the
Encyclopædia Britannica, for instance, describes
rock 'n' roll as 'insistent savagery'.) By the late
1950s, the sheer quantity of unreliable entries
evading correction so angered an American
physicist named Dr Harvey Einbinder
(1926–2013) that he spent five years combing
through the volumes to collect and publish the
mistakes. Einbinder's *Myth of the Britannica*
appeared in 1964, a furious 390-page litany
of errors. *Science Magazine* praised Einbinder
as a 'dedicated prince of iconoclasts' who
'rips into his subject from all angles and with
devastating effect'. Critics even suggested
that the editorial board of the *Encyclopædia
Britannica* hire Einbinder as a factual
watchdog, but apparently this was not an idea
that appealed to either irritated party.

Such a degree of fact-checking was obviously
not possible for the compilers and readership
of the medieval bestiary, an ancestor of the
modern encyclopedia; and thank goodness,
because gone would be their fantastical
charm. These 'book of beasts' collections are

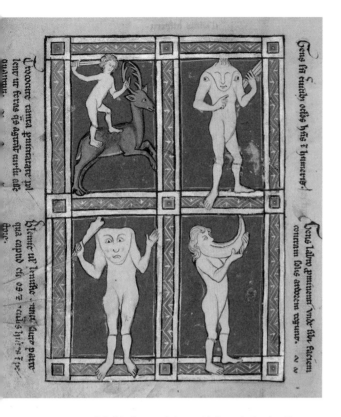

Mythical races of the world, from the bestiary De Natura Avium; De Pastoribus et Ovibus; Bestiarium; Mirabilia Mundi; Philosophia Mundi; On the Soul *by an unknown Franco-Flemish artist, 1227 or after.*

'A Man Without Knowledge of Fire, A Man Riding a Crocodile, A Centaur, Sanrus' from the same Franco-Flemish bestiary

filled with illustrated descriptions of animals, plants and distant peoples, and were among the most popular books of the 1100s and 1200s. The bestiary was an attempt to make sense of the living world by drawing on the highly fanciful and unreliable classical authors (Pliny the Elder, Aristotle, Herodotus etc.), via earlier encyclopedias like the massively influential *Etymologiae* of Isidore of Seville (*c.* AD 560–636). Each entry usually concludes with some moral lesson found in the animal's behaviour: the pelican, for example, was believed to tear open its chest to bring its young to life with its own blood, and therefore served as a living representation of Jesus.

Ducks and geese are shown sprouting from trees, crocodiles devour hydras, the

phoenix bursts from the fire and griffins, basilisks, dragons and unicorns with a variety of horns are assembled with scientific thoroughness. Occasionally one finds Pliny's story of a battle between an elephant and a dragon, the blood of which combined to create the red mineral and pigment cinnabar. Common too is his description of the *bonnacon* or *bonasus*, a bull-like creature that lived in the ancient kingdom of Paeonia (modern-day Macedonia). As its horns curled inward the animal instead relied on its bottom for defence,

OPPOSITE: *A hydra refusing to be digested bursts out of a crocodile's side, and a battle elephant, from a twelfth-century bestiary with details from Gerald of Wales's* Topographia Hibernica *(c.1188).*

ſt animal in nilo flumine q̃d dicit̃ ydru̅ in aqua ydri
uuiens. Grea enim ydros aquã uocant. Inde dr̃

ſt animal quod dicitur elephanſ in quo non eſt con
cupiſcentia coituſ. Eſephantẽ grei a magnitudine

H afia animal naure qd bonnaton dicunr. cut tautirnu ca

The mythical bonnacon sprays its flaming dung on three unfortunate hunters.

spraying boiling hot dung that set fire to anything and anyone it touched. (It's also from Pliny that we have the expression 'lick into shape', from his claim that bear cubs are born as shapeless lumps of white flesh, which their mothers must lick until they take cub form.)

It's easy to chuckle at the apparent gullibility of these writers but occasionally there is truth at the root of even the wildest rumour, distorted by misobservation or the great distances that notions travel between cultures. Having said that, Pliny had no problem indulging in mockery himself. 'It is amazing how far Greek gullibility goes,' he snickers in his *Natural History* as he describes the Greek fear of werewolves, while in the same work recommending the smearing of mouse faeces on one's head to cure baldness. The mythical component of bestiaries would not be swept out for centuries. Leonardo da Vinci (1452–1519) wrote his own, repeating the same fantastic stories, like the origin of the phrase 'crocodile tears': 'The crocodile will seize a man and kill him immediately with his jaws,' da Vinci wrote. 'Then he will weep for him and wail in a mournful manner. When he has finished his lament,

he will devour him cruelly. So it is with the hypocrite, who weeps when he is happy, showing a tearful countenance while in his ferocious heart he is rejoicing all the while.'

Wonderful early modern examples of these books are Edward Topsell's heavily illustrated *The History of Four-Footed Beasts* (1607) and *The History of Serpents* (1608). The English cleric and author provides himself with the disclaimer 'I would not have the Reader … imagine I have … related all that is ever said of these Beasts, but only [what] is said by many', then proceeds to repeat every superstition from antiquity about the animals of the world. Topsell's is a cartoonish natural world: weasels give birth from their ears, lemmings graze in the clouds, elephants worship the Sun and the Moon, and fall pregnant by chewing on mandrake. Toads have a toadstone in their heads that protects people from poison, and apes are terrified of snails. And then there are the mythical creatures assembled beside the real animals, including the Persian manticore, described as having 'a treble rowe of teeth beneath and above … his face and eares like unto a mans, his eyes grey, and collour red, his taile like the taile of a Scorpion of the earth … his voice like the voice of a small trumpet or pipe'.

The first to collect together all of these enduring superstitions, myths and folklore and purge them with relentless scientific rationale was Sir Thomas Browne (1605–82), an English author whose written works stretch across science, medicine, religion and the esoteric. Every day, modern English speakers use words and phrases coined by Browne. The *Oxford English Dictionary* drew on 4156 quotations from his works, and he is credited with the first usage of around 700 words including amphibian, approximate, aquiline, biped, cadaverous, causation, coexistence, coma, disruption, elevator; as well as follicle, hallucination, illustrative, migrant, participating, ruminating, selection, transgressive, undulation, variegation and vitreous.

Most famously, he coined the word electricity in his book *Pseudodoxia Epidemica: or Enquiries into very many received tenets and commonly presumed truths* (1646), a comprehensive encyclopedia of 'vulgar errors'

or misconceptions. With a subtly humorous tone, Browne addresses the 'obstinate adherence unto Antiquity' before specifically targeting a wild variety of misbeliefs: 'That a Diamond is made soft, or broke by the blood of a Goate'; 'That the roote of Mandrakes … givs a shreeke upon eradication'; 'That an Elephant hath no joints'; 'Of the musicall note of Swans before their death'; 'That the flesh of Peacocks corrupteth not'; 'That Storkes will only live in Republicks and free States'; 'That a Beaver to escape the Hunter bites off his testicles or stones'; among many others.

On the mythical unicorn, for example, he points out that such a feature does indeed exist in nature with the rhinoceros and the narwhal, but suggests that with such a large horn projecting at the angle with which it is commonly drawn, the animal would be prevented from grazing and surely starve. But Browne did not merely dismiss the errors offhand: he tested them practically, no matter how ridiculous the notion nor eccentric the experiment required. In regard to the belief

The Persian manticore, from Edward Topsell's 1607 The History of Four-Footed Beasts.

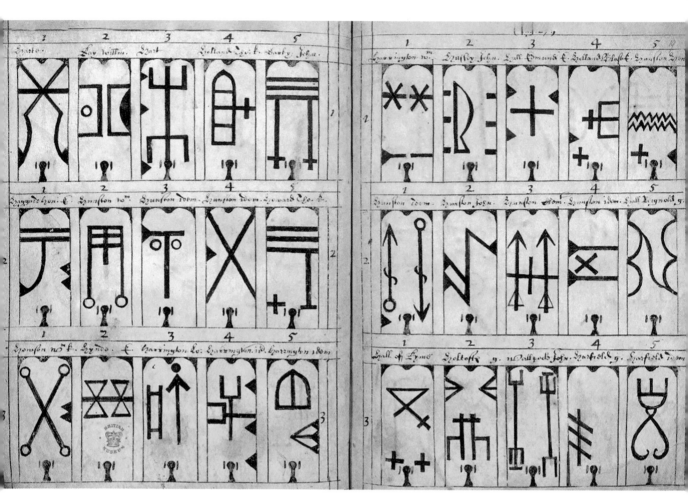

BRITISH MUSEUM

ABOVE: *Pages from a sixteenth-century 'swan marks' book. These registers collected the ownership symbols of those granted by the Crown the privilege of owning mute swans. The marks were cut or branded into the birds' upper-bills.*

that a dead kingfisher suspended with a thread served as an accurate weather vane, Browne spent an afternoon hanging the dead birds from a ceiling beam, and noted how they twirled in different directions with no discernible pattern. Probably best to use an actual weather vane, he concluded.

Where bestiaries and compendiums like those of Topsell and Browne focus on the marvels of the natural world, some of the most curious compilations obsess over a single area of wonder. For Adriaen Coenensz, this

was fish. The Dutch wreck master, official fish auctioneer of Scheveningen and amateur ichthyologist, began work on his extraordinary 800-page *Visboek* ('Fish Book') in 1577 at the age of sixty-three. Over three years, he amassed material on the fishing grounds and marine animals of the seas and coastal waters to form an illustrated fish database of sorts, taking as much from works like Olaus Magnus's *Historia de Gentibus Septentrionalibus* as he did from local folk tales. A curious example of the latter is the legend of the magically tattooed tunnyfish (see pages 120–121), a creature caught in 1561 in the Mediterranean Sea near Ceuta, which reportedly had images of ships magically ingrained in its scales – vessels, it was thought, that it had encountered on its journeys.

Another weird entry is the sea bishop, or bishop-fish, a sea creature popularly featured in sixteenth-century writing that is dressed in a mitre, slippers and gloves, and clutching a wand and chasuble. According to legend it had once been brought to the King of Poland, and when it gestured towards the Catholic bishops, appealing for its release, freedom was granted. From the records of court sessions at Leiden in 1583, we know that Coenensz certainly recognized the appeal of his beautiful book. He asked permission for both his manuscript and collection of dried fish 'to be shown on the coming free annual fair and the festival of the relief of the city' of Scheveningen. Viewers were charged five cents to see the dried fish, and twenty-five cents to see the book.

When it comes to colourful sea creature spectacle, however, nothing beats the first coloured, published study of fish species. In 1719, Europeans knew very little of Indonesian wildlife – Louis Renard knew even less, but that didn't stop this Amsterdam bookseller from confidently producing the vibrant two-volume collection *Fishes,* *Crayfishes, and Crabs, of Diverse Colours and Extraordinary Form, that are Found Around the Islands of the Moluccas and on the Coasts of the Southern Lands* (1719). Thirty years in the making, the 100 plates of *Poissons, ecrevisses et crabs …* carry 460 illustrations of marine biology. In the second volume, however, scientific accuracy swiftly becomes a casualty of artistic licence. Or, as Renard himself explains in the Editor's Advertisement at the front of the book: 'the second volume, less correct, in truth, in the exactitude of the drawings, but very curious for the innovations of which it is filled and the Remarks which are beside each Fish.'

BELOW: *The* Libro de los Epítomes *('The Book of Epitomes'), running to over 2000 handwritten pages, had lain unidentified for over 300 years when in 2019 it was discovered in the Arnamagnæan Collection in Copenhagen. It catalogues part of the enormous library of Hernando Colón (1488–1539), son of Christopher Columbus, who attempted to gather a copy of every book in the world. His collection of around 20,000 works was the greatest of its day. Only a quarter of the books survive, housed in Seville Cathedral since 1552, and so the* Libro *… is the sole source of information for many titles that no longer exist.*

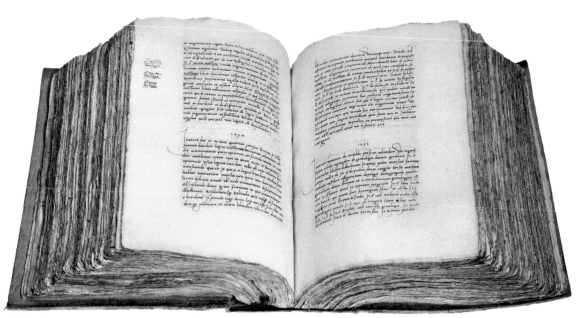

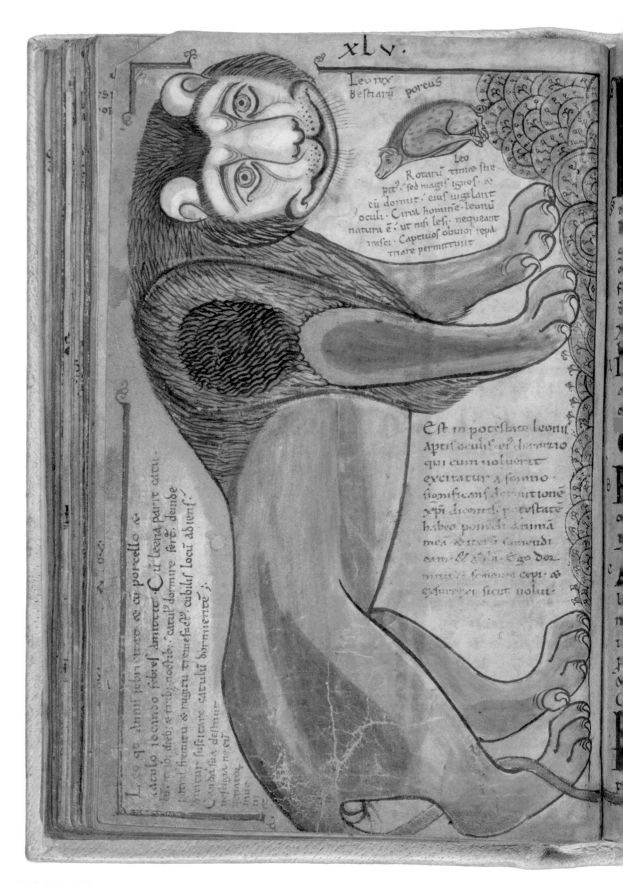

IISIDORVS SPALESS

EPS DE NATVRIS BESTIARVM;

LEO cauda ppria operiens uestigia ne uenator eu
inueniat. leonem ortu de tribu iuda significat. q in fine sclom
humanitatis sue cauda ne auenatore diabolo agnosceretur
glam deitatis occuluit. Leo rex bestiaru & dns. rugitu suo
& fremitu catulu suu excitat triduo dormiente. ds deoz & dns.
filiu suu die tercia amorte suscitat incolum. Leo cauda
tra peutiendo circulu faciens. que desiderat inde abstrat.
Xps di filiu fine sue mortis que p cauda notat que finis est
bestie. peutiens baruthru quos uoluit inde eripuit. Ite de leone
LEO sibi resistentes occidit & deuorat ac peregrinos repatri
are pmittit. Xps u supbos destruens. humiles exaltat ingra
& peregrinos pauperes spiritu ad paradysi gaudia repatare cedit;
Tygris bestia uariis distincta maculis. uirtute De tygride
& uelocitate mirabis crudelis est nemini parcens;
Pantera bestia nigra ut alba uarietate distinguitur.
fuluis depicta orbiculis. Hec semel omino parit. nam
onerata fetib; uuluam taq obstante partu unguib; lacerunt
ita ut semen infusum postea retinere non possit; De antalope
Antalops animal nimis acerrimu auenatorib; capi non
potest. Habet aute longa cornua ferri similitudine ha
bentia. ita ut possit etiam arbores secare altas. & ad tra psterr
nere Du u int ueniet ad eufraten... bium. Est aute frutex
iuxta fluuiu que dr hericina hab... uirgulta subtilia...
plixa. Cuq incipit ludere obligat... nib; muirgultis...
& cu diu pugnauerit & se liberare ii possit. exclamat...
Cuius uoce uenator audiens. ueniet & tinuo a...
Pardus uarietate distinctus. ueloz nimis & p...
guinem. saltu ad mortem ruit festinanter...
Leopardus ex adulterino concubitu leoni...
pardo & leena nascitur. faluis ut leo. nigris ut p...

The lion that guards the bestiary chapter of the *Liber Floridus* ('Book of Flowers'), a medieval encyclopedia compiled by Lambert, Canon of Saint-Omer, between 1090 and 1120, chronicling the history of the world and the cosmos.

The tattooed tunnyfish in Adriaen Coenensz's grand Fish Book *of 1580.*

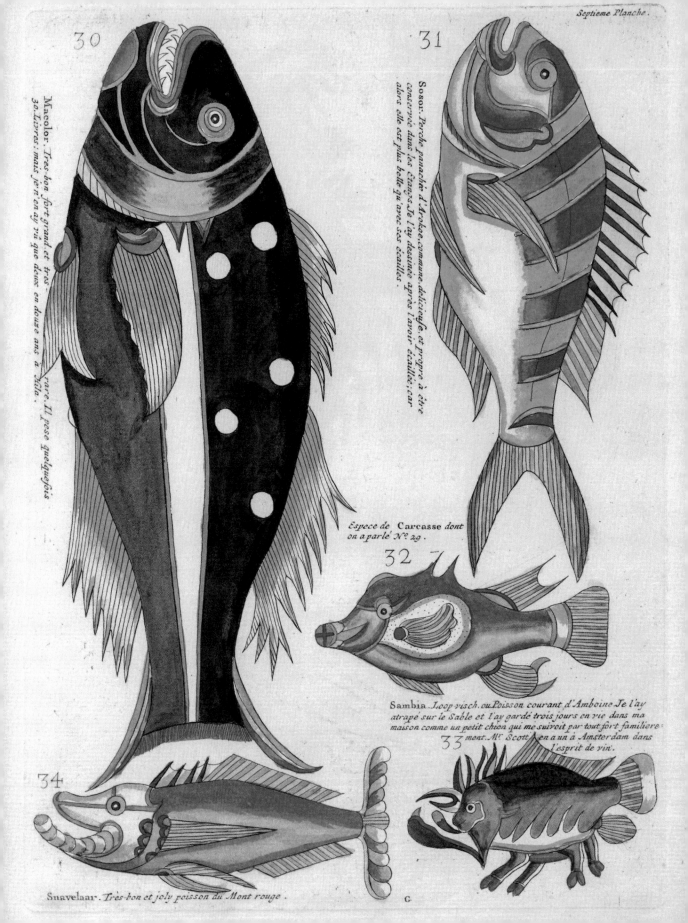

30

31

Macolor. Trés-bon fort grand, et trés
30.Livres: mais jé'n'en ay vû que deux en douze ans à
rare. Il pese quelquefois
Héla.

Sosor. Perche panachée d'Amboine, commune, delicieuse, et propre à être
conservée dans les étangs. Je l'ay dessinée après l'avoir écaillée: car
alors elle est plus belle qu'avec ses écailles.

Espece de Carcasse dont
on a parlé N.º 29.

32

Sambia. Loop visch. ou Poisson courant d'Amboine Je l'ay
atrapé sur le Sable et l'ay gardé trois jours en vie dans ma
maison comme un petit chien qui me suivoit par tout fort familiere-
ment. M.ᵣ Scott en a un à Amsterdam dans
33   l'esprit de vin.

34

Snavelaar. Trés-bon et joly poisson du Mont rouge.

G

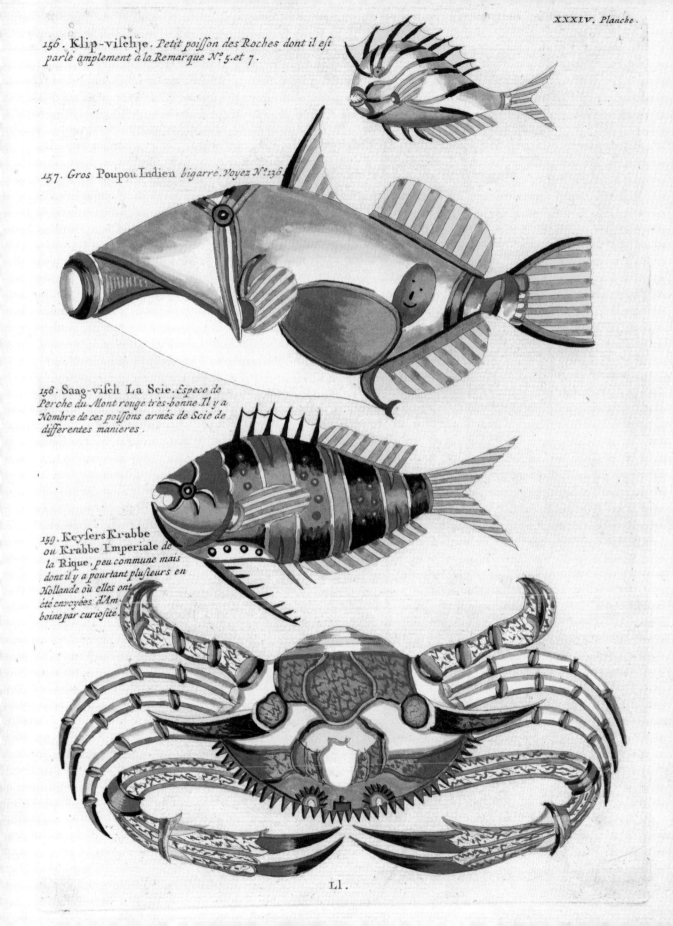

156. Klip-vischje. Petit poisson des Roches dont il est parlé amplement à la Remarque N.º 5. et 7.

157. Gros Poupou Indien bigarré. Voyez N.º 136.

158. Saag-visch La Scie. Espece de Perche du Mont rouge très-bonne. Il y a Nombre de ces poissons armés de Scie de differentes manieres.

159. Keysers Krabbe ou Krabbe Imperiale de la Rique, peu commune mais dont il y a pourtant plusieurs en Hollande où elles ont été envoyées d'Amboine par curiosité.

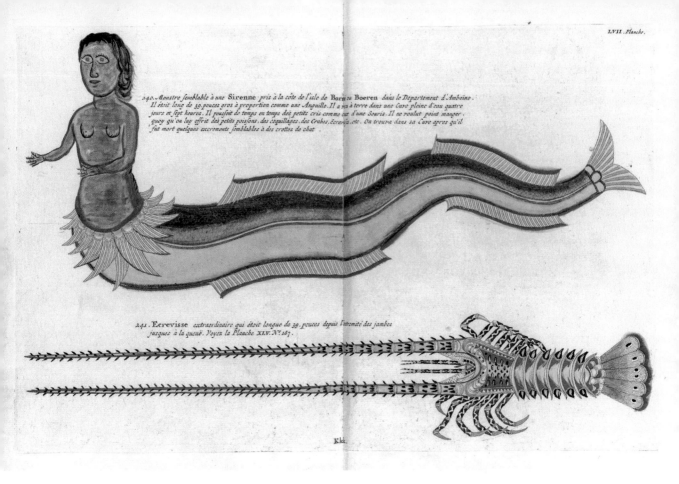

240. Monstre semblable à une Sirenne pris à la côte de l'isle de Boru ou Boeren dans le Departement d'Amboine.
Il etoit long de 59.pouces gros à proportion comme une Anguille. Il y a eu à terre dans une Cuve pleine d'eau quatre
jours et sept heures. Il poussoit de temps en temps des petits cris comme eus d'une Souris. Il ne vouloit point manger
quoy qu'on luy offrit des petits poissons, des coquillages, des Crabes, Ecrevisses etc. On trouva dans sa Cuve apres qu'il
fut mort quelques excremens semblables à des crottes de chat.

241. Ecrevisse extraordinaire qui etoit longue de 59.pouces depuis l'extremité des jambes
jusques à la queuë. Voyez la Planche XLV. No. 187.

Kkk.

PREVIOUS PAGES: LEFT: *The four-legged* Poisson courant *(Running Fish) that followed its discoverer around 'like a little dog'. From Louis Renard's* Fishes, Crayfishes, and Crabs… *(1719).*
RIGHT: *The* Krabbe Imperiale*, along with three other impossibly coloured creatures from Louis Renard's* Fishes, Crayfishes, and Crabs… *(1719).*

ABOVE: *The mermaid, the coup de (dis)grâce of Renard's work. 'A monster resembling a Siren,' reads the original caption. 'It was 59 inches long with the proportions of an eel.' (Suggesting, perhaps, that it was a large eel.)*

Many of the fish bear at least some resemblance to real specimens found in the waters of the East Indies, but others have distinctly avian and even human features, as well as decorations of sun, moon, star and even top-hat motifs. The artist's designs become increasingly experimental, and the vivid colours that become almost fluorescent in some examples are as wonderful as they are misrepresentative.
Highlights include the spiny lobster, *Panulirus ornatus*, reported to favour a

mountain habitat and possessing a penchant for climbing trees and laying red-spotted eggs 'as large as those of a pigeon'. The *Crabbe-Criarde*, we are told, mews like a cat. Another crab with a perfect crucifix marking on its body is said to be a subject of local worship, since one of its kind emerged from the sea to return a cross to St Francis Xavier after a furious king had thrown it into the waters in disgust. The four-legged fish shown on page 122 is, according to its caption, the '*Loop-visch* or *Poisson courant* (Running Fish) of Ambon', of which the writer notes: 'I trapped it on the beach and kept it alive for three days in my house, where it followed me around like a very friendly little dog. Mr Scott has one in Amsterdam pickled in wine.' The *Krabbe Imperiale* (see page 123) is truly dazzling, but the best is saved for last. The final plate of the volume features a delightfully detailed diagram of a captured mermaid, which reportedly cried like a mouse.

Fishes, Crayfishes, and Crabs ... gave the European reader some sense – albeit misinformed – as to what lay in the waters of the East Indies; but imagine the potency of a book that allowed the reader to see, touch and even smell the material of cultures at the opposite end of the world. Appearing in 1787, *A Catalogue of the Different Specimens of Cloth Collected in the Three Voyages of Captain Cook, to the Southern Hemisphere* ... offers just such an experience, for the books collect neatly cut samples of various forms of 'tapa' cloth (manufactured from tree bark) that was used for dress, bedding and other traditional purposes by the native societies encountered by Captain James Cook during his exploration of the South Pacific. Opening up Captain Cook's tapa cloth 'atlas' is to embark on a transpacific island tour of the eighteenth century, when tapa was processed across the region, from New Zealand, Samoa and Tongatabu to Fiji and the Solomon Islands. In Hawaii it was referred to as 'kapa', and much of the material collected in the book is taken from there, where Cook would eventually meet his grisly end.

It goes without saying that the tapa cloth book is a rare item. Only forty-five examples are known to exist, and each one is unique. It seems that Alexander Shaw, the credited compiler, produced custom copies in small batches to meet demand as it came through the door of his little shop on the Strand, London. Perhaps the grandest example is that of the Welsh naturalist Thomas Pennant,

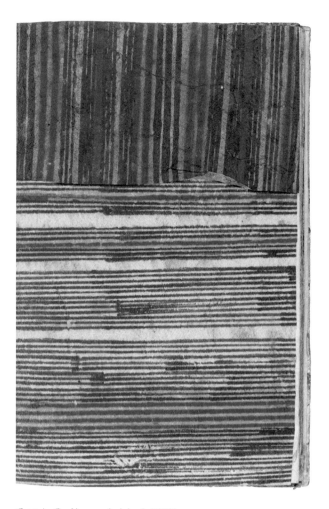

Captain Cook's tapa cloth book (1787), a collection of exotic materials from the many cultures encountered on the explorer's travels around the Pacific.

who on first seeing the book immediately offered to purchase Shaw's entire stock of the exotic cloth. He built his own plump edition, binding Shaw's text with interviews with Cook's crew and ninety-two samples of tapa, cut to full-page size. The book is one of the most evocative artefacts from the entire history of European exploration.

While Britain mourned the death of the heroic Cook in Hawaii, one man was conducting his own unusual explorations without leaving London, plunging into the

FRANCIS GROSE ESQ? F.A.S.

bowdlerized for later editions in line with Britain's transition from Georgian bawdiness to Victorian primness. No longer could the author get away with entries like: 'BURNING SHAME, a lighted candle stuck into the private parts of a woman' (to which Grose added in his own copy: 'certainly not intended by Nature for a candlestick'). He also reluctantly removed 'FUN THRUSTER, a Sodomite', and 'APPLE DUMPLING SHOP, a woman's bosom', among others. A few other notables from the first edition include:

ARSY VARSEY, *to fall arsy varsey,*
    i.e. head over heels.
BEARD SPLITTER, *a man much*
    given to wenching.
BLINDMAN'S HOLIDAY, *night, darkness.*
A BLOWSABELLA, *a woman whose hair is*
    dishevelled and hanging about her face.
CACKLING FARTS, *eggs.*
CASTING UP ONE'S ACCOUNTS, *vomiting.*
CUP OF THE CREATURE, *a cup of good liquor.*
CURTAIN LECTURE, *a woman who*
    scolds her husband when in bed, is
    said to read him a curtain lecture.
DUKE OF LIMBS, *a tall, awkward,*
    ill-made fellow.
DUTCH FEAST, *where the entertainer*
    gets drunk before his guests.
FRENCHIFIED, *infected with the*
    venereal disease.
LOUSELAND, *Scotland.*
MARRIAGE MUSICK, *the squalling*
    and crying of children.
MILK THE PIDGEON, *to endeavour*
    at impossibilities.
PUFF GUTS, *a fat man.*
SHAG BAG, *a poor sneaking fellow,*
    a man of no spirit.
SLUBBER DE GULLION, *a dirty nasty fellow.*
TORMENTOR OF CATGUT, *a fiddle player.*

city's seedy underbelly late at night, armed only with a notebook and a nervous assistant. Francis Grose (1731–91), who once described himself as 'Too fat to ride a horse and too poor to keep a carriage', gathered material for his most famous work, *A Classical Dictionary of the Vulgar Tongue* (1785), on midnight strolls through London's darkest quarters, fearless in his pursuit of forming a comprehensive collection of crude and criminal slang – the kind of vocabulary omitted from Johnson's dictionary. Grose and his assistant Tom Cocking frequented slums, drinking dens and dockyards in the name of research, collecting the vernacular of 'soldiers on the long march, seamen at the capstern [*sic*], ladies disposing of their fish, and the colloquies of a Gravesend boat', to curate the greatest dictionary of obscenities, or 'non-standard words', and linguistic oddities ever assembled.

Over 9000 entries feature in the first edition of 1785, of which almost 100 were

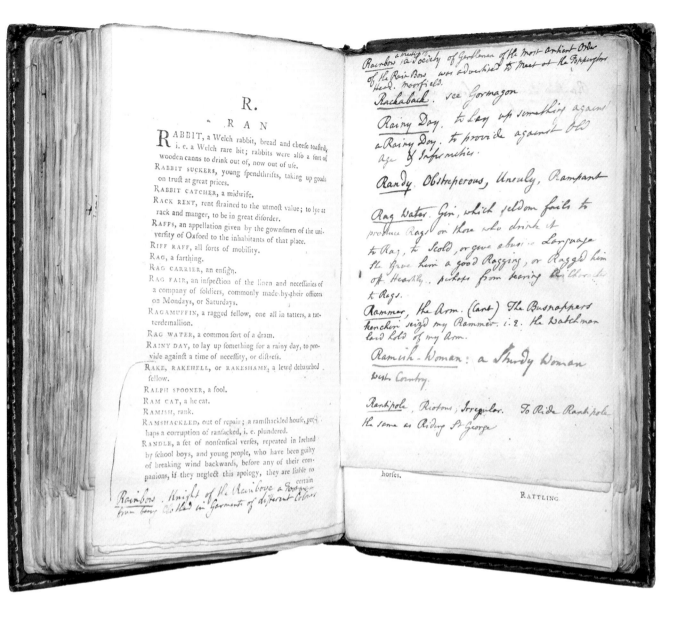

Opposite: *Portrait of Francis Grose, from his*
A Provincial Glossary *(1787).*

Above: *Francis Grose's own annotated copy of his*
Dictionary of the Vulgar Tongue.

One set of phrases in the *Dictionary of the Vulgar Tongue* concerns a particular area of London: 'COVENT GARDEN AGUE, the venereal disease,' wrote Grose, 'COVENT GARDEN ABBESS, a bawd [madam of a brothel]; COVENT GARDEN NUN, a prostitute.' Covent Garden was a notorious hub of prostitution in the eighteenth century, and its nightly male wanderers, possessed

of less academic interests than Grose, were assisted by a guide of their own. *Harris's List of Covent-Garden Ladies* was a pocketbook of around 150 pages printed annually between 1757 and 1795, cataloguing the 120–190 prostitutes working in the Covent Garden and West End areas of the city. Around 8000 copies were sold annually for two shillings and sixpence each, but its author was never

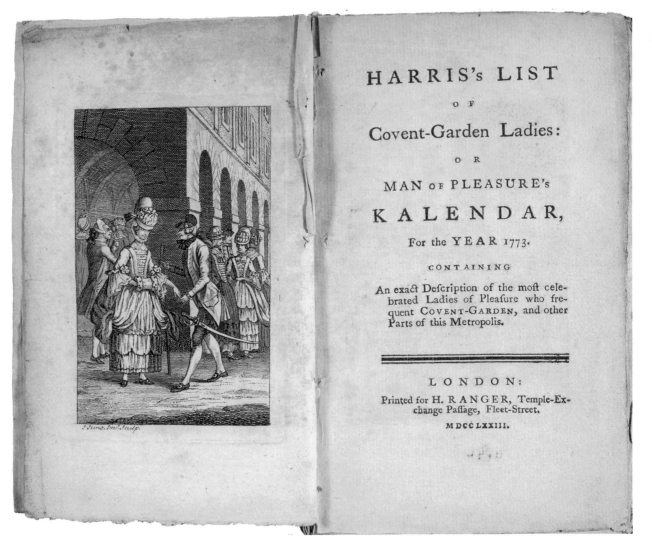

HARRIS's LIST

OF

Covent-Garden Ladies:

OR

MAN OF PLEASURE's

KALENDAR,

For the YEAR 1773.

CONTAINING

An exact Description of the most celebrated Ladies of Pleasure who fre-
quent COVENT-GARDEN, and other
Parts of this Metropolis.

LONDON:

Printed for H. RANGER, Temple-Ex-
change Passage, Fleet-Street.
MDCCLXXIII.

Title page of the 1773 edition of Harris's List
of Covent-Garden Ladies.

discovered (although Samuel Derrick, a Grub
Street hack, and a Covent Garden pimp
named Jack Harris are commonly identified
as likely culprits.)

What makes the lurid *List* … so
interesting to browse is the information
we learn of these ladies of the second half
of the eighteenth century – not just their
names, ages and physical attributes, but
their specialties and talents both in and out
of the bedroom (including their singing and

dancing skills), their quirks of personality
and snatches of personal background. The
'genteel agreeable' Miss B—nd of No.28 Frith
Street listed in the 1788 edition, for example,
is 'distinguished more by the elegancy of her
dress, than the beauty of her person, which
might perhaps have been ranked in the list of
tolerable's, had not the small-pox been quite
so unkind; she is, nevertheless, a desirable
well tempered piece'.

Miss Davenport's entry concludes: 'Her
teeth are remarkably fine; she is tall, and so
well proportioned (when you examine her
whole naked figure, which she will permit

you to do, if you perform the Cytherean Rites like an able priest) that she might be taken for a fourth Grace, or a breathing animated Venus de Medicis.' Miss Clicamp, of No.2 York Street near Middlesex Hospital, is noted as 'one of the finest, fattest figures as fully finished for fun and frolick as fertile fancy ever formed … fortunate for the true lovers of fat, should fate throw them into the possession of such full grown beauties.'

Eventually, however, the same shift in public attitudes to indecency that saw Grose expurgate his *Vulgar Tongue* also led to a more robust intolerance of the sex trade and calls for reform, and the 1795 edition of *Harris's List …*, the crudest of all, was the last to be put out, as those responsible for its printing were fined and imprisoned.

While Francis Grose and *Harris's List* were chronicling London's nocturnal skulduggery, a contemporary American notebook known as the *Journal of College Disorders* (1788) collected records of an altogether more dangerous world: teaching. The Harvard Library holds the papers of a former teacher, Eliphalet Pearson (1752–1826), who in 1785 took up the position of Hancock Professor of Hebrew and other Oriental Languages at the university. In his miserable diary Pearson records the cruel and often violent acts of student rebellion, or 'disorders', suffered by the university tutors on a daily basis. The book paints a picture of a staff under constant siege, reporting thefts of food, firewood, candles, bibles and pretty much anything not bolted to the floor; outrageous drunkenness; the drawing of weapons; the drowning of a dog in a well; the breaking of locks; the graffitiing of lecture room walls with gravel; and even the melting down of the kitchen's pewter plates to be poured into – and thereby wreck – the school bell. Some choice extracts that caught my eye include:

December 4, 1788: 'P.M. - A disorderly, riotous noise called up Mr. Webber who desired them to be still. Immediately upon his leaving them, the noise became more violent, which occasioned his return. He then ordered all to their chambers; but none withdrew. He then ordered them individually & by name. The two Sullivans declined going, & James said he would go, when he pleased. - After this the two Sullivans conducted improperly towards Mr. Smith, & disobeyed a positive order of Mr. James.'

December 5, 1788: 'A snowball was thrown at Mr. Webber, while he was in the desk at evening prayers. Upon complaint, a meeting was called 6 Dec. And, upon pleading, as others had done before, that he was intoxicated, Sullivan 2d was admitted to a public confession; which was exhibited at a meeting 8 Dec.'

December 9, 1788: 'The President read the confession of Sullivan 2; but there was such a scraping, especially in the junior class, that he could not be heard. He commanded silence, but to no purpose. Disorders coming out of chapel.'

December 9, 1788: 'Also … at breakfast … Bisket, tea, and a knife thrown at the tutors.'

December 12, 1788: 'Many of the chapel windows also were broken.'

December 16, 1788: 'Still greater disorders at Dr. Wigglesworth's public lecture. As he was passing up the alley, two volleys of stones, one from each side, were thrown at him … before he reached another pew, another volley of stones was discharged from the north side of the alley … While the Doctr. & two tutors were walking down the alley, a stone was sent into the chapel through a window, the glass of which was driven against one of the gentlemen.'

Finally, Pearson notes with palpable relief:

January 7, 1789: 'Vacation commenced.'

Eliphalet Pearson, a teacher under siege.

One of the most enjoyable collections of all to browse, however, was written later, in the mid-nineteenth century, when the Portuguese writer Pedro Carolino set out to produce the finest Portuguese-to-English phrasebook the world had ever seen – an admirable ambition, for Carolino could speak not a word of English. What he had instead was a Portuguese-to-French phrasebook and a French-to-English dictionary. Phrase by phrase he diligently translated his Portuguese sentences into French, and then fed these results through the second dictionary into English. Of course, like anything passed through multiple digestive systems the result is a complete mess.

Jettisoning all idiomatic nuance, Carolino succeeded in birthing the world's worst language guide, a mad bag of nonsense titled *O Novo Guia de Conversação, em Portuguez e Inglez* ('The New Guide to Conversation in Portuguese and English'), published in Paris in 1855. The book slowly picked up a cult following of literary rubberneckers, which led to printings in both London and Boston under the revised title *English as She is Spoke*. Mark Twain was an avid fan, writing in the introduction of the American edition:

'Nobody can hope to produce its fellow; it is perfect, it must and will stand alone: its immortality is secure … One cannot open this book anywhere and not find richness … this celebrated little phrase-book will never die while the English language lasts.'
It remains, of course, a great read. In the section 'Familiar phrases' we find such unintelligibles as: 'At which is this hat?', 'One she is ugly, at-least she is gracious' and 'All trees have very deal bear'. 'Dress your hairs' must have caused considerable confusion, along with 'Take care to dirt you self', 'Yours parents does exist yet?' and 'He refuse to marry one-self'. What, one wonders, must readers have made of other unintentionally blunt phrases for conversation, like: 'You break my head', 'You don't dance well', 'Your guitar is it tuned?' and 'You interompt me'. 'You make grins', however, is rather charming. The arrangement of the phrases can be curious, too. For example, 'It is almost nine o'clock' follows 'They are all dead'; while 'I have learned the French language' is followed by 'My head is sick'. That apparently well-known English expression 'To craunch the marmoset' appears to be the result of Carolino mangling the genuine French phrase *croquer le marmot*, which means to wait patiently for someone to open a door.

And then there are the example dialogues. 'Dialogue with a Launderess' features the command: 'You shall bend my shirts'; while the scenario titled 'For to ride a horse' presents a guide to demanding a refund, apparently at gunpoint: 'Here is a horse who have a bad looks. Give me another; I will not that. He not sall know to march, he is pursy, he is foundered. Don't you are ashamed to give me a jade as like? he is undshoed, he is with nails up; it want to lead to the farrier.' To which the horse dealer nervously replies: 'Your pistols are its loads?'

O NOVO GUIA

DA

CONVERSAÇÃO,

em Portuguez e Inglez,

OU

ESCOLHA DE DIALOGOS FAMILIARES

SÔBRE VARIOS ASSUMPTOS;

precedido
d'um copioso Vocabulario de nomes proprios,
com a pronuncia figurada das palavras inglezas,
e o accento prosodico nas portuguezas, para se poder aprender com perfeição
e a inda sem mestre, qualquer dos dous idiomas.

OFFERECIDO
A' ESTUDIOSA MOCIDADE PORTUGUEZA E BRAZILEIRA

por JOSÉ DA FONSECA
E PEDRO CAROLINO.

PARIS.

Vª J.-P. AILLAUD, MONLON E Cª.

Livreiros de suas Magestades o Imperador do Brasil
e el Rei de Portugal,

RUA SAINT-ANDRÉ-DES-ARTS, Nº 47.

1855

O Novo Guia de Conversação (1855), *which was republished in English and became known as*
English as She is Spoke.

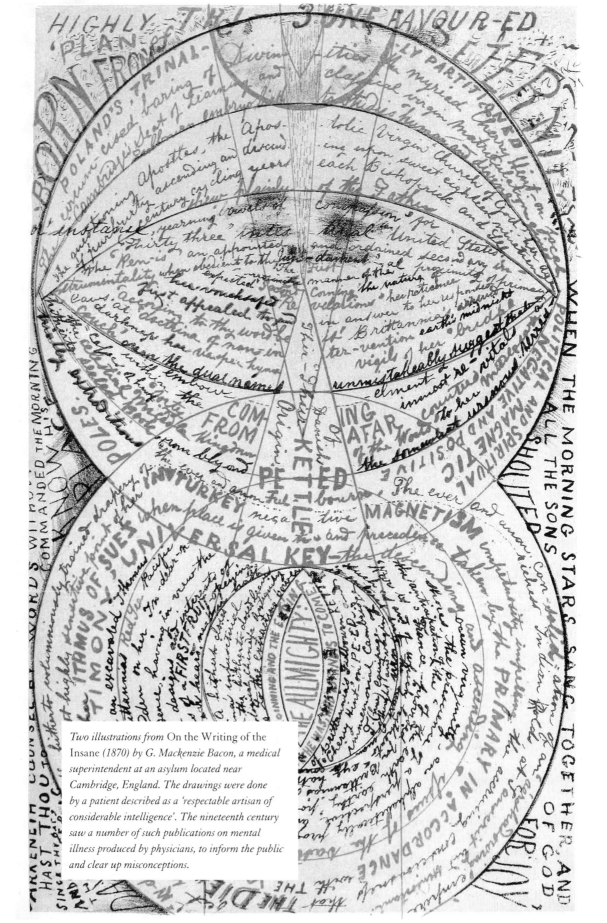

Two illustrations from On the Writing of the Insane *(1870) by G. Mackenzie Bacon, a medical superintendent at an asylum located near Cambridge, England. The drawings were done by a patient described as a 'respectable artisan of considerable intelligence'. The nineteenth century saw a number of such publications on mental illness produced by physicians, to inform the public and clear up misconceptions.*

Beautiful and deadly, the American volume Shadows From the Walls of Death *(1874) is a collection of nineteenth-century wallpapers that contain a high amount of arsenic. Over 100 copies of the book were distributed by the State Board of Health, Michigan, to public libraries to raise awareness of poisonous wallpaper.*

PECULIAR TYPEWRITERS

Left: *A Japanese typewriter from 1976 by the Nippon Keieiki Company, with several thousand printing 'slugs' individually embossed with kanji characters (one set of ideograms of the three used in written Japanese).*

Below: *The Victor typewriter, patented in the USA in 1889. Like the Mignon, this used an index (here semi-circular) with a pointer and an enter key.*

Above: *Entering the market in 1896, the unique and beautiful Lambert is a collectors' favourite. Typing was done by rotating the disk to the correct letter and pressing it down, which would tilt the entire disk until contact was made with the paper.*

Right: *The AEG Mignon typewriter model 4, the mother of all index typewriters. It appeared in 1905 and remained popular until its final production year in 1934. The operator moved the pointer to a desired letter on the interchangeable index card and hit the enter key. With a bit of practice operators averaged 100 strokes per minute.*

ABOVE: *The Keaton Music Typewriter, first patented in 1936 by Robert H. Keaton from San Francisco, California; it allowed the copying of music notation at speed and in quantity.*

RIGHT: *The Hansen Writing Ball, a rare early typewriter invented in Denmark in 1865, and the first commercially produced typewriter. The distinctive design features fifty-two keys on a large brass hemisphere, with the vowels to the left and consonants to the right.*

WORKS OF THE SUPERNATURAL

For centuries, one of the most popular tools in the medieval European magician's box of tricks was the Bible. Scraps of its pages served as healing charms; its prayers and passages were read out as magical incantations in rites, while the book itself served as a protective talisman, hidden under pillows to ward off witches and malicious spirits. But the most curious magical use of the Bible is that of literally eating and drinking its words and pages, in the hope of absorbing its divine power for healing effect. A number of medieval religious manuscripts show signs of having been washed with water for the inky solution to then be drunk. The Book of Durrow, an illuminated manuscript of the Gospels created between AD 650 and 700, somehow survived into the late seventeenth century to be given to the library of Trinity College, Dublin, despite at one point having been dunked in a bucket of water by a farmer trying to make a magical medicine for his ailing cows.

To this day in Islamic West Africa, parts of the Qur'an are similarly rinsed and drunk to treat illness and protect against witchcraft. The *fakis* (teachers and healers) of the Berti of northern Dafur provide their patients with bottles of the Qur'anic ink-water to drink throughout the day, while the students of the Batak *datu* carve a spell dictated by their teacher into bamboo held over boiled rice. The boys eat the splinters that fall into the rice, ingesting 'the soul of the writing'.

To find curious magical literature written even earlier than the Bible we can go all the way back to the Old Kingdom of ancient Egypt (*c*.2686–2181 BC).[1] The Egyptians attributed the invention of writing to the lunar god Thot, and so thought of hieroglyphics as crackling with a magical energy. The most famous ancient Egyptian literature is the Book of the Dead, the funerary text of magic spells compiled by numerous priests over about 1000 years to assist the deceased's safe journey through the Duat, or Underworld, into the afterlife. But before the first copies of the Book of the Dead appeared (the original title of which actually translates to the slightly chirpier 'Book of Emerging Forth into the Light'), there were the Pyramid Texts, the oldest known body of Egyptian magical writing; and in particular, an extraordinary work known as the 'Cannibal Hymn'.

The Cannibal Hymn comprises two spells known as Utterances 273 and 274, carved into the antechamber of the tomb of Pharaoh Unas (sometimes Wenis, *c*.2378–2348 BC), in praise of the dead king as he hunts and eats parts of the gods. In a metaphor of transcendence, the deceased pharaoh is

OPPOSITE: *Sketch of the reported levitation of the spiritualist medium D. D. Home. From Louis Figuier's* Les mystères de la science, *Paris 1880.*

---

1 To contextualise the earliness of this period, Egyptians at this time still shared the planet with woolly mammoths, which had not yet gone extinct. Though mostly wiped out in the Ice Age 6000 years before, a small population of the animals existed on Wrangel Island off the northern coast of far eastern Siberia until 1650 BC.

assisted by the god Shezmu in a butchery ritual, slaughtering, cooking and eating the gods in their sacrificial bull form. In doing so, he absorbs their divine powers in order to negotiate his passage to the afterlife, and ensure his transformation as a celestial divinity ruling the heavens. 'The sky pours water, the stars darken ...' sings the Cannibal Hymn. 'Unas is the bull of heaven, who rages in his heart, who lives on the being of every god, who eats their entrails, when they come, their bodies full of magic, from the Island of Fire.' The magical hymn was reproduced in the later Coffin Texts as Spell 573, but by the time the Book of the Dead (*c*.1550 BC) began to be copied, the hymn was abandoned to the dust of tombs.

With the rise of Christianity in Europe, non-Biblical magical texts – or 'grimoires' as they would be known from the eighteenth century – became a target of authorities for suppression and burning. The difficulty, though, was defining what exactly magic

ABOVE: *A Talismanic shirt of the early sixteenth century with the entire Qur'an written inside, bordered by the ninety-nine names of God written in gold. The shirt was believed to be imbued with protective powers and was likely meant to be worn under armour in battle.*

was – its overlap with science and religious study meant it could never be entirely distinguished. Take the 'leechbooks' of late Anglo-Saxon England, for example, medical handbooks which offer spells and charms for healing alongside scientific instruction – magical or medicinal? One approach, adopted by the Spanish-born Archbishop of Lyon, Agobard (*c*. AD 779–840), was to puncture superstition with reasoned argument. Agobard wrote several works against pagan practices, as well as a curious treatise *De Grandine et Tonitruis* ('On Hail and Thunder'), rediscovered in 1605. In this book, he methodically argues against popular beliefs in weather magic, particularly the conviction

that there were ships that flew above the clouds, carrying villainous sky-pirates who routinely descended to steal crops damaged by storms (conjured by *tempestarii* – storm sorcerers), to take back to their land of 'Magonia'.[2]

Allegations of the use of magical texts were also used to smear figures of the Catholic Church, including two popes. Silvester II (*c.*946–1003), the first French Pope, was a prolific scholar who endorsed the study of Arabic texts, yet found himself the subject of a bizarre legend propagated by the English monk William of Malmesbury and the rebel Cardinal Beno. According to this legend, as a younger man Silvester had stolen an Arab book of spells while studying in the Muslim cities of Córdoba and Seville, and taught himself sorcery. He was also said to have owned a bronze robotic head that would prophetically answer his questions with a booming 'yes' or 'no', and to have made a Faustian pact to magically help him ascend to the Papal throne.[3]

Accusations against Pope Boniface VIII, on the other hand, resulted in him being

ABOVE: *A magical appeal to the Baltic Doom-God for control over lightning: 'Birch-bark letter no.292' is written in the Karelian/Baltic-Finnic language from the early thirteenth century. A translation was made by the Russian linguist Eugene Helimski in 1986: 'God's arrow, ten your name(s) / Arrow sparkling, arrow shoots / The Doom-God guides/ directs (leads/rules?)'.*

posthumously brought to trial between 1303 and 1311 for having used a grimoire for demonic conjuration, controlling three pet demons and – with testimony from a witness – sacrificing a cockerel in a magic ring in his garden. Protestant reformers, of course, delighted in these stories. The mathematician John Napier (1550–1617) wrote that as many as twenty-two Catholic popes were 'abominable Necromancers'.

The scarcity of surviving early magic texts is hardly surprising given the frequency with which they ended up on a pious fire, especially during the witch-hunts of the sixteenth and seventeenth centuries, and how the threat of that fate induced an

---

2 This fantastical notion of a sea above the sky is echoed later in the English author Gervase of Tilbury's *Otia Imperialia* ('Recreation for an Emperor'), nicknamed the *Book of Wonders*, created *c.*1214 for his patron, Emperor Otto IV. Gervase reports of a ship's anchor falling from the sky and crashing into a churchyard. Sailors slid down the line, but retreated to their aerial ship when confronted by startled churchgoers. The villagers manage to capture one of the men, but he promptly 'drowned' on the ground.

3 Part of the inscription on the tomb of Pope Silvester II reads *Iste locus Silvestris membra sepulti venturo Domino conferet ad sonitum* ('This place will yield to the sound [of the last trumpet] the limbs of buried Silvester II, at the advent of the Lord'). Historically this was misread as 'will make a sound', which gave rise to the curious legend that his bones rattle in the tomb just before the death of a Pope.

understandable reluctance in scribes to copy and distribute the manuscripts lest they join their works in the flames. Also, the manufacture of a medieval grimoire required rarer ingredients. For purity, 'virgin' parchment from animals not yet sexually developed, or 'unborn' parchment, fashioned from an amniotic sac, was stipulated. This continued well into the modern period, even when paper was a considerably cheaper and less disgusting option.

ABOVE: *Pope Silvester II and the Devil, illustrated c.1460.*

OPPOSITE TOP: *A Chinese oracle tortoise plastron (underside of shell), with an inscription featuring the ancient form of* zhēn *'to divine'. From the Shang dynasty, dating to the reign of King Wu Ding,* c.1200 BC.

OPPOSITE BOTTOM: *The* I Ching *is an ancient Chinese divination manual and the oldest of the Chinese classics, from the Western Zhou period (1000–750 BC). The book uses a type of fortune-telling called cleromancy – six randomly selected numbers are turned into a hexagram, whose meaning is then sought in the book.*

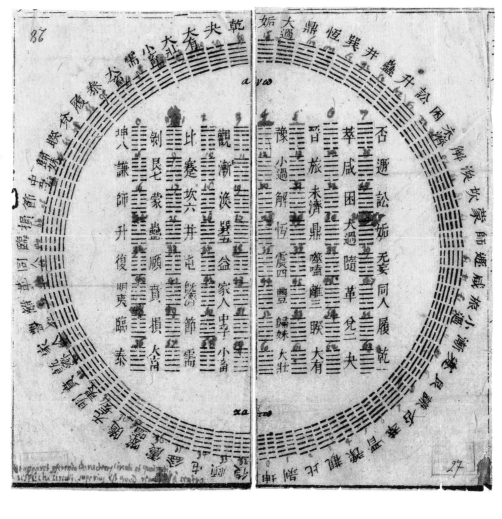

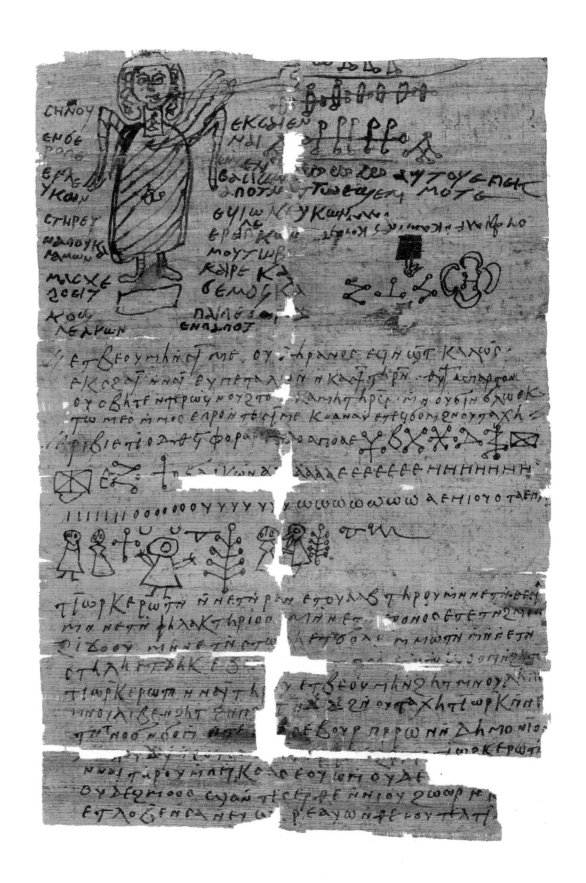

OPPOSITE: *A Coptic magical papyrus, from sixth- or seventh-century Egypt. Two spells are written on it: the top one grants a beautiful singing voice, and the second is a love spell incorporating the froth of a jet-black horse and the body of a bat. The object of your desire will fall in love with you 'like a dog that is crazy for its pups'.*

Of the surviving examples, there are a few stand-out items for the curiosity collector undaunted by Satanic association. The *Picatrix* is a 400-page encyclopedic work of magic and astrology, and a primary source for alchemists. Originally written in Arabic under the title *Ghāyat al-Ḥakīm* ('The Aim of the Sage'), estimates for its date of creation have been made as early as the first half of the tenth century. For the copy with the most powerful historical aura, see the *Picatrix* in the collection of the British Library, a volume once owned by the sixteenth-century occultist Simon Forman. This Elizabethan astrologer physician kept detailed casebooks (held by Cambridge University) that make for an entertaining insight into Shakespearean English life, as he draws on magical works like the *Picatrix* to treat complaints like the patient 'thrust with a rapier in his privy parts', a woman who suckled puppies and evil spirits that caused one gentleman to shout 'Kisse myne arse' at every passer-by. Forman used magical works to consult with angels for advice, and used bizarre treatments that included the 'pigeon slippers' cure, which involved cutting open the birds and attaching them to the feet of the patient.[4]

An infamous grimoire of angelic magic well circulated on the Continent was the *Heptameron*, which lays out the rituals for conjuring the angels associated with each of the seven days of the week, for which one needed perfume, a sword and a whistle. Inside are tables that break down which angel rules over each of the twenty-four hours: the third hour of the day is the domain of Nasnia, for example, while the magician conjuring at 8 p.m. should call on Tafrac for best results. The *Heptameron* was falsely attributed to a famous author, the Italian astrologer Pietro d'Abano (1257–1316), a professor of medicine at Padua who was reputedly such a passionate hater of milk that he would throw up at the sight of anyone drinking it.

For distinguishing magic from astrology, d'Abano twice came before the Inquisition, the second time dying in prison in 1315 (or 1316 according to some sources) before he could face trial. 'The general opinion of almost all authors is, he was the greatest magician of his time,' wrote the French scholar Gabriel Naudé in the seventeenth century, 'that by means of seven spirits, familiar, which he kept inclosed in chrystal, he had acquired the knowledge of the seven liberal arts, and that he had the art of causing the money he had made use of to return again into his pocket.' A likely candidate for the authorship of the *Heptameron*, then, were it not for the 250-year disparity between the learned d'Abano's death and the earliest evidence of the book's existence in the mid-sixteenth century.

Somewhat ironically, we learn crucial details of magical texts from those protesting the loudest against their popularity at the time. In Johann Weyer's *De praestigiis daemonum* ('On the Illusion of Demons', 1577), the sceptic Dutch physician rationally analyses incidences of witchcraft and demon

---

4 This stemmed from the belief in the dove as a messenger of the afterlife – if the patient was strapped with such feathers, he or she could not pass on. Catherine of Braganza, wife of Charles II, was given the treatment by her desperate Portuguese palace medics, but died on 31 December 1705.

conjuring. He dismisses the *Heptameron* as a 'pestilential little book', but by repeating sources now lost, we learn, from the appendix of his book for example, of the *Pseudomonarchia daemonum*, or 'False Monarchy of Demons', a hierarchical list of the sixty-nine demons of Hell. Such criticism could backfire on the critic. In attempting to demonstrate the nonsense of popular spells, charms, rites and exorcism techniques by describing them in detail, the Protestant Weyer himself inadvertently drew much hostility from both Reformed and Catholics,

like the French jurist Jean Bodin, who accused him of propagating witchcraft – and the Church swiftly banned his book too.

The Vatican sought to know their enemy, and the Vatican Secret Archives, a records office that had existed in some form from as early as the first century, swelled

BELOW: *A German copy of the* Heptameron *grimoire written sometime between 1750 and 1799, with instructions for conjuring angels for the seven days of the week, information on magical circles and prayers to recite for conjurations.*

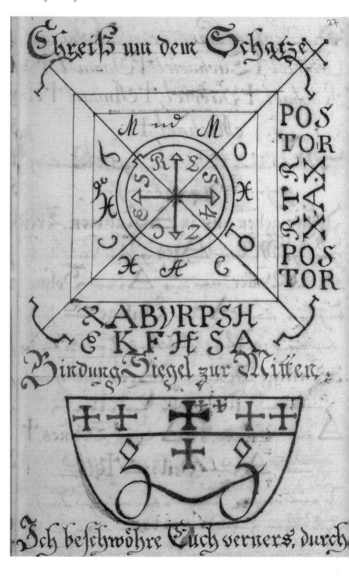

Within the illustration, the following text appears:

J make a cercle large and round.
With karettis and ffygures.
And knowe not the aventures.
For the dirkenesse hyode with June.
Off the karettis whanne J gynne.
To emprynte til they be seue.
J wote neuere what they mene.

Aue J conjecte yt may so be.
That spirites scholde obeye to me.
By my invocacyouns.

ABOVE: *How to conjure a demon, and order it to fetch treasure for you. From the manuscript* The Pilgrimage of the Life of Man *by John Lydgate (second quarter of the fifteenth century).*

with contraband in a collection that was only opened to scholars in the late nineteenth century by Pope Leo XIII (1810–1903).[5] One book that has been confirmed by the archivists as sitting on their shelves is the *Grand Grimoire* (which would go on to be a sensationally popular mass-market publication), a guide to summoning the Devil's prime minister of Hell, Lucifugé Rofocale. The manuscript was said to be adapted from writings by the probably mythical medieval character Honorius of Thebes, who many claimed had written his grimoire while possessed by the Devil. The *Grand Grimoire* is said to contain proof of demonic evocation and occult spells, as well as the process whereby newly elected popes are slowly won over by Satan's greatness.

---

5 Vatican scholars have also produced their own literary curiosities. Keeper of the Vatican library Leo Allatius (1586–1669), for example, wrote *De graecorum hodie quorundam opinationibus* ('On the Popular Beliefs of the Greeks', 1645), a letter in which he presents the first methodical discussion of vampires, specifically a peculiar Greek type known as the Callicantzaros vampire, active around Christmas. Allatius, though, is perhaps most famous for his unpublished, entirely rumoured essay *De Praeputio Domini Nostri Jesu Christi Diatriba* ('Discourse on the Foreskin of Our Lord Jesus Christ'), which posits that the recently observed rings of Saturn were formed from the foreskin of Jesus Christ.

The frontispiece engraving of Iugum ferreum Luciferi, seu exorcismi terribles *(1676), a Spanish manual for performing exorcisms by Didaco Gómez Lodosa, showing a priest successfully banishing an evil spirit.*

The rite for conjuring Lucifugé to appear within a magic circle to grant requests was particularly enticing because of his knowledge of the whereabouts of buried treasure. The *Grand Grimoire*, rumoured to be impervious to fire, was claimed to have been discovered in the tomb of Solomon in 1520, but records date its first appearance to about 1750, when across Europe one could hear treasure-hunters chanting its 'Great Call' to Lucifugé: 'Emperor LUCIFER, master of all the rebel spirits, I beg you to favour me in the call that I am making to your grand minister LUCIFUGÉ ROFOCALE, desiring to make a pact with him.' In nineteenth-century Paris the diabolic *Grand Grimoire* was republished as *Le Dragon rouge* ('The Red Dragon'). You could find it openly displayed in the windows of high-street bookshops, which is where the English book collector Thomas Frognall Dibdin bought two copies, after asking for 'anything old and curious'.

Where most authors and readers of grimoires were preoccupied with demonic assistance, Britain's most famous occult philosopher, Dr John Dee, was more focused on establishing communication with angels. This he sought to achieve with the assistance of a scryer, an intermediary who could gaze into a crystal ball or other device and interpret spiritual responses. In 1582, he found his man in Edward Kelley, who at the time operated under the name of Edward Talbot to disguise his conviction for 'coining', or forgery.[6] Through Kelley, Dee was finally able to seek celestial help in interpreting a magical manuscript with which he was obsessed, known as the *Book of Soyga*. With 147 pages of incantations, astrological instructions, demonology, lists of lunar mansions and the genealogies of angels, it was the mysterious last thirty-six pages with which Dee was obsessed. Each carried a square table of letters in thirty-six rows by thirty-six columns, all indecipherable.

Happily, Kelley managed to patch him through to the archangel Uriel, and Dee, who recorded the session in his diary, wasted no time in asking the minister of grace: 'Is my book, of Soyga, of any excellency?' Through Kelley, Uriel replied in Latin that the book had been

Frontispiece illustration of the Devil, from a copy of Le Dragon rouge *grimoire, printed c.1820.*

6 Kelley held Dee under his own spell for years, even when Kelley revealed to Dee in 1587 that the angels – namely a spirit called Madimi – had ordered them to swap their wives for a night. Dee was anguished by the command of the 'angels', and ceased any further spiritual conferences. He did, nevertheless, share his 32-year-old wife, Jane: the 'cross-matching' is noted in Dee's diary as occurring on 22 May 1587. The two men eventually parted ways in 1589.

Edward Kelley in the act of invoking the spirit of a dead person. From Ebenezer Sibly's New and Complete Illustration of the Celestial Science of Astrology ..., *from 1784.*

revealed to Adam in the Garden of Eden by the good angels of God. Quite excellent, then. 'Will you give me any instructions, how I may read those Tables of Soyga?' asked Dee. Alas, Uriel's reply was disappointing: 'Only the Archangel Michael himself can interpret this book.' The *Book of Soyga* was long thought lost, until in 1994 the American scholar Deborah Harkness discovered not one but two copies – MS Sloane 8 in the British Library, and Bodley MS 908 in the Bodleian Library. Both had been catalogued under the work's *incipit* (starting word) Aldaraia.

Of all of these magical manuscripts, though, a personal favourite is MS1766 of the Wellcome Collection in London, more commonly referred to as the *Compendium of Demonology and Magic*. The work is written in both Latin and German, and its author and date of creation are unknown. The date of 1057 is given on the title page (as well as the warning *Noli me tangere* – 'don't touch me'), but this is clearly in the tradition of presenting grimoires to seem much older than they actually are, and it is usually dated to 1775. With the witch-hunting hysteria having subsided by this time, you can see the artist relishing the freedom to exercise (or perhaps exorcise) his imagination.

Over thirty-five extraordinary illustrated pages the author paints conjurations, devils devouring limbs, flames and snakes bursting from crotches, as well as pages of inked sigils and mystical symbols, and bright red demonic character sheets, displaying the influence of earlier grimoires including the seventeenth-century *Book of Abramelin* and Agrippa's *Three Books of Occult Philosophy*. One image shows a man performing necromantic arts within a protective circle, with a grimoire and a corpse of a hanged man beside him. Another shows a magician digging for treasure, only to find that his accomplice has been seized by a 2.7-metre (9-ft) cockerel-headed demon that is also casually urinating on their lantern. A pretty unambiguous warning against the 'fashionable crime' of magic-based treasure-hunting that would remain popular across Europe for some time.

OPPOSITE: *A pact signed by Lucifer and the French Catholic priest Urbain Grandier, who was executed for sorcery in 1634 following the 'Loudun Possessions' affair, in which he was accused of summoning evil spirits to possess a convent of Ursuline nuns. The pact, written in backward Latin and signed by Lucifer and his demons, was later published as proof.*

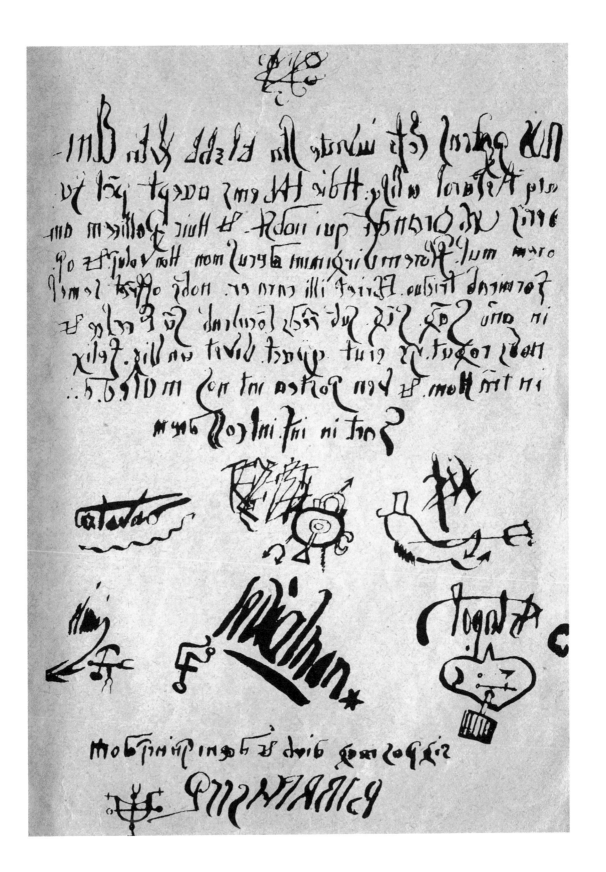

The Mowing-Devil:
Or, Strange *NEWS* out of
Hartford-fhire.

Being a True Relation of a Farmer, who Bargaining
with a Poor *Mower*, about the Cutting down Three Half
Acres of *Oats*; upon the *Mower*'s asking too much, the *Farmer* fwore, *That the Devil fhould Mow it*, rather than He:
And fo it fell out, that that very Night, the Crop of *Oats*
fhew'd as if it had been all of a Flame; but next Morning
appear'd fo neatly Mow'd by the Devil, or fome Infernal Spirit, that no Mortal Man was able to do the like.
Alfo, How the faid *Oats* ly now in the Field, and the Owner
has not Power to fetch them away.

Licenfed, *Auguft* 22th. 1678.

ABOVE: *The Mowing-Devil: Or, Strange News out
of Hartford-Shire (1678). The pamphlet relates how
a Hertfordshire farmer refused to pay a labourer for
mowing his field, swearing he'd rather the Devil
mowed it instead. He awoke to see the field in flames
that night, and in the morning found it perfectly
mowed, that no mortal man was able to do the like.
Crop circle researchers consider it the earliest record
of the phenomenon.*

BELOW: *A Batak amulet against bullets and with
magical drawings on the reverse, inscribed on the rib
bone of a water buffalo.*

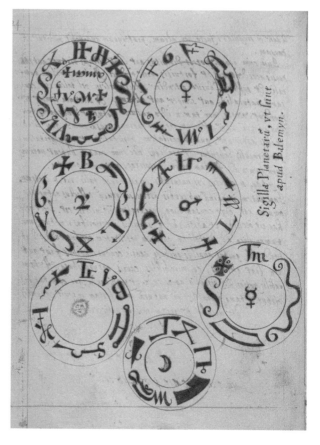

ABOVE: *Magical sigils invoking the planetary
spirits, from a copy of the* Book of Balemyn,
mid-seventeenth century.

OPPOSITE TOP: *A 1750 Ethiopian magical recipe
manuscript, containing protective amulets, talismans
and charms. This would have been the manual for a*
däbtära *or exorcist.*

OPPOSITE BOTTOM: *A folding spell manual (*pustaha*)
used by wizards of the Toba Batak tribe, north
Sumatra, Indonesia. In the collection of the
Rijksmuseum, Netherlands. For the Batak, writing
was primarily to preserve magical knowledge, handled
by the* datu *or priest-magician writing on the bark of
the* alim *tree and folding the book like an accordion.*

Seine Raupen A.:
Harn von gespuckt
und Zwischendruck.

Der fürst der finsternis: Dagol:

FOLLOWING FOUR PAGES: *Images from the*
Compendium of Demonology and
Magic *(c.1775). The Devil devouring the*
limbs of sinners; treasure-hunting with a
demon; a seemingly friendlier bat-eared
demon; and an advancing snake-demon.

Frevelhaftes Schaz=Graben.
ohne Kdntnis der Operation. A: 1668.
zu N:

So erscheinet der Belzebub.
Seine Raupsist Mandragora mit Meuschen Zann.

Magots.   Turitel.
Carufar   Nelion
Prisop.   Eloson.

So gefällt das Astharoth zu verrinnen.

Oriens. Baimon. Ariton. Gogaleson. Zugula.

Asa

Vezol

Chuz

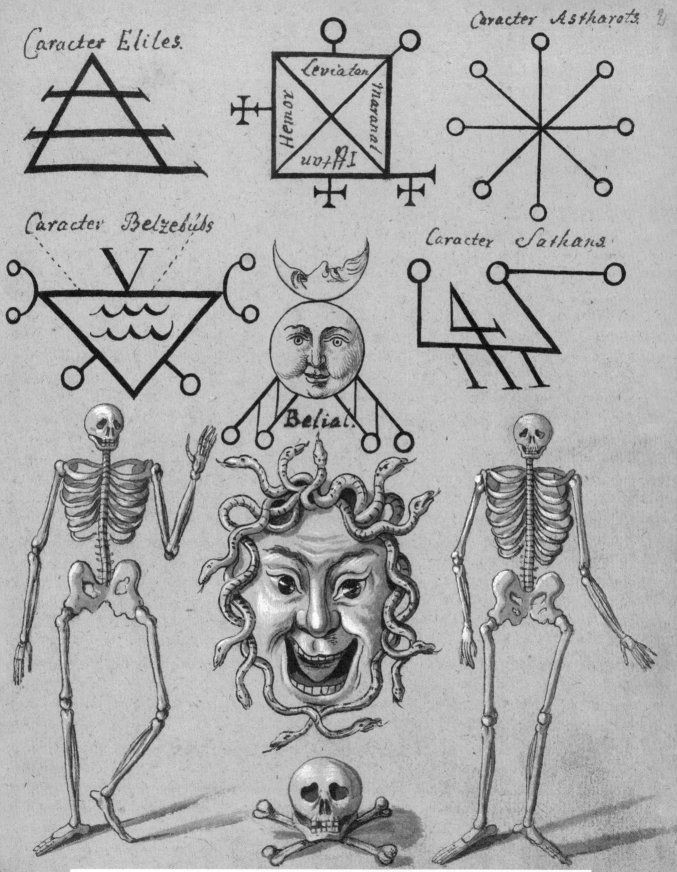

Another image from the Compendium of Demonology and Magic *(c.1775): snake demon and demonic characters.*

Nowhere, though, was the consultation of grimoires for finding buried treasure more damaging than in Egypt, where a medieval Arab tomb-robbing grimoire had 'guided' local opportunist excavators since the fifteenth century. The *Kitīb Kanz al-'ulūm wa-al-durr al-manzūm fī ḥaqā'iq 'ilm al-sharī'ah wa-daqā'iq 'ilm al-ṭabt'ah* ('Treasure of Knowledge and Orderly Pearls on the True Meaning of Revealed Knowledge and the Intricacies of Natural Science'), sometimes known as *The Book of Buried Pearls*, offers a list of burial sites together with supernatural information on how to remove their treasures and dispel the *djinn* and spirits that guard their secrets. The book was responsible for centuries of grave-robbing that left the landscape riddled with countless holes. In an effort to negate

The Clavis inferni *('Key of Hell'), a late eighteenth-century black magic text by 'Cyprianus', a common pseudonym. The work is said to have been a textbook of the Black School at Wittenburg, a German school for the dark arts. This image shows the Kings of the North, South East and West with their associated beasts.*

the destructive effect of the book, which remained popular into the twentieth century, in 1907 the Director of Antiquities in Egypt, Gaston Maspero, ordered cheap Arabic and French reprints of the book, in the hope that ubiquity would counteract its mystery and credibility. This was largely in vain. The editor of this new edition, Ahmed Bey Kamal, claimed that *The Book of Buried Pearls* had caused more damage to Egyptian antique heritage than wars and natural erosion combined.

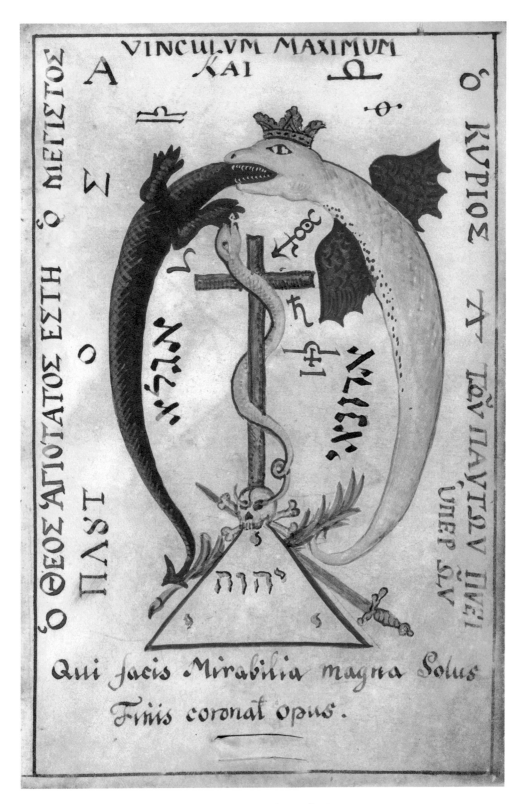

A crowned red-wing dragon devours a lizard, also from the Clavis inferni.

ABOVE: *Portraits from Francis Barrett's* The Magus
*(1801) of Apollyon, or Abaddon, the angel of Death
and king of a locust army; and the fallen angel
Belial, also known as the Devil.*

BELOW: *Adramelech, 'king of fire', eighth of the ten
arch-demons and Grand Chancellor of Hell. From the
1863* Dictionnaire infernal, *an alphabetically indexed
compendium of demonology first published in 1818.*

Adramelech, grand chancelier des enfers

By design most grimoires tell us very little of their authors, the anonymity offering both protection and marketable mystery. In contrast, in the literary genre of 'spirit writing' which we turn to now, it is the author that is of primary interest, principally because they managed to write the book while dead. Guided by a supernatural wordsmith, mediums would write out messages, predictions and even entire books, either through a planchette (a small wheeled board fitted with a vertical pencil), a standard pen or through dictation to an assistant. As luck would have it, the psychic connection seems to be strongest with the great titans of literature, but their skills invariably prove to have rusted somewhat post mortem. 'Strange perversions of style occur,' the book historian Walter Hart Blumenthal noted dryly in 1955, 'and lapses into the commonplace, even the maudlin, give rise to the suspicion that the afterlife is not especially stimulating to the literary spirit.'

According to *Essential Cataloguing: The Basics* (2002), the authoritative guide followed by the British Library and the American Librarian Association, books written by the ghosts of authors must be catalogued under the name of the post-mortem personality, not the name of the medium who recorded the work. This means, for example, that technically speaking Shakespeare's final work was not *The Two Noble Kinsmen* (1613–14), but *For Jesus' Sake – By Shakespeare's Spirit* (1920). You can find it catalogued under 'Shakespeare, William (Spirit)'. Shortly after his death in 1870, having written only half of *The Mystery of Edwin Drood*, the ghost of Charles Dickens chose to reach out to one T. P. James, a small publisher in Brattleboro, Vermont, USA, to dictate the second half of his tale. *Part Second of the Mystery of Edwin Drood, by the Spirit Pen of Charles Dickens* was published in 1873. Alas, a callous world paid little attention.

THE BOSTON PLANCHETTE.

From the Original Pattern, first made in Boston in 1860.

RETAIL PRICES OF THE BOSTON PLANCHETTE.

Black Walnut Board, neatly finished, durable castors . . . $1.00
Polished Board, silvered castors. 1.50
Holly Wood, handsomely painted 2.00

Advertisement for a planchette, a piece of wood with wheeled castors and a pencil-holding aperture, used by mediums channelling dead authors, among other spirits.

In 1884, American writer and 'humble instrument' Olive Pettis really went for gold and produced *Autobiography by Jesus of Nazareth*, from which we learn that Christ is as generous with interminable sentences and exclamation marks as he is with fish and loaves. 'Mark Twain (Spirit)' is credited with authoring a book seven years after the author's death, titled *Jap Herron: A Novel Written From the Ouija Board* (1917); while Sir Arthur Conan Doyle, whose ridiculed belief in the supernatural cost him a peerage, got back in touch in 1983 to relay *The Great Mystery of Life Beyond Death*. (Doyle, incidentally, published a collection of his wife's own automatic writing, *Pheneas Speaks*, in 1927. Lady Doyle receives a mere mention in the acknowledgement.) If you are so inclined, you can also browse the *Post-Mortem Journal* of T. E. Lawrence (1964), 'Recorded through automatic writing by Jane Sherwood', and *Psychic Messages from Oscar Wilde* (1934), in which Wilde avoids any in-depth discussion of his works in favour of launching an unexpected and lengthy attack on James Joyce.

Approaching the twentieth century, things get wilder, with the rising popularity of science fiction and astronomical discovery. One fascinating book from this period is *From India to the Planet Mars* (1899) by the University of Geneva psychologist Theodor Flournoy. The book is effectively a case report on the French medium Hélène Smith, whose psychic satellite dish was attuned not just to the dead (both Marie Antoinette and a fifteenth-century Indian princess say hello) but living, breathing Martians. Between 1894 and 1901 she held over sixty séances relaying the Martian language and biology, and filing a Martian traffic report: 'How funny, these cars!' says Smith. 'Hardly any horses or people that are on the move. Imagine different kinds of armchairs that slide but don't have wheels. It is the tiny wheels that produce the sparks … One also sees the people walking. They are built like us and hold onto each other with the little finger.'

In the late 1940s, Mary Stephenson Barnes of California followed suit with her writings of 'clairaudient' transcripts of new poetry from Robert Browning, broadcast from the fourth dimensional plane. 'It seems a little strange that Browning would choose me as a collaborator,' she admits, somewhat pre-

JAP HERRON

A NOVEL WRITTEN FROM THE OUIJA BOARD

WITH AN INTRODUCTION
THE COMING OF JAP HERRON

Mark Twain

NEW YORK
MITCHELL KENNERLEY
MCMXVII

The title page of Jap Herron, *the book Mark Twain wrote seven years after his death.*

emptively, 'but that's the way it is.' And in 1953, an American woman named Florence Anspacher transcribed poems transmitted by her deceased husband in *Enigma: A Poetic Mystery*, via an Ouija board. The sessions were conducted with the help of two family friends, Joseph Auslander and Audrey Wurdemann – who just happened to be, respectively, a Columbia professor of poetry and a Pulitzer prize-winning poet.

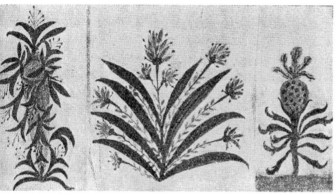

OPPOSITE AND ABOVE: *A passage of Martian writing channelled through the hand of the French psychic Hélène Smith, and her sketches of the Martian landscape. Found in* From India to the Planet Mars *(1899).*

ABOVE: Occult Crime: Detection, Investigation, and Verification*, a 1992 advisory text for American law enforcement on supernatural crime.*

Literature to help defend against the dark arts appeared with greater frequency with the moral panics of more recent times. One worth tracking down is *A Basic Guide to the Occult for Law Enforcement Agencies* (1986), although copies are so rare that the assistance of a treasure-hunting demon might be your only hope of finding one. The pamphlet is the work of the god-fearing housewife Mrs Mary Ann Herold of Colorado, whose advice for police officers is to treat with suspicion scenes of dried blood, human skulls – 'with or without candles' – and 'rooms converted into dungeons or torture chambers'. Tattoos, black make-up and shaved heads are also dead giveaways of Satanic murderers. 'It is my hope,' concludes Mrs Herold (and may I say that I share the sentiment for this chapter, also), 'that the information contained in this guide will prevent not only personal harm to you, but also will serve to preserve and protect the general public. If just one innocent child is saved from being used as a human sacrifice … then my purpose will have been accomplished.'

RELIGIOUS ODDITIES

On 23 June 1626, a suspiciously fat codfish caused quite the stir at Cambridge market. When its belly was sliced open, out slid a parcel of folded cloth cut from a ship's sail. Wiping away the guts, the fishwife peeled back the soggy layers to reveal the contents: a small, slim book. Though almost disintegrated by the juices of its unorthodox presentation case, it was found to be a curious collection of religious treatises with the title *Preparation to the Crosse*. In a letter that was later handed to the British Museum, Dr Joseph Mead of Christ's College, Cambridge, excitedly confirmed the discovery to Sir Martin Stuteville: 'When I first saw it, it seemed almost turned into a jelly, and consumed … I saw all with mine own eyes – the fish, the maw, the piece of sail-cloth, the book … He that had had his nose as near as I yester morning, would have been persuaded there was no imposture here without witness.'

The book was said to have been written almost 100 years earlier by the Protestant priest John Frith, while he was held prisoner by Cardinal Wolsey in a fish cellar – an environment so noxious that it had fatally overwhelmed several of his fellow captives. Frith was burnt at the stake shortly afterwards, on 4 July 1533 'for his soul's salvation'; but a century later, when the circumstances of its discovery at the fish market became known, his *Preparation to the Crosse* took on a new life. It was reprinted with a huge run under the title *Vox Piscis [Voice of the Fish]; or, the Book-Fish; contayning three Treatises which were found in the belly of a Cod-fish …* (1627), with a woodcut depicting the fish stall, the book and the fishwife's knife. How the book had miraculously appeared inside the fish was never established. A young Cambridge scholar in *Notes and Queries* quipped that the book

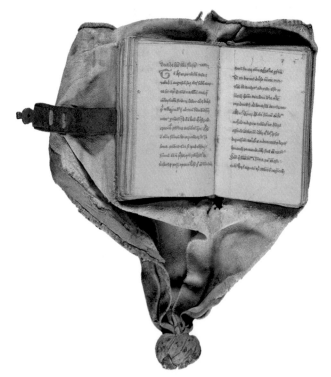

LEFT: *A c. fifteenth-century 'girdle book', which accessorized the dress of medieval European monks. The leather bindings of these small portable books were tied in a Turk's head knot which tucked into the belt, for the book to swing from the waist.*

OPPOSITE: *A page of the* Luttrell Psalter *(Add MS 42130 in the British Library), a psalter (book of psalms) created in 1320–45 for the wealthy landowner Sir Geoffrey Luttrell. The book is uniquely strange with its illustrations of everyday fourteenth-century life that enter the surreal and grotesque, apparently at the whim of the artist.*

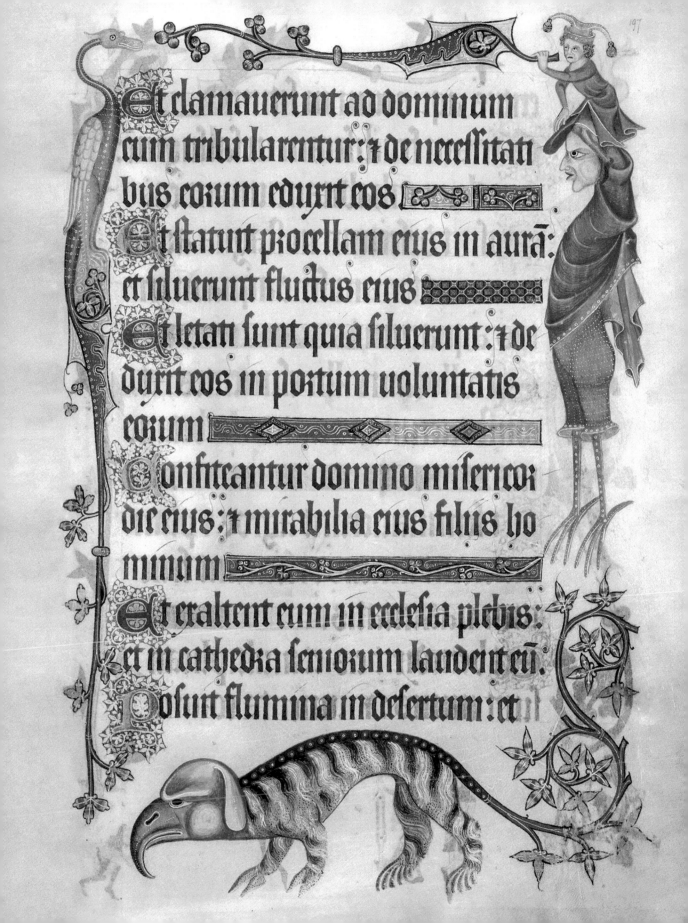

Et clamauerunt ad dominum
cum tribularentur: ꝛ de necessitati
bus eorum eduxit eos

Et statuit procellam eius in aurā:
et siluerunt fluctus eius

Et letati sunt quia siluerunt: ꝛ de
duxit eos in portum uoluntatis
eorum

Confiteantur domino misericor
die eius: ꝛ mirabilia eius filiis ho
minum

Et exaltent eum in ecclesia plebis:
et in cathedra seniorum laudent eū.
Ponut flumina in desertum: et

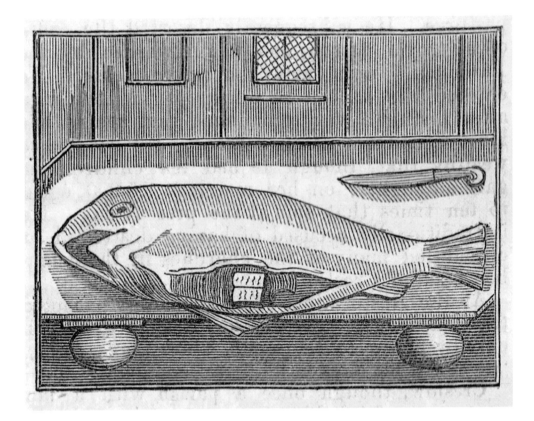

The book-fish, as engraved in Vox Piscis… *(1627).*

'might be found in the Code, but could never be entered in the Digest'.

While many writers can claim the same 'devoted' following as *Vox Piscis* eventually found, as far as I'm aware the instance of a reader demonstrating their affection by legally *marrying* a book has happened only once. Sabbatai Zevi (1626–76) was a Sephardic ordained rabbi who, from the age of twenty-two, claimed to be the long-awaited Jewish Messiah. This he proved by pronouncing the Tetragrammaton, the four-letter name of the God of Israel, which was strictly forbidden to do by anyone other than the Jewish high priest in the Temple in Jerusalem on the Day of Atonement.

He also told his followers that he could fly, but explained he couldn't do it in public because they weren't worthy of witnessing

Sabbatai Zevi (1626–76), lawfully wedded husband of the Torah.

A later replica of the cumdach *of the Stowe Missal (written after* AD *792).*

it. As a stunt to reinforce his authority he then organized a wedding ceremony between himself (the *Ein Sof* or 'One Without End'), and the Torah, the Scroll of Law. The ceremony was solemnly performed at Salonica (at the time part of Turkey) sometime between 1653 and 1658. With the holy text dressed in bridal vestments, the ceremony was performed before witnesses in the manner of a traditional Jewish wedding. Sabbatai Zevi lovingly placed the ring upon one of the wooden rollers around which the scroll is wound. The groom beamed. The crowd cheered. The rabbis of Salonica promptly banished Zevi from the city.

As we'll also see with the miniature copies of the Qur'an worn under armour and on battle flags for protection (p. 221), the combination of religious devotion and the magical power of books was a powerful amalgam. In early medieval Ireland, the great texts associated with significant Christian figures were protected with *cumdachs*. These luxuriously decorated metal reliquary cases, or book-shrines, usually feature tooled metalwork dominated by a crucifix design on the cover, and can be finely bejewelled. They were carried on a cord or chain to wear around the neck, placing them close to the heart, which was thought to offer protective and medicinal benefits to the wearer, and so the cumdachs and their 'battle bibles' were worn in warfare. Only five examples

The Joshua Roll, a Byzantine illuminated manuscript of probably the tenth century, is unique in Christian manuscripts in that it is in the form of a single horizontal rotulus *(scroll) measuring 10 metres (33ft) long; the form is more common in Chinese art.*

of *cumdachs* survive. The most famous is the copper and silver-plated one for the *Cathach of St Columba*, an important psalter and likely the oldest Irish book in existence, probably created just after the death of Columba in AD 597. That historic text and its cumdach belonged to the O'Donnell clan, an old Gaelic royal family whose members bore it aloft as a battle standard (*Cathach* means 'Battler' and it was also used as a rallying cry). The custom was for a monk to wear it around his neck and walk three times around the O'Donnell forces to activate its protective charm.

Contrary to what one might assume, a large-format Bible, in either one or several volumes, was a relatively rare production in the manuscript era. With it being so labour-

and cost-intensive to produce carefully copied manuscripts, it made sense to prioritize the texts most frequently used; thus it was much more common during those 1500 years for artisans to reproduce just the four Gospels. But, of course, even the most careful scribe (and later, printer) was not immune to error — the Word of God might be infallible, but its mortal transcriber was decidedly not so. When it was noticed while re-reading that words and sentences had been skipped over, the scribe would write them in above or next to the line. If the omission was greater, a *signe de renvoi* or 'tie mark' symbol (typically a cross, line or set of dots) would be added, to connect to a

OPPOSITE: *From 1641–43 the London writer John Taylor engaged in a 'pamphlet war' with rival author Henry Walker, in which the two men attempted to humiliate each other in print. Here Walker is depicted in an intimate situation with the Devil, on the title page of John Taylor's* A Reply as true as Steele, To a Rusty, Rayling, Ridiculous, Lying, Libell *(1641).*

A Reply as true as Steele,

To a Rusty, Rayling, Ridiculous, Lying, Libell; which was lately written by an impudent unsoder'd Ironmonger and called by the name of *An Answer to a foolish Pamphlet Entituled, A Swarme of Sectaries and Schismatiques.*

By IOHN TAYLOVR.

The Divell is hard bound, and did hardly straine,
To shit a Libeller a knave in graine.

Printed Anno Dom. 1641.

Painted miniature of Titivillus, 'patron demon' of scribes, from a c.1510 French manuscript.

gloss (notation) in the margin – this is the ancestor of the modern footnote. If the wrong word was added, then it would be erased (from the Latin *eras*, literally 'scraped away') from the surface of the vellum skin with a knife, and the bare patch written over.

It is fascinating to examine the mistakes that weren't caught. Even the famed *Book of Kells* (created *c.* AD 800), the greatest treasure of insular manuscript art[1], with its breathtakingly ornate illustrations, offers traces of human error among its 340 leaves of high-quality calf vellum. For example, its scribe created an extra ancestor in the genealogy of Jesus. In the Gospel of Luke at 3:26, the transcriber misread 'QUI FUIT MATHATHIAE' as 'QUI FUIT MATHATH *IAE*'. On the assumption that IAE (the Latin ending of Matthew's name) was an entirely separate person, the mysterious IAE was recorded as such.

---

1 The monastic art of the British Isles from *c.*500 to 900 AD.

So vexing was the possibility of error for even the most accomplished scribe that we find references and illustrations of it personified in demon form. Titivillus, known as 'the patron demon of scribes', was said to be sent by Lucifer to torment the tired scribe and trick him into bringing errors into his work, and is first referenced *c.*1285 by Johannes Galensis (John of Wales) in *Tractatus de penitentia*. The demon was also said to steal monks' idle chatter and their mumbled delivery during church services to bring back to Hell. Apparently, Titivillus's work is not yet done: Marc Drogin notes in *Medieval Calligraphy: Its History and Technique* (1980) that 'for the past half-century every edition of the *Oxford English Dictionary* has listed an incorrect page reference for, of all things, a footnote on the earliest mention of Titivillus'.

As well as the corrections and commentary offered in glossed margins, scribes could also embellish works in the borders with illuminations. An extraordinary example of just how far this enlivening could be taken is the *Smithfield Decretals*, one of approximately 675 surviving copies of the glossed *Decretals* (Papal decrees concerning points of canon law) of Pope Gregory IX (*r.*1227–41). Every one of its 626 pages of text is bustling with imagery. The manuscript was first copied out in the early fourteenth century somewhere in the south of France; by 1340, it was in the hands of a London owner, who hired a team of artists to fill its margins with images and symbols to help elucidate the information. The *Decretals* was a key text for legal study in the Middle Ages – it isn't hard to imagine how grateful the reader must have been for these distractions from the monotony of the text. Another great feature to be found is in the text itself. On the recto of folio 314, the exhausted scribe sneaks in his own appeal, having by this point written out (with his colleagues)

The Virgin Mary rides the Satanic Serpent at the end of the world. From Heinrich Kircher's Prophetia Apocalyptica … *(1676), a rare German work.*

1971 Papal letters and accompanying documents across 310 folios. 'The whole thing is finished,' he cries triumphantly, 'give the man who wrote it a drink.'

With the introduction of printing, a curious collector's pursuit on this theme was created with incidents of Bible printers' errata (typos and other reproduction errors), which have led to certain editions, referred to today with nicknames based on these mistakes, being highly sought after. Many are unintentionally comical, especially when one considers the horror they must have provoked in their makers. The *Wicked Bible*, *Adulterous Bible* or *Sinner's Bible*, from 1631, for example, by Barker and Lucas, omits a crucial 'not' from Exodus 20:14 to proclaim the seventh commandment as being, 'Thou shalt commit adultery'. The printers were fined £300 for this, and the bulk of the books were destroyed. Only eleven surviving copies

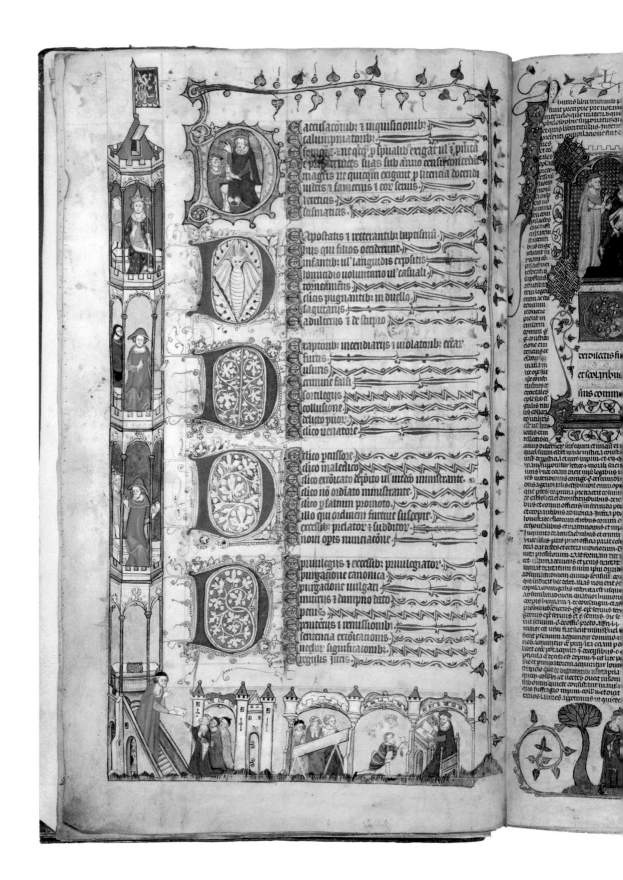

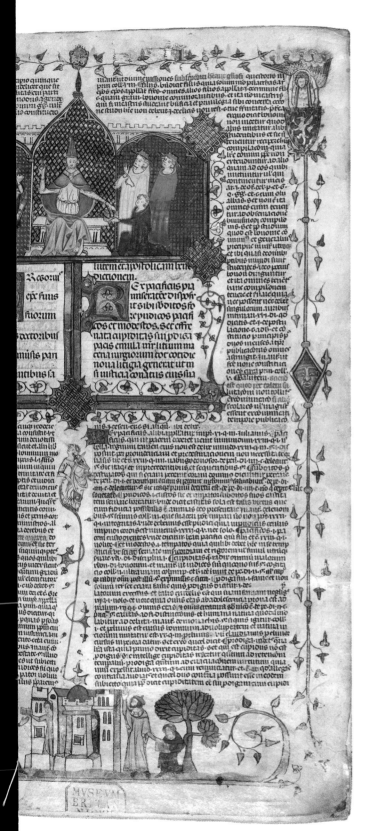

are known. Similarly, the *Sin On Bible* from 1716 commands, in Jeremiah 31:34, to 'sin on more' rather than 'sin no more'; 8000 copies were printed before the mistake was noticed.

Edmund Becke's Bible of 1549 is notable for Becke inserting his own notes, most famously his addition to 1 Peter 3:7's command to the husband to honour his wife, which reads 'And if she be not obediente and helpful unto hym, endevoureth to beate the fear of God into her heade, that thereby she may be compelled to learne her dutye and do it.' This has led to it being known as the *Wife-Beater's Bible*. The *Judas Bible*, from 1613, has Judas, not Jesus, saying 'Sit ye here while I go yonder and pray' (Matthew 26:36). This remained in the second edition printed by Robert Barker, printer to King James I – in a copy held in St Mary's Church, Totnes, Devon, UK, the misprint was long ago covered with a small piece of paper (see image overleaf). And finally, thanks to a damaged printer's letter n, the *Owl Bible* from 1944 swaps 'own' with 'owl' in 1 Peter 3:5 to slightly confusing effect: 'For after this manner,' it reads, 'in the old time the holy women also, who trusted God,

LEFT: The Smithfield Decretals. *The central illustration on the right-hand page shows Gregory IX, surrounded by his cardinals, organizing the distribution of the work.*

BELOW: *'The whole thing is finished; give the man who wrote it a drink,' writes the worn-out scribe of the* Smithfield Decretals.

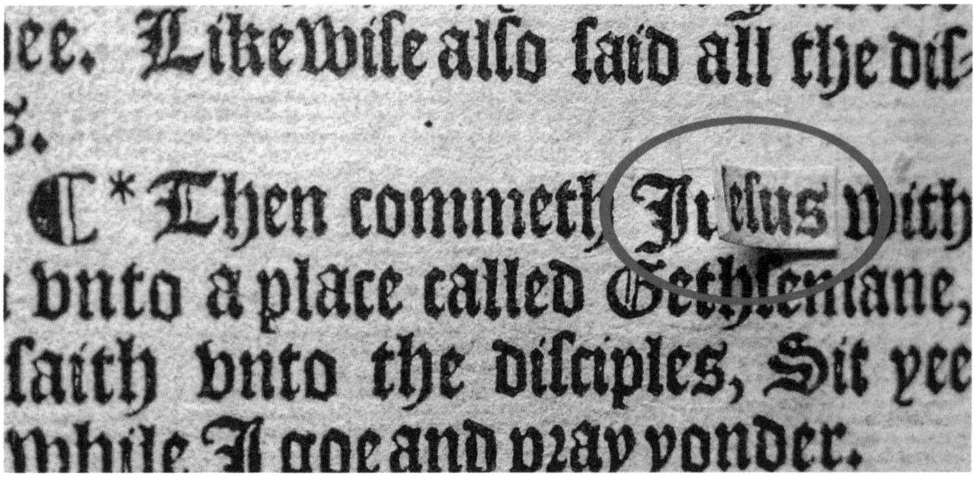

ee. Likewiſe alſo ſaid all the diſ
. ¶ *Then commeth Judas with
vnto a place called Gethſemane,
ſaith vnto the diſciples, Sit yee
while I goe and pray yonder.

adorned themselves, being in subjection to their owl husbands.'[2]

Visions of the landscapes, tortures and demonic workforce of Hell in medieval manuscripts have lost none of their startling gruesomeness for the modern viewer, with strange ideas that have since fallen by the infernal wayside. Take the 'Hell-mouth', a terrifying doorway to Satan's subterranean kingdom in the form of a giant animal's maw, from which tortured souls and demons reach out in agony. The idea appears to originate from the Anglo-Saxon period, with surviving literature describing the entrance to Hell in this bestial way. Sometimes it's the mouth of the Devil himself. 'Came they never out of the pit of snakes and of the throat of the dragon which is called Satan,' writes the author of Homily 4:46–8 in a late tenth-century volume of religious writings known as the *Vercelli Book*. One of the most spectacular depictions is in the *Winchester Psalter* ('Cotton MS Nero C IV' in the British Library), shown here, from the twelfth century. The Archangel Michael locks up the gaping jaws of the scaled Satanic dragon, as it reveals a wriggling pile

A copy of the Judas Bible with misprint covered over later.

of miserable souls (including a speared king and queen) and overseer demons within, in a scene of the Last Judgement. This was the eternity that awaited those who failed entrance to Heaven's paradise – the effect remains as startling to the modern reader.

At roughly the same time, across the world an unknown Japanese scribe was putting the finishing touches to an equivalent manuscript scroll and masterwork, bearing the same hellish warnings. Today preserved in the Nara National Museum, the *Hell Scroll* (jigokuzōji) has officially been designated one of the National Treasures of Japan. It shows seven of the lesser hells mentioned in the *Kisekyō* ('Sūtra of the World Arising'), describing six of them in the accompanying text, with each entry beginning 'There is yet another hell'.

OPPOSITE: *The Archangel Michael locks the Hell-mouth, in this miniature depiction from the* Winchester Psalter *(Cotton MS Nero C IV, f. 39r), in the collection of the British Library.*

---

2 Outside of Biblical printing, a most unfortunate printing error can be found in *The Vocabulary of East Anglia: an Attempt to Record the Vulgar Tongue of the Twin Sister Counties, Norfolk and Suffolk* … by Robert Forby (1830) in which the title PREFACE had its R accidentally replaced with a second E.

DESENGANNO

DOS

PECCADORES

Descendant in infernum uiuentes Ne descendant morientes S. Bern.

OPPOSITE AND ABOVE: *Title page and illustration from* Desenganno dos Peccadores (*'Disillusion of Sinners', 1724) by the Jesuit priest Alexandre Perier. The book features graphic depictions of the sense-based tortures awaiting sinners in Hell, from demons hammering metal bolts through one's eye to the sounds of Satanic trumpets and the barking of hellhounds.*

TORMENTO DOS OVVIDOS

Top: *'Hell of the Flaming Rooster', the eleventh of the sixteen hells and fourth section of the Japanese work known as the Hell Scroll.*

Above: *The 'Hell of Measures', the second section of the scroll and the tenth of the sixteen hells.*

Here we learn details of the punishments meted out in the Hell of Excrement, the Hell of Measures, the Hell of the Iron Mortar, the Hell of the Flaming Rooster (presided over by a giant fire-breathing cockerel), the Hell of the Black Sand Cloud, the Hell of Pus and Blood and the Hell of Foxes and Wolves. The entire scroll unrolls to an overwhelming demonic panorama of 4.55 metres (14ft 11in) in length.

If we turn to Italy while following this theme, we find Jacobus Palladinus de Teramo (1349–1417) – bishop, canon lawyer and member of the powerful family of Palladini. While de Teramo is better known for more sober works like his commentary on Peter

Lombard's *Libri quatuor sententiarum* ('Sentences', printed at Augsburg, 1472), I am particularly fond of his bizarre tract of *c.*1382 titled *Consolatio peccatorum, seu Processus Luciferi contra Jesum Christum*, the 'Consolation of Sinners', which is also known as the *Liber Belial* or *Book of Belial*.

The work takes the form of a lawsuit filed by Lucifer and the forces of Hell against Jesus Christ, in which the Devil accuses the Son of God of trespassing into Hell, and is suing for damages. The case is presided over by King Solomon, with Moses defending Jesus Christ and the juridically trained demon Belial appearing for the Devil. At a second trial, Joseph acts as judge, and Aristotle and Isaiah

appear on Jesus Christ's legal team, facing off against the Emperor Augustus and Jeremiah for the Devil. Both verdicts are found in favour of Jesus, but a concession is made to grant the Devil right of possession over the souls of the damned at the Last Judgement.[3]

ABOVE: *From a 1461 copy of Jacobus de Teramo's* Liber Belial. *Here the Devil returns to Hell, triumphantly waving the writ of his lawsuit against Jesus Christ, to the delight of his minions.*

---

3 Incidentally, both God and the Devil have been the recipients of real lawsuits in recent history. *United States ex rel. Gerald Mayo v. Satan and His Staff*, for example, was filed in 1971 by Gerald Mayo, an inmate at Western Penitentiary, Pittsburgh, who complained that Satan had 'deprived him of his constitutional rights' – it was dismissed after the court noted that as a foreign prince Satan could claim sovereign immunity. In 1970, Arizona lawyer Russel T. Tansie sued God for $100,000 for 'negligence' on behalf of his secretary, Betty Penrose, whose house had been damaged by lightning. When the defendant 'failed to turn up in court', Penrose won the case by default.

OPPOSITE: *Leaves from a Thai* samut khoi, *or folding-book manuscript, telling the story of the monk Phra Malai travelling to Hell.*

The 1461 manuscript copy shown on page 181 is the only one to feature full colour miniatures, which have been associated with the 'Master of the Housebook', the most prestigious illuminator and graphic artist of the late Middle Ages in the Middle Rhine region. The book follows the formal requirements of canon law and was much read in the Middle Ages, printed numerous times and translated into several languages.

In Thai literature, the setting of Hell features prominently in *samut khoi*, or folding-book manuscripts, which from as early as the eighteenth century were commissioned by relatives of the recently deceased to earn merit for their loved ones in the afterlife. The better the artist and the more money spent on the book, the higher the rate of spiritual return. The beautifully illustrated books usually tell the legend of Phra Malai, a Buddhist monk of the Theravada tradition who is said to have achieved supernatural powers through meditation and worthiness. The monk flew to Hell (*naraka*), where he granted mercy and gave comfort to those he encountered. He returned to the land of the living with warnings from the deceased, who encouraged those alive to do all they can to avoid Hell by living a meritorious life through meditation and adherence to Buddhist principles. (The story itself is likely much older than the earliest surviving eighteenth-century manuscript examples, as it's based on an ancient Pali text.)

The books are written mostly in black ink on sturdy paper made from the bark of the khoi tree, with higher-grade examples featuring gold ink and luxurious gilt and lacquered covers. *Samut khoi* are truly amazing objects when completely unfolded. A typical example measures 69cm (27in) wide by 14cm (5½in) tall, but fully extended can reach 13.41 metres (44ft) in length. Traditionally, Thai monks used the books to recite aloud the legend of Phra Malai in fun, dramatic performances, flouting their strict rules for behaviour; but by the end of the nineteenth century they were officially

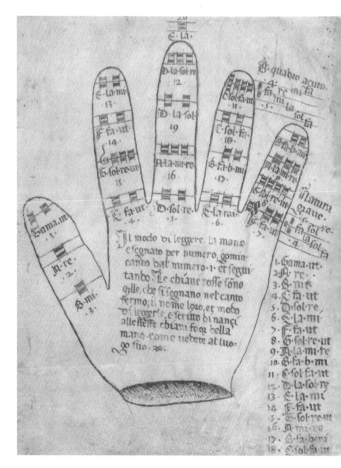

BELOW: *A 'Guidonian hand'. The Italian music theorist Guido of Arezzo (c.991–1033) devised the diagram to illustrate his own technique for choristers to learning songs. With codifying that had developed through various Greek, Roman and early medieval iterations, Guido assigned each note from a hexachord, or six-part, system of musical notation, to one of nineteen points around the hand.*

banned from conducting this undignified entertainment, and the books' popularity sadly faded away.

Visions of the afterlife serve as effective reminders as to why believers should keep to the straight and narrow, but there are also books of equal curiosity that served as more practical *aides-mémoire* for the pious, to help grease the hinges of the pearly gates. One such peculiarity is the *Ars memorandi per figuras evangelistarum* ('The Art of Memorizing the Evangelist Figures', Nuremberg, *c*.1470), a memory tool especially popular with the Dominican Friars, as its symbolic representation helped those with more limited education to memorize the Gospels. The images are wonderfully weird. The four Evangelists are each represented by the angel, the eagle,

the lion and the ox, and are decorated with symbols alluding to events in the life of Christ, helpfully decoded by explanatory text on the opposing page.

We can also include here the seventeenth-century 'memory tickler' pocket book devised by the French cleric Christophe Leuterbreuver. *La Confession Coupée ... ou la méthode facile pour se preparer aux confessions* ('The Cut-out Confession; or the easy method of preparing for confession') first appeared in 1677, and was so popular that it was reprinted in further editions as late as 1751. The book is a godsend to the forgetful sinner (and perhaps also the virtuous confessor in need of some sinful conversation material), as it comprises an enormous catalogue of every seventeenth-century sin conceivable, divided into chapters headed by the ten commandments.

Below: *A Tibetan musical score used in Buddhist monastic ritual, with the notation for voice, drums, trumpets, horns and cymbals.*

Opposite: *The strange symbolism of the* Ars memorandi ... *(Nuremberg, c.1470), designed to help people learn the Gospels by heart.*

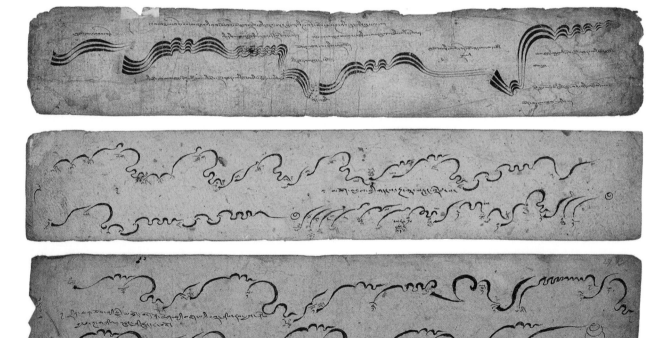

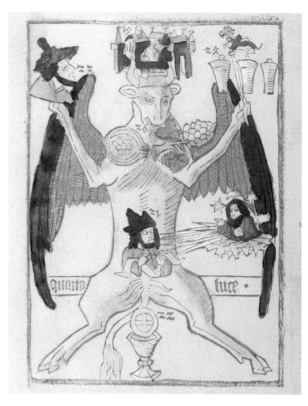

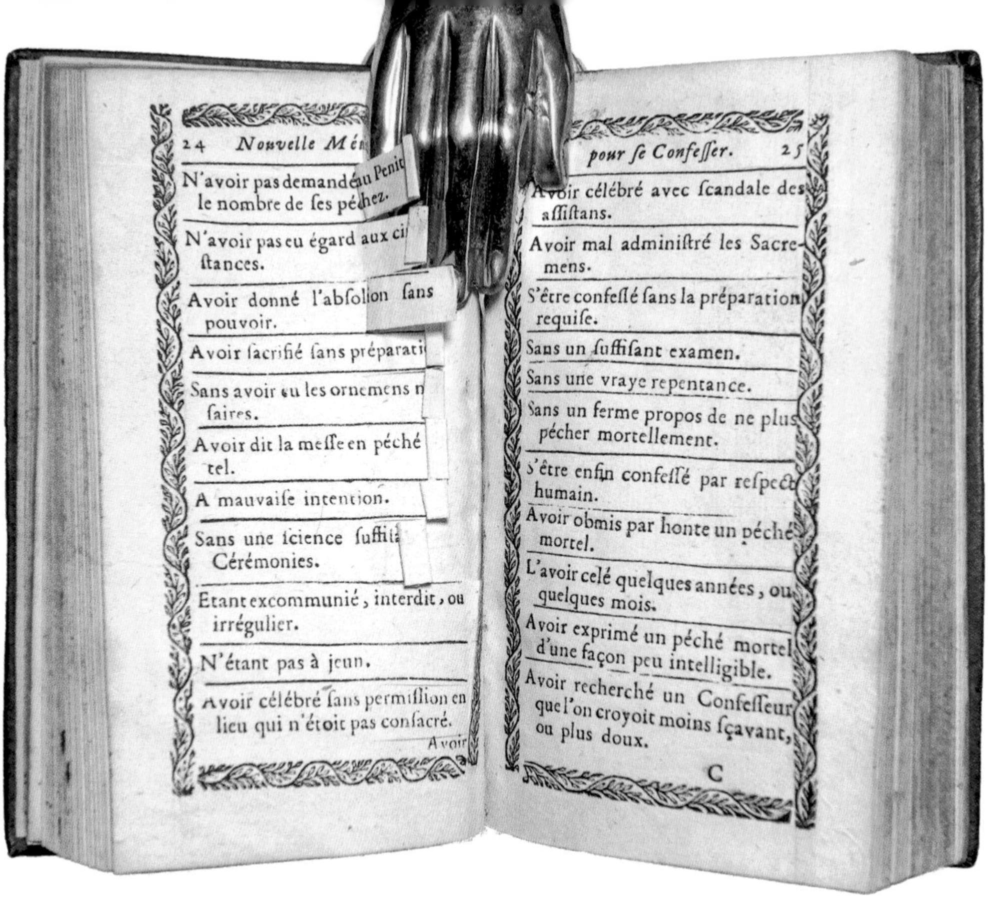
24 Nouvelle Mé
N'avoir pas demandé au Penit
le nombre de ſes péchez.
N'avoir pas eu égard aux ci
ſtances.
Avoir donné l'abſolution ſans
pouvoir.
Avoir ſacrifié ſans préparati
Sans avoir eu les ornemens n
ſaires.
Avoir dit la meſſe en péché
tel.
A mauvaiſe intention.
Sans une ſcience ſuffi
Cérémonies.
Etant excommunié, interdit, ou
irrégulier.
N'étant pas à jeun.
Avoir célébré ſans permiſſion en
lieu qui n'étoit pas conſacré.
Avoir
pour ſe Confeſſer. 25
Avoir célébré avec ſcandale des
aſſiſtans.
Avoir mal adminiſtré les Sacre-
mens.
S'être confeſſé ſans la préparation
requiſe.
Sans un ſuffiſant examen.
Sans une vraye repentance.
Sans un ferme propos de ne plus
pécher mortellement.
S'être enfin confeſſé par reſpect
humain.
Avoir obmis par honte un péché
mortel.
L'avoir celé quelques années, ou
quelques mois.
Avoir exprimé un péché mortel
d'une façon peu intelligible.
Avoir recherché un Confeſſeur
que l'on croyoit moins ſçavant,
ou plus doux.
C

The tear-out sins of the confessional pocket book La Confession Coupée *(1721 edition).*

Each misdeed is printed on a tab that can be peeled away from the page to stand out. (See image above.) In this way the confessor can prepare ahead of time, and in the confessional quickly flick through the book to find the relevant wrongdoings. Just as manuscript notations bring alive the personalities of previous readers, so too do used copies of these holy registers give an intriguing sense of penitents past. I notice in my copy from 1721, for example, that the sins picked out by its original owner include: *N'avoir apris et exercé que de vanité* – 'Having learned and exercised only vanity'; *N'étant pas à jeun* – 'Not fasting'; *S' être obstiné dans la péché* – 'Having been stubborn in sin'; and *Avoir vomi des blasphèmes* – 'Having spewed blasphemies'.[4]

The proliferation of printing would open up opportunities for every religious scholar and fringe thinker nursing their own eccentric theory to distribute it as far as literacy and curiosity could be found, as we shall see; but there are, of course, earlier manuscript examples on strange themes to examine. Take beard theology – not a subject one often considers, but one with an extensive history. The British Library holds the only surviving copy of the first book on beards, *Apologia de Barbis* ('In Defence of Beards'), written *c.*1160 by Abbot Burchard of Bellevaux Abbey, France.

4 Incidentally, one ingenious literary aid for the cleric in the preaching of sermons was the invention of John Trusler, who in *c.*1790 published complete sermons that he printed in a font mimicking natural handwriting. Should a parishioner happen to glance at the printed notes, they would appear to be the original manuscript work of the priest.

The work is an attempt to quell a furious squabble between the Cistercian monks of the abbey, who were clean-shaven, and the lower-ranked lay brothers, who were bearded. The abbot had gently reprimanded some poorly behaved lay brothers in a letter, writing that the bearded men were metaphorically 'fuel for the fire', referencing a quote of the prophet Isaiah. The lay brothers took this to mean that the abbot was threatening to literally burn off their beards, and revolted. The book is the abbot's soothing response, extolling the virtues of beards to a ridiculous extent. 'A beard is appropriate to a man as a sign of his comeliness,' he coos, 'as a sign of his strength, as a sign of his wisdom, as a sign of his maturity, and as a sign of his piety.' So what did this mean for his monks, who shaved? The abbot had to think quickly. The answer was 'inner beards'. It was what was grown on the inside, he said, that matters more than the external appearance. Just as it was more important to *have* faith than to *act* as if one did, so it was better to have the virtues of the bearded than to have the beard itself.

The Swedish scientist Olaus Rudbeck (1630–1702) had his own entirely different idea. A professor of medicine at Uppsala University, Rudbeck was one of the first to discover the lymphatic vessels of the human body, and established Sweden's first botanical garden. But in *Atlantica* (1679), a 3000-page four-volume treatise, he presents his proudest discovery – that the lost civilization of Atlantis was real and had been settled by Noah's descendants in central Sweden. It was Sweden that was the original cradle of civilization, he claimed, and Swedish the first language, spoken by Adam, from which Latin, Hebrew and all other languages evolved. He spent years touring the country and applying his own unique interpretations on archaeological evidence, finally publishing

ET NOS HOMINES

Olaus Rudbeck, accompanied by Father Time, peeling back the skin of the globe and pointing to his discovery of the real location of Atlantis – Sweden.

his conclusions between 1679 and 1702. Isaac Newton reportedly requested a copy, but on the whole, Rudbeck's incorporation of myth with science and documented history was heavily criticized. Rudbeck was undeterred however, and continued to develop the text with further research; but during Uppsala's great fire of 1702 his manuscripts were destroyed while he reportedly stood on the roof of his blazing building, shouting directions to help others escape the flames.

Just as eccentric was John Murray Spear (1804–87), an American Spiritual clergyman notable for two things: one, his admirably fierce abolitionism; and two, his attempt to build an electrically powered Messiah called 'the New Motive Power' that he claimed would herald a new Utopia. In his book *Messages From the Superior State; Communicated by John Murray, Through John M. Spear* (1853), Spear relates the instructions for humanity and other messages he received from a coterie of spirits he called 'The Association of Electrizers', a group that included the ghosts of Benjamin Franklin, Thomas Jefferson, John Quincy Adams, Benjamin Rush and Spear's namesake, the minister John Murray.

The year the book was published, Spear and a troupe of devoted followers withdrew to a secluded wooden lodge atop High Rock Hill in Lynn, Massachusetts, and began building the mechanical Messiah from copper, zinc, magnets and a dining-room table. After nine months of work, Spear ordered a female follower, whom he hailed the 'New Mary', to give birth to the machine in an elaborate ritual. Reader, would you be shocked to learn that the electric Messiah failed to rise? Spear then claimed to have received a message from the Association of Electrizers instructing him to immediately retire, and he disappeared. 'Dearly have I loved the work in which I was engaged,' he wrote. 'I have been helped to see that beyond the clouds that were round about me, there was a living, guiding, intelligent, beneficent purpose – the elevation, regeneration and redemption of the inhabitants of this earth.'

Those disappointed by the failed genesis of Spear's robot Jesus would, however, have been fascinated by the news that came from Japan later, in 1933, when a Shinto priest in the Ibaraki Prefecture discovered written documents that turned out to be the last will and testament of Jesus Christ. What's more, the papers (which disappeared just before the outbreak of World War II) identified the nearby village of Shingō in Aomori Prefecture as his last resting place.

Jesus, it turns out, did not die on the cross – that was his previously unreported brother Isukiri, who had secretly taken his place. As Isukiri suffered the crucifixion, Jesus secretly fled for Japan, taking with him his brother's severed ear and a lock of the Virgin Mary's hair as keepsakes. On a journey of four years, he crossed the Siberian tundra to reach Alaska, then sailed for Hachinohe, and finally reached Shingō. There, he made a fake identity for himself and enjoyed a quiet life, marrying a farmer's daughter named Miyuk and raising three children, farming garlic and tending to those in need. Described as bald with features of a 'long-nosed goblin', Jesus Christ died in Japan at the age of 106. The documents also recorded Christ as having first visited Japan at the age of twenty-one to study theology (which fits neatly into the twelve unaccounted years of his life in the New Testament). He apparently studied under a great master near Mount Fuji, picking up the Japanese language and immersing himself in Eastern culture. Then, at the age of thirty-three, he returned to Judea by way of Morocco.

The most remarkable aspect of this story is that you can visit the grave of the Japanese Jesus to this day. 'Daitenku Taro Jurai', as Jesus is known in Shingō, was buried in a mound of earth marked with a large wooden cross and bordered with a white picket fence. Every year around 20,000 pilgrims make the seven-hour train journey northwards from Tokyo to visit the grave, which is maintained by the local yoghurt factory. Payment of just 100 yen (about 70p) will gain you entrance to the Legend of Christ Museum, where you can examine related relics and buy Jesus coasters and coffee mugs. The villagers of Shingō are certain of their godly heritage. 'I'm not really planning

'Christ's Grave' in Shingō, Japan. 'When Jesus Christ was 21 years old, he came to Japan and pursued knowledge of divinity for 12 years,' reads the sign. 'His younger brother, Isukiri, casually took Christ's place and ended his life on the cross. Christ, who escaped the crucifixion, went through the ups and downs of travel, and again came to Japan. He settled right here … and died at the age of 106.'

anything at all for the 25th [of December], as it doesn't really matter to us,' a 52-year-old villager named Junichiro Sawaguchi told a reporter in 2008. 'I know I am descended from Jesus, but as a Buddhist, it's just not all that important.'

Of course, the various religious notions that have so inspired the authors in this chapter continue to maintain a hold over popular imaginations – we need only look at the success of more recent books like *23 Minutes in Hell* (2006) to find this in evidence. 'I wasn't yet aware of it,' begins the American author, Bill Wiese, 'but I had fallen into hell.' On an otherwise unremarkable Sunday night, on 22 November 1998, the southern California realtor was in bed with his wife when suddenly 'without any notice, I found myself being hurled through the air … I landed in what appeared to be a prison cell. I was completely naked … This was not a dream.' Wiese details his encounter with two odorous beasts of Evil who spoke in a blasphemous language, and then a meeting with Jesus, who told him to share his story. Then he awoke screaming on his living room floor.

Both Christian and secular critics came together in scepticism. On Wiese's description

of Hell being so hot that it was 'far beyond any possibility of sustaining life', Rob Moll of *Christianity Today* pointed out that, you know, it being Hell, this wasn't so much of a problem. John Sutherland, writing about the book in the *New Statesman*, also took issue with Wiese's writing, especially his description of the sound of billions of tortured souls screaming in infinite agony as 'annoying'. Naturally the book sold well regardless, spending three weeks on the extended *New York Times* bestseller list for paperback non-fiction, despite the criticism and Wiese's oblivious statement that his book 'will be the closest you will ever come to experiencing hell for yourself'. As for why God would choose an estate agent to be thrown into Hell for a torturous episode – well, how can we possibly fathom His mysterious ways?

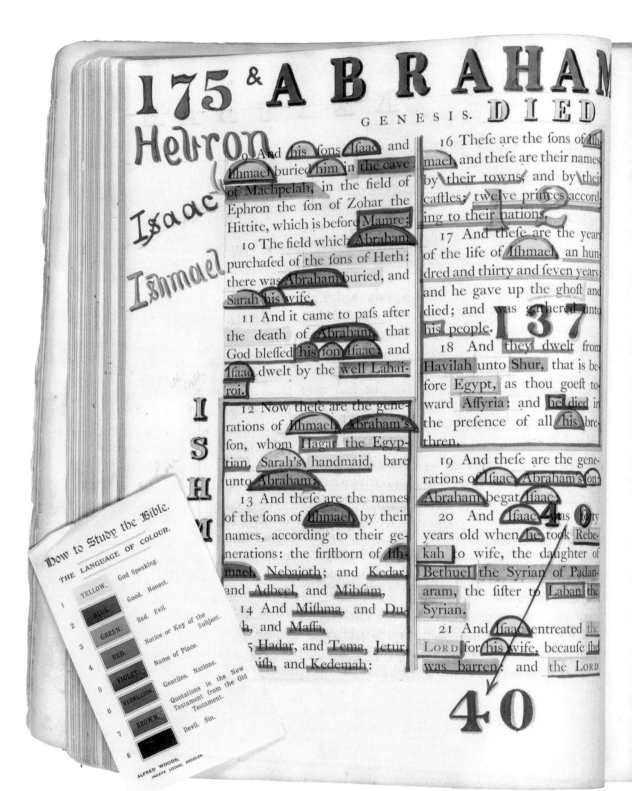

JACOB

CHAP. XXV.

was entreated of him, and Rebekah his wife conceived.

22 And the children ſtruggled together within her; and ſhe ſaid, If it be ſo, why am I thus? And ſhe went to inquire of the LORD.

23 And the LORD ſaid unto her, Two nations are in thy womb, and two manner of people ſhall be ſeparated from thy bowels; and the one people ſhall be ſtronger than the other people; and the elder ſhall ſerve the younger.

24 And when her days to be delivered were fulfilled, behold, there were twins in her womb.

25 And the firſt came out red, all over like an hairy garment; and they called his name Eſau.

26 And after that came his brother out, and his hand took hold on Eſau's heel; and his name was called Jacob: and Iſaac was threeſcore years old when ſhe bare them.

27 And the boys grew: and Eſau was a cunning hunter, a man of the field; and Jacob was a plain man, dwelling in tents.

28 And Iſaac loved Eſau, becauſe he did eat of his veniſon: but Rebekah loved Jacob.

29 And Jacob ſod pottage: and Eſau came from the field, and he was faint:

30 And Eſau ſaid to Jacob, Feed me, I pray thee, with that ſame red pottage; for I am faint: therefore was his name called Edom.

31 And Jacob ſaid, Sell me this day thy birthright.

32 And Eſau ſaid, Behold, I am at the point to die: and what profit ſhall this birthright do to me?

33 And Jacob ſaid, Swear to me this day; and he ſware unto him: and he ſold his birthright unto Jacob.

34 Then Jacob gave Eſau bread and pottage of lentiles; and he did eat and drink, and roſe up, and went his way: thus Eſau deſpiſed his birthright.

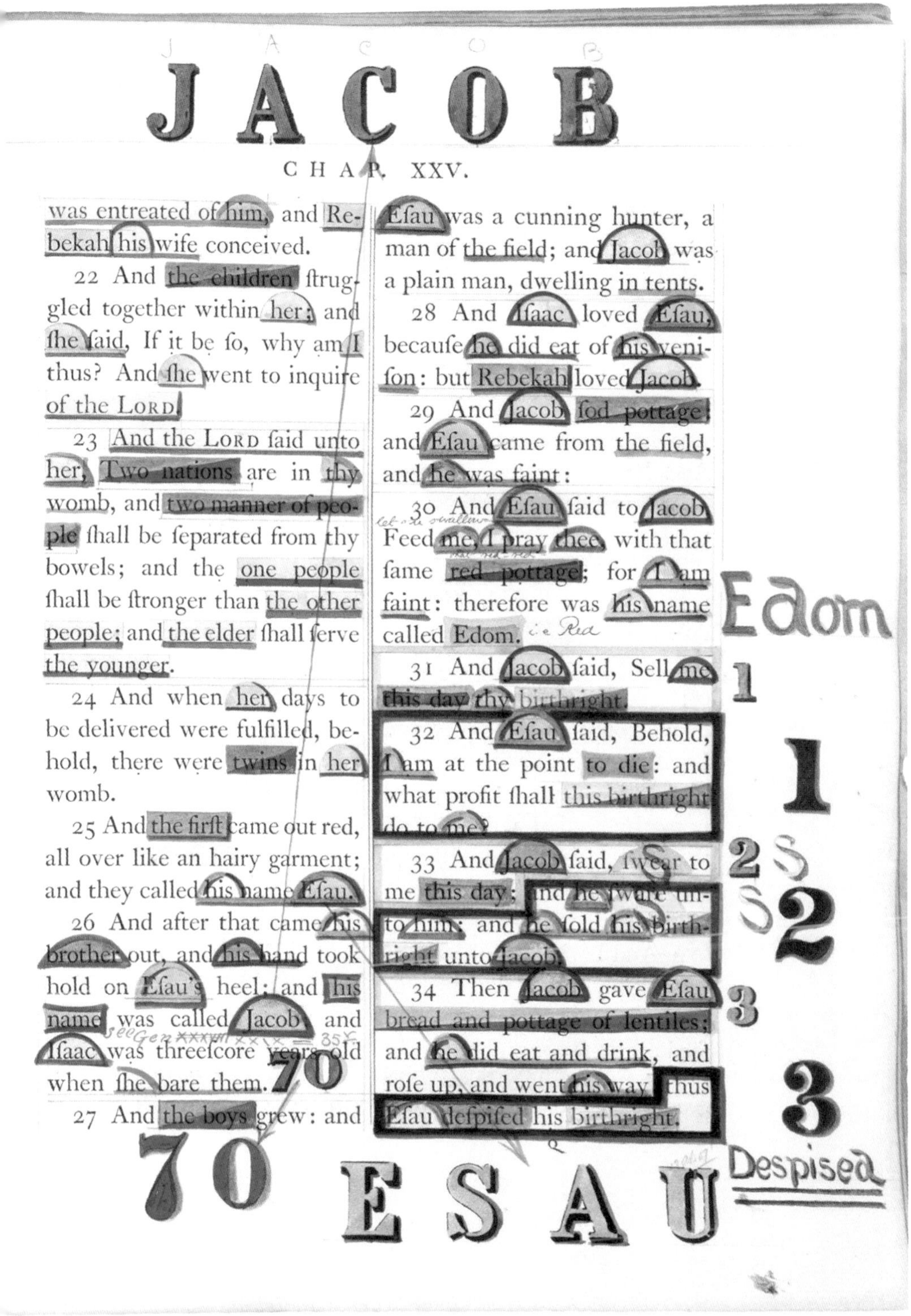

Over twenty years, the East Anglian merchant Alfred Woods (1836–1912) filled his unique Bible with brilliantly colourful annotations, following a painting system of his own invention (see the guide at bottom left). Yellow (God Speaking), Blue (Good. Honest), Green (Bad. Evil), Violet (Name of Place), Black (Devil. Sin) etc. Occasionally Woods records his reading progress, for example: 'Read through in 4 hrs 45 mins, 1888', and 'Read through & painted various colours & finished 10th Feby 1909 (age 73)'.

CURIOSITIES OF SCIENCE

One of the greatest scientific scholars in the history of the world was the man known as Galen (AD c.129–216). The Greek physician travelled and studied extensively before settling in Rome and producing many written works, eventually rising to the role of personal physician to several emperors. He is also, in terms of literary curiosities, a goldmine. Galen had many strange theories that endured for far too long. In part, these originated from the fact that Roman law in his time forbade the dissection and autopsy of the human cadaver, and so his writings of the body are based on dissections of pigs, Barbary macaques and other primates, with the whopper of an assumption that their anatomy was essentially similar to that of humans. The basis of much of his science, espoused in works like *Ars medica* ('Arts of Medicine') and *De naturalibus facultatibus* ('On the Natural Facilities') was the theory of 'humourism', which considered the workings of both the body and the mind to be governed by a quartet of internal chemicals – black bile, yellow bile, blood and phlegm; a system that Hippocrates (*c*.460–*c*.370 BC) is usually credited as first applying in medicine.

Galen was particularly fascinated with the circulatory system. Blood, he wrote, was constantly being consumed by the body, and replaced with new supplies created by the liver, to be circulated by two separate bloodstream systems. (The story goes that Galen's fascination with the pulmonary system originated from his early career as chief physician to the gladiators in Pergamon, when he would see the exposed beating hearts of fighters as they lay dying.)

In fact, the discovery of the circulatory system would only be made centuries later by William Harvey, published in his *Exercitatio anatomica de motu cordis et sanguinis in animalibus* ('Concerning the Motion of the Heart and Blood') of 1628. This would inspire a series of curious scientific episodes. Sir Christopher Wren, more famous for his design of St Paul's Cathedral, was inspired to test Harvey's claim by dissolving opium in wine and injecting the solution into the ligatured vein of a dog. In a separate event, from correspondence with Robert Boyle in 1666, we learn that the Cornish physician Richard Lower (1631–91) was inspired to inject *soup* into the veins of dogs to see if this would nourish them. Unfazed by the instant failure of these experiments, Lower decided to transfuse blood from a lamb into a volunteered lunatic named Arthur Coga whose brain was 'a little too warm', believing the patient would be cured because 'sheep's blood has some symbolic power, like the blood of Christ, for Christ is the Lamb of God'. Somehow Coga survived the experiment, as did his lunacy.

OPPOSITE: *From Diderot's* Encyclopédie *(1751–66), a skeleton plate used as writing paper by an eighteenth-century Italian lawyer with a sense of humour – the scribbled notes are his records of last wills and testaments drawn up for clients.*

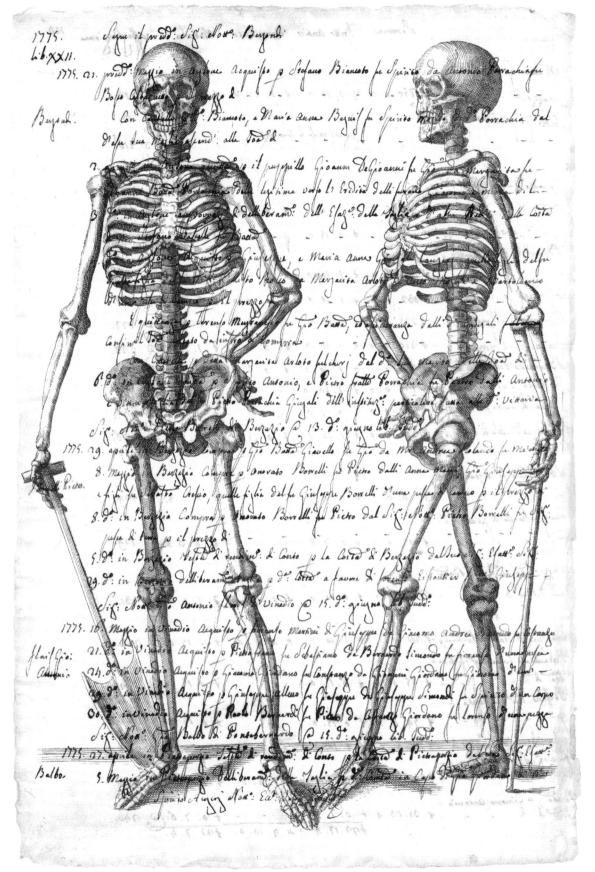

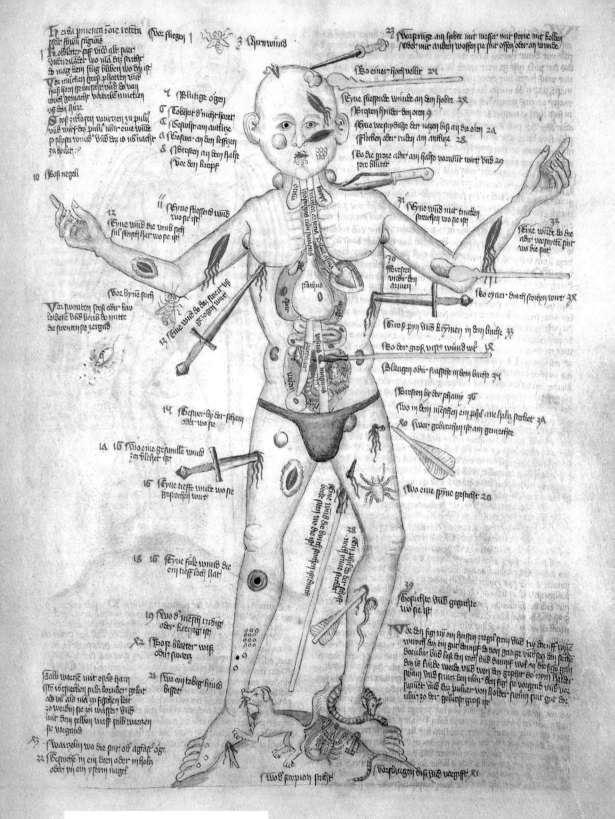

A medical 'Wound Man' illustration from a Bavarian manuscript made around 1420, showing the range of injuries commonly suffered by patients.

CLIII
SI AMBAS
MANUS EI FORIS
Invenerit quidfacere
debeat duob; humer is et manu
sinexutraq; insigens restinger
rei reueal et sicut superis
dua manib; compositis adpherisse
capropaulatim et leuit ei foris adducat. p gene sia.

CLIII ET SI BREUISSIMU
caput habeat et ambas manus foris
exerit et oporcet obsterceapru smissa
manu sua caput infantiadorificii cor
rigat et compohensis manib; infantis
la coribz et componat et sic conar nixbz
p sibreuitas caput orificii uuluae
n adiuuat unde eiciendus. e. p qua pri
or emanus exteriit.

CLUSIIN PEDIBz DESCENDENS
In aliqua parte uuluae reli cu corp;
reli cu corp; inclinauerit quid facere debeat
sicuti retrorsur dixi obstetrix missa
manu suam eum componat et si adduca
adducat foris.

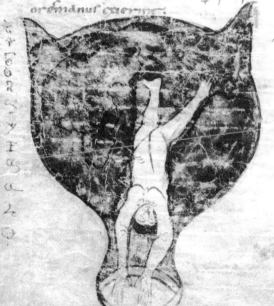

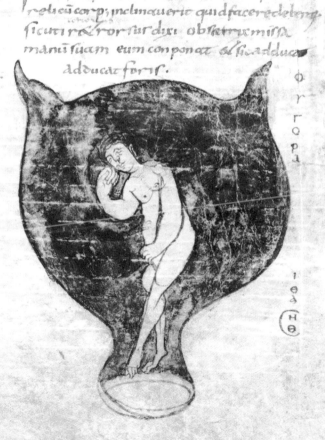

Four depictions of the foetus in the womb,
from a ninth-century Latin manuscript.

*An early blood transfusion from lamb to man,
by Matthäus Gottfried Purmann.*

But back to Galen, who also wrote that the skin's pores became blocked with sooty smoke particles generated by warm blood, until so much pressure built up that the soot erupted out of the skin in a solid string: this was how hair was made. Following through with this idea of humans as walking smokestacks, he believed hair colour indicated internal body temperature – the darker the hair, the higher the soot level, and therefore the hotter the temperature. Blond people therefore lacked natural warmth.

It wasn't until 1523, some 1300 years later, that Galen's *De naturalibus facultatibus* was published in Latin in London, and another twenty years until the validity of his descriptions would be overturned with the landmark publishing of Andreas Vesalius's *De humani corporis fabrica* in 1543. In Britain, surviving examples of medical texts in this intermediary period of about AD 700–1200 are few and far between. Most people were illiterate, and knowledge was passed down orally. But one type of work produced at this time was the 'leechbook', its name originating not with the bloodsucking annelid but a modernization of the Old English word læce-bōc, translating as 'book of medical prescriptions'.

The most famous example is the manuscript in the British Library known as *Bald's Leechbook* (AD c.925–950), whose recipes are taken from Greek and Roman authors, and Anglo-Saxon physicians with names like 'Oxa' and 'Dun'. This work is a fascinating read for its contemporary cures listed in order of relevance to the body from head to toe, before opening up to all sorts of injuries, diseases and disorders, from spider bites to baldness cures. 'If blood run from a man's nose too much,' advises the author, 'poke into the ear a whole ear of barley, so he be unaware of it.' The various remedies for 'mickel hicket' (hiccups) principally involve getting the patient to drink warm water and throw up – 'put a feather in oil, poke him frequently in the throat [with it] that he may spew'. For shoulder pain one should 'Mingle a turd of an old swine which be a fieldgoer with old lard' and wipe it on to the sore spot. For warts, apply a concoction of dog urine and mouse blood. For demonic possession, the affected party is given the rather wonderful recommendation of drinking a herbal medicine out of a church bell.[1]

---

1 Though the majority of its potions and rudimentary treatments should be safely consigned to history (like treating cataracts with raw hare's liver), in 2015 Christina Lee, a professor in Viking studies at the University of Nottingham, translated the recipe for an eye salve involving garlic, allium, wine and cow bile, and tested its antibiotic effects on the notoriously resistant 'superbug' bacterium MRSA. To the team's astonishment, they found that the Anglo-Saxon remedy succeeded in destroying much of the virus that modern antibiotics fail to treat.

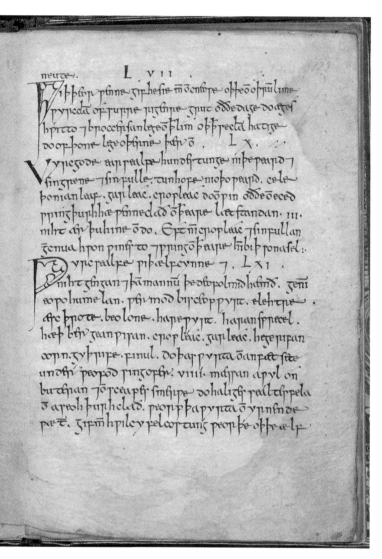

The elegant lettering of Bald's Leechbook, *from the mid-tenth century.*

an alternative treatment analysing the liquid believed to be a 'filtrate' of the humours, with its own spectrum of colour, that the patient could produce without the help of scorching metal.

A 'piss prophet' was, as Francis Grose neatly defines in his *Dictionary of the Vulgar Tongue* (1785), 'A physician who judges of the diseases of his patients solely by the inspection of their urine.' The piss prophet examined, smelled and cheerfully tasted the urine to diagnose ailments, consulting works like Theophilus Protospatharius's seventh-century text *On Urines*, with the most helpful books containing coloured urine wheels to compare with the patient's sample and advise diagnosis. The method continued into the seventeenth century, but with medical advancements rendering it obsolete, and the heavy drubbing it took from satirical works like Thomas Brian's *The Pisse Prophet, or Certain Pisse-pot Lectures* (1637), the popularity of the piss prophets soon began to dry up.

All of this emerging diagnostic science did not exactly bring a shift away from the types of crude popular remedies seen with the much earlier leechbooks. 'Mouse rotted and given to children to eat, remedieth pissing the bed,' advises John Partridge in *The Widow's Treasure* (1595), which also contains the advice to steam your clothes with boiling mercury to get rid of lice (and with them, your higher brain function). To jolt the comatose awake, the French physician Bernard de Gordon (*c.*1258–1318) recommended full-throated screaming at the patient, or the loud playing of musical

In Western Europe's so-called 'twelfth-century Renaissance', monks desperately sought out the texts of antiquity and Islamic knowledge to enrich their libraries. Among the stacks of this new knowledge pile were 'cautery' texts, which advised physicians on how to draw out the previously mentioned four humours by pressing white-hot metal implements against the skin. Surviving examples are scarce – it seems treatment by burning poker wasn't wildly popular with patients. In place of this, medieval diagnosticians had much greater success with

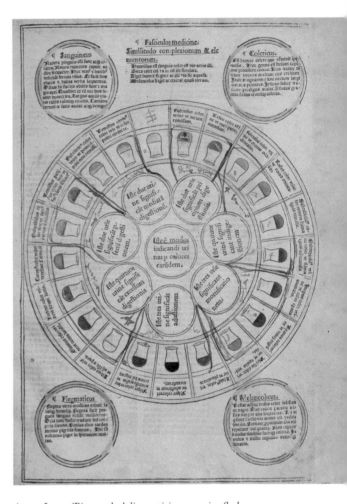

instruments by their head, or holding squealing pigs in their face. If all else fails, pluck their chest hairs.

In *A Most Excellent and Perfect Homish Apothecarye* (1561), Europe's most popular apothecary (medical recipe book) of the fifteenth and sixteenth century, the German physician and alchemist Hieronymus Brunschwig has a foolproof test for determining whether a patient is possessed by a demon: 'It is good to take the harte and liver of a fishe called a Pike and put the same into a pot with glowing hot coales and holde the same to the patient so that the smoke may enter into him. If he is possessed he can not abide that smoke but rageth and is angry.'

ABOVE LEFT: *'Piss prophet' diagnosticians examine flasks of urine, from* Fasciculus Medicinae, *a physician's manual of six medical treatises first printed in 1491.*

ABOVE RIGHT: *Also from* Fasciculus Medicinae *(1491), a large 'urine wheel' of twenty-one thin-necked, urine-filled flasks, with guides for the physician to the different colours.*

OPPOSITE TOP: *The guild book of the barber-surgeons of York, c.1475–99. Left, an illustrated 'zodiac man', with astrological symbols linked to the parts of the body. Right, a volvelle, or paper dial, with the months and their zodiac symbols. Physicians were required to consider factors like lunar position before attempting surgical procedures.*

OPPOSITE BOTTOM: *The muscles of the human body, and the anatomy of the pregnant woman, from an English medical treatise of the mid-fifteenth century by 'Pseudo-Galen'.*

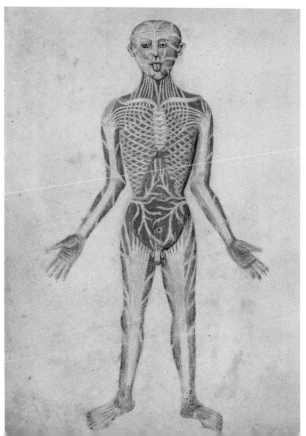

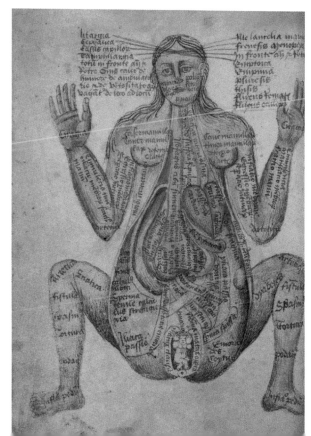

ALCHEMY MANUSCRIPTS

THIS PAGE: *The majestic Ripley Scroll is an alchemical manuscript with instructions to create the Philosopher's Stone, which would allow one to transmute matter – especially base metals like lead – into noble metals like gold. Approximately 6 metres (19ft 9in) long, the scroll is covered with mystical symbolism. The scroll takes its name from the English alchemist George Ripley (c.1415–90), whose writings were pored over by famous figures like John Dee, Robert Boyle and Isaac Newton.*

OPPOSITE TOP LEFT: *An alchemist holding a flask, from a 1582 German copy of the anonymous* Splendor solis (*'Splendour of the Sun', 1532–35), one of the most beautiful alchemical manuscripts ever made. The Latin scroll unfurling from the flask reads 'Let us ask the four elements of nature'.*

OPPOSITE TOP MIDDLE: *From an eighteenth-century copy of the* Book of the Seven Climes *by Abū al-Qāsim al-'Irāqī al-Simāwi, a Muslim alchemist from Baghdad, who wrote on alchemy and magic in the 1200s. His work is the earliest study to focus solely on alchemical illustration.*

OPPOSITE TOP RIGHT: *A Chinese illustration of an alchemical furnace and tools needed to create a mercury-based elixir. From the Chinese text* Waike tushuo (*'Pictorial Manual of External Medicine'), 1856. In ancient China, drinking precious materials was recommended, in order to acquire their durability. The Jiajing Emperor (1507–67) likely died from drinking a mercury-based 'Elixir of Life' provided by his alchemists.*

ABOVE AND LEFT: *The Clavis Artis* is a German
alchemical manuscript of wonderful watercolour
paintings produced sometime in the late seventeenth
to early eighteenth centuries. The text credits
authorship to Zoroaster, and claims that the original
text 'was written by the author over a skin of dragon'.
Next to nothing is known about the origins of the work.

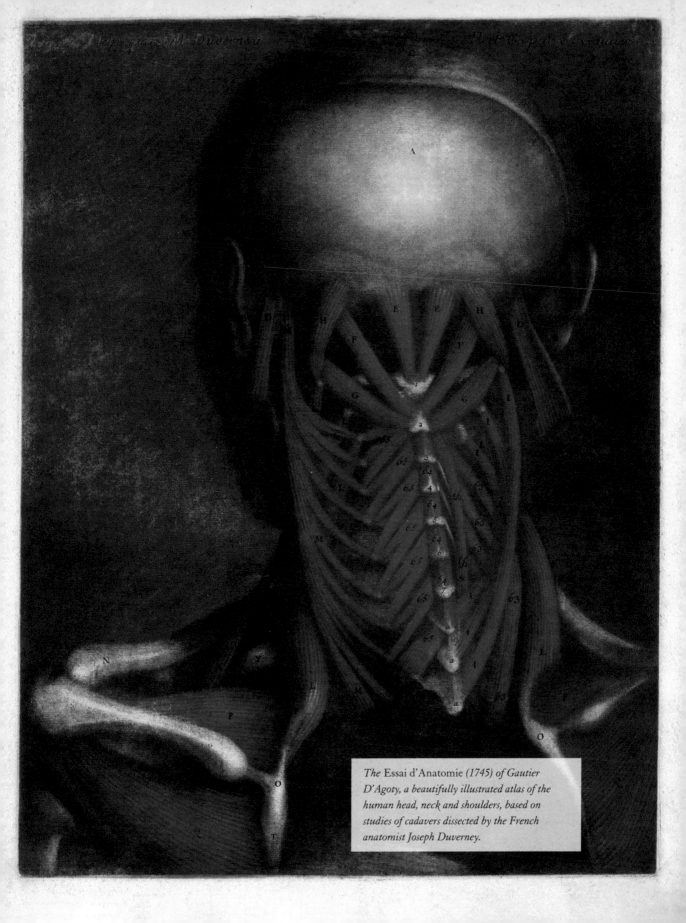

The Essai d'Anatomie *(1745) of Gautier D'Agoty, a beautifully illustrated atlas of the human head, neck and shoulders, based on studies of cadavers dissected by the French anatomist Joseph Duverney.*

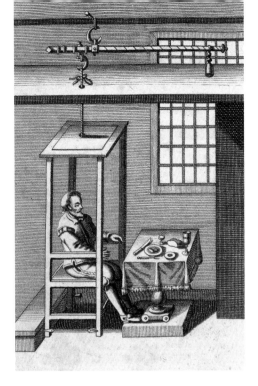

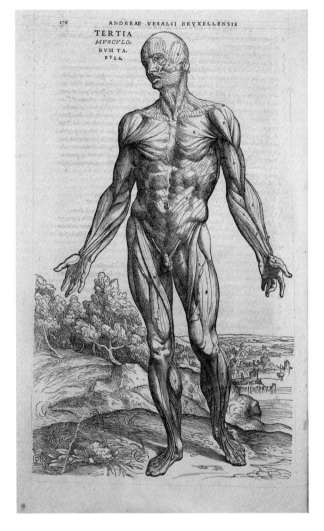

ABOVE: *The frontispiece engraving from Santorio Santorio's* De statica medicina *(1614), showing the Venetian physiologist in his weighing-chair balance device. Every day for thirty years Santorio ate, worked and slept on the giant furnished scale, recording his every ingestion and excretion, to study the fluctuations of his body weight against his solid and liquid waste. In doing so he originated the study of the metabolism.*

RIGHT: *Vesalius's '*Tertia musculatorum' *(third muscle man).*

With their basis in original observation, the anatomical books that appeared in the sixteenth century overthrew the classical writers, and presented a grand unveiling of the interior of the human body. The first to draw back the curtain was Andreas Vesalius (1514–64), a Flemish physician at the University of Padua, with his *De humani corporis fabrica* ('On the fabric of the human body', 1543), a landmark work of seven volumes with magnificent anatomical illustrations.[2] Vesalius also benefited from the Renaissance improvements in woodcut engraving, and so was able to publish drawings of unprecedented detail. *De humani ...* was based on Vesalius's lectures at Padua, where he distinguished himself by illustrating his discussions with a live dissection of a corpse before his students, a work of manual labour that academics

---

2 The notion that dissection was forbidden by the medieval Church, and that Vesalius, Leonardo da Vinci and their fellow anatomists risked great danger by performing dissections, is an enduringly pervasive myth. 'I know of no case in which an anatomist was ever prosecuted,' notes Professor Katharine Park of Harvard University, 'and no case in which the Church ever rejected a request for a dispensation.'

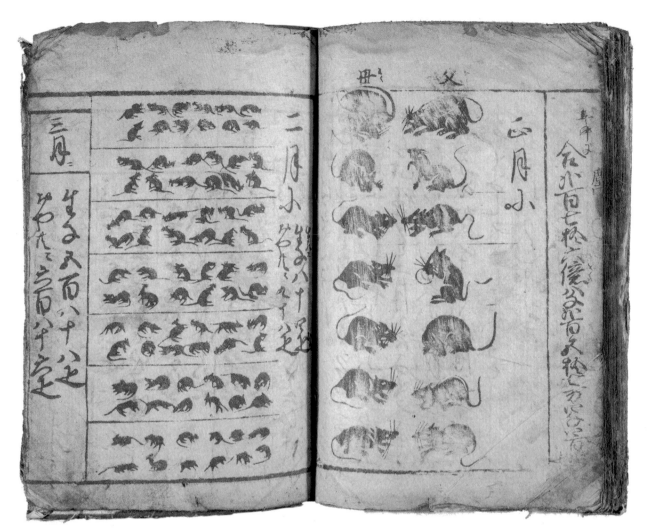

ABOVE: A Manual of Mathematics (Jinkōki), *an extraordinary book by an unknown Japanese author of the early seventeenth century. Instead of using line diagrams, this author uses rats to illustrate complex geometric progression and the calculation of the volume of 3D figures.*

FAR LEFT: *The 'monster of Ravenna', a monstrous birth in Italy in 1512 said to be an omen for the nearby battle in which the French drove the Papal-Spanish armies from the field. From Ambroise Paré's* Des monstres et prodigies … *(1585), one of the most famous prodigy volumes.*

LEFT: *A two-headed human from Ambroise Paré's* Des monstres et prodigies … *(1585).*

An illustration from Fortunio Liceti's De monstruorum causis, natura et differentiis, *originally published in Padua in 1616, then reprinted in 1634 with elaborate artwork.*

were not expected to perform. Part of the reason why his illustrations are so striking is the allegorical posing with which Vesalius portrays his dissected models, which were usually the corpses of executed prisoners (a fact used by his pro-Galen critics, who pointed to the criminal nature as the reason for their 'abnormality' from the established understanding). The undead figures stand in the foreground of rural backdrops, animated and gesturing, as haunting reminders of human frailty and mortality.

In the sixteenth century, scientific interest in 'prodigies' saw a flood of popular literature on the subject. 'Prodigy books' were studies of miraculous events and medical cases of 'marvels', which ranged from 'monstrous' births and natural defects to pygmies, mermaids and any other curiosity of nature. The case files of the French surgeon Ambroise Paré are full of these strange

instances, like the report of a two-headed human and the birth of the 'monster of Ravenna' in Italy in 1512, shown here.

In his *Praxis medica admiranda* (1637), Zacutus Lusitanus reports a woman giving birth to a salamander and a man who attempted to urinate but instead expelled a cloud of flies. The frontispiece illustration of Georg Abraham Mercklin's thesis *De incantamentis* (1715) includes a detail of the 1694 case of a German twelve-year-old named Theodorus Döderlein who began vomiting insects. After a few weeks he had produced 162 woodlice, thirty-two caterpillars, four millipedes, two worms, two butterflies, two ants and a beetle. Then came

Above: *Theodorus Döderlein vomits a torrent of animals.*

the amphibians: twenty-one newts, four frogs and the occasional toad. Clearly the pastor's son was possessed by the Devil. Nothing, not even prayer, had any effect, until the boy's doctors tried an old treatment for clearing magical animals from the stomach: horse urine. Vat upon vat of stinking equine water was poured down the poor boy's throat until, miraculously, he announced he was cured. Good work everyone, many thanks, the horse piss really did the trick – no need for another round of treatment.

Britain had its own famous curiosity case in 1726. The pamphlet *A Short Narrative of an Extraordinary Delivery of Rabbets, Perform'd by Mr. John Howard Surgeon at Guilford* (1727) is an account written by Nathaniel St André, court anatomist of King George I, of an extraordinary case that he personally witnessed, known as the 'Godalming miracle'. On the evening of 27 September, Mr John Howard, the Man Midwife of

Guildford, had attended a patient of his named Mary Toft when she went into labour and gave birth to parts of a pig. In October, Toft bore a rabbit with a cat's paws and head, and later a series of rabbits. The king ordered his secretary, Samuel Molyneux, and St André to investigate.

The men arrived in time to witness Toft give birth to the fifteenth rabbit. A skinless doe of about four months' growth was delivered, and later that evening a large ball of fur and the creature's head. The king's men inspected the rabbits, examined Toft, and concluded the animals grew in her ovaries and then hopped over to the Fallopian tubes. St André published his pamphlet in verification, and it became an instant bestseller. 'The Surrey rabbit-breeder' was the talk of London: some declared Toft a witch, others a Satanic rabbit in human form, or perhaps she had merely had romantic liaisons with a buck. Mary was brought to London, and the prestigious obstetrician Sir Richard Manningham was brought in to examine her. He immediately noticed that one of the rabbit placentas was in fact a hog's bladder, at which

Below: *Mary Toft giving birth to a litter of rabbits in an etching by W. Hogarth, 1726.*

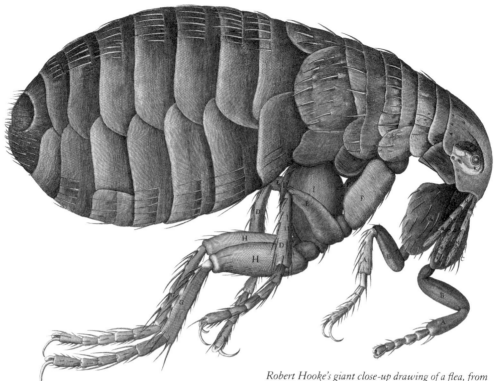

Robert Hooke's giant close-up drawing of a flea, from Micrographia *(1665). Hooke built up the image of the insect through separate examinations of its various regions. The plate was often plagiarized in the next two centuries.*

observation Toft – slightly suspiciously – burst into tears. She eventually admitted to hiding rabbit parts in a secret pocket in her dress. Her confession to the imposture can be found today in the Hunterian Library in Glasgow.

The Toft affair is all the stranger given that the power of the scientific gaze had been amplified greatly in the preceding decades, following the introduction of two ground-breaking inventions – the compound microscope, which appeared in Europe around 1620, and the telescope, a few years before. In 1665, two scientific works appeared at roughly the same time – one German, one English – which make for a great double-act in the curiosity collector's catalogue, despite the fact that the scale of their subject matter could not be more opposed.

How can one do justice to Robert Hooke's *Micrographia: or Some Physiological Descriptions of Minute Bodies Made by*

Magnifying Glasses with just a short description? The book quite simply broke open the world, pouring its secrets out across pages of descriptions and over thirty finely engraved illustrations. Hooke was the first to illustrate insects, plants and everyday objects seen through the eyepiece of a microscope. Before, the smallest object the naked human eye could observe was the width of a human hair. With the *Micrographia*, the reader toured the microcosmic wonders of the world's most mundane residents – the delicate wings of 'The great Belly'ed Gnat'; the intricate arrangement of the 'eyes of the Grey drone-fly', and most famously Hooke's drawing of that prolific pest, the flea, which was gloriously reproduced in a fold-out engraving measuring half a metre wide (see above).

Examining a thinly sliced piece of cork, he coined the term 'cell' for the minute structures he saw within, as they were reminiscent of the bare cell rooms of monks. In browsing the contents list of *Micrographia*, you can *feel* Hooke's excitement at discovering the unseen world: 'Of the Point of a sharp small Needle; Of the Edge of a Razor; Of the fiery Sparks struck from a Flint or Steel; Of Figures observ'd in small Sand …' It conjures the image of a man drunk with delight, grabbing every object, plant and insect around him to transform with unexpected detail under his lens. 'Of Charcoal, or burnt Vegetables; Of Moss; Of the curious texture of Sea-weeds; Of the stinging points and juice of Nettles, and some other venomous Plants; Of the Seeds of Poppy; Of the Feet of Flyes, and several other Insects; Of the Sting of a Bee; Of the Teeth of a Snail …' One can't help but envy the thrill of such endless discovery.

That same year, readers were presented with the magnificent, macroscopic contrast of Athanasius Kircher's illustrated *Mundus Subterraneus* (1665), which the German Jesuit scholar presents as a masterful understanding of the Earth's geologic secrets, but which is in fact a raucous zoo of wonderfully crackpot ideas. For one, Kircher pinpoints the location of the lost island of Atlantis, even providing a map, following Plato's description to depict it in the centre of the Atlantic Ocean. He also identifies the long puzzled-over source of the Nile as being the 'Mountains of the Moon'; discusses fossils that he interprets as the buried remains of giant humans; examines cave-dwelling societies and theorizes on creatures of the underground world including dragons.

A highlight is the illustration featured opposite, Systema Ideale Pyrophylaciorum, a study of the volcanic system of Earth, a planet 'not solid but everywhere gaping, and hollowed with empty rooms and spaces, and hidden burrows', with terrible volcanoes being 'nothing but the vent-holes, or breath-pipes of Nature'. Kircher had been developing these ideas ever since his curiosity had led him up Mount Vesuvius just seven years after it had erupted, and where he examined the crater, perched on its rim. 'I thought I beheld the habitation of Hell,' he wrote, 'wherein nothing seemed to be much wanting besides the horrid fantasms and apparitions of Devils.'

While Hooke explored the microscopic world and Kircher the cosmic theatre, the science of the inner universe of the mind progressed at a more sluggish rate, although there are notable titles to mention. A most remarkable volume in the history of psychiatry is *Illustrations of Madness: Exhibiting a singular case of insanity* (1810) by John Haslam. This was the first published study of a single psychiatric case, telling the extraordinary story of John Tilly Matthews, who was admitted to London's notorious Bethlem (popularly designated 'Bedlam') psychiatric hospital in January 1797, after being arrested for shouting 'Treason!' at Lord Hawkesbury (later Lord Liverpool) from the public gallery during a debate at the House of Commons. In 1809, his family began petitioning for his release, and Haslam

OPPOSITE TOP: *Athanasius Kircher's depiction of the 'fire canals', or volcanic system, of the subterranean world, from his* Mundus Subterraneus *(1665).*

OPPOSITE BOTTOM: *A later illustration of the 'Cat Piano' described in Athanasius Kircher's* Musurgia Universalis *(1650), which he describes in Book 6, Part 4, Chapter 1. 'In order to raise the spirits of an Italian prince … a musician created for him a cat piano. The musician arranged [cats] in cages side by side, so that when a key on the piano was depressed, a mechanism drove a sharp spike in the appropriate cat's tail. The result was a melody of meows that became more vigorous as the cats became more desperate.'*

Hoc Schema exprimit Caloris sive Ignis usus, vel quod idem est, pyrophylaciis per universa Geocosmi viscera admirando DEI opificio, varie distributa ne alicubi deesset, quod conservationi Geocosmi tantopere fore necessarium; Nemo autem sibi persuadeat quin revera hoc pacto quo schema refert, constitutum est; cosq prorsa ordine disposita aestuaria, nequaquam. Quis enim hoc observavit? quinam illuc penetravit unquam ex hominibus; Hoc itaq Schemate solummodo ostendere voluimus, Telluris viscera plena esse aestuariis et pyrophylaciis; sive ea jam hoc modo, sive alio, disposita sunt: ex centro igitur Ignem per omnes Subterrestris mundi sinitus usq ad ipsas exterioris superficiei montes Vulcanos deduximus; Ignis Centralis Signatur A litera. Reliqua sunt aestuaria Naturae, signata B. Canales pyragogi C. minimi vero rivi sunt fissurae Petrae, per quas Ignei spiritus pervadunt.

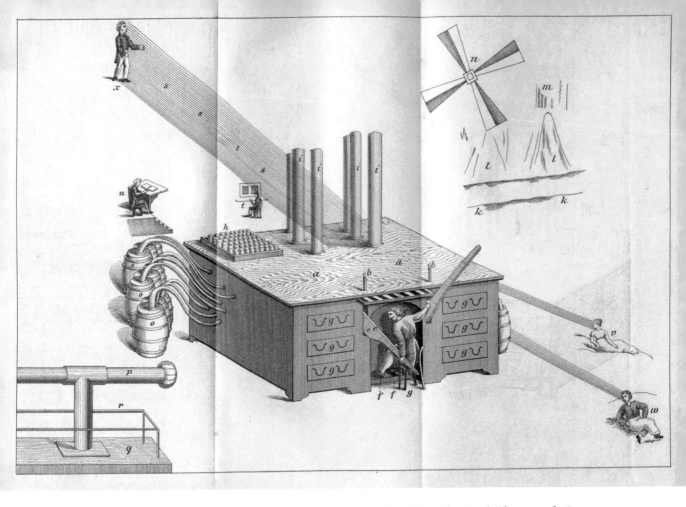

The giant mind control device known as the 'Air Loom', as imagined by James Tilly Matthews.

published *Illustrations of Madness* to support his case for continued treatment.

Matthews's delusions centred around an insidious device he called the 'Air Loom'. He was convinced that a villainous gang adept in pneumatic chemistry (studying gases and chemical reactions) had set up the machine, a kind of gaseous charge generator, close to Bethlem, and were torturing him daily by zapping him with harmful rays. He described the effects of these rays as 'Lobster-cracking', 'Stomach-skinning' and 'Apoplexy-working with the nutmeg grater'. Members of the Air Loom Gang included the machine's principal operator, the Middleman, Catherine, Jack the Schoolmaster and Sir Archy. They were led by a

man called Bill, or 'the King'. The gang of spies controlled modern politics, Matthews claimed, with countless other units armed with Air Looms around London, each with 'pneumatic practitioners' who prepared suitable candidates for brainwashing by 'premagnetizing' them with 'volatile magnetic fluid'. Key figures of the British government including William Pitt were affected, their minds being read and manipulated by the gang.

The idea is recorded meticulously by Haslam but is most effectively conveyed by Matthews's drawing of the Air Loom that Haslam included in the book, the first published work of art by an asylum inmate (shown above). The Middleman sits operating the giant machine, its rays striking a victim (top left), while Jack the Schoolmaster is drawn just above the barrels of gas on the left, and Sir

Archy and Catherine are found in the bottom-right corner. In 1814, Matthews was relocated to 'Fox's London House', a private institution in Hackney. Away from Bethlem, his delusions seemed to cease almost immediately and he became a popular and trusted patient, helping with the asylum bookkeeping and gardening until his death in 1815.

So what else can one add to the shelves of the strangest of scientific collections, as we barrel towards the twentieth century? Among the books that reject the scientific consensus with bonkers theories is *Omphalosan: an Attempt to Untie the Geological Knot* by the respected zoologist Philip Gosse (inventor of the seawater aquarium and world's leading expert on butterfly genitalia), written in 1857, two years before Charles Darwin's *On the Origin of Species*.

A devout Christian, Gosse's central hypothesis is that the conflict between the ancient age of the Earth proposed by geologists of the Victorian era, and the much more recent creation date given in the Bible, could be resolved with a simple explanation he called the Omphalos (Greek for 'navel') hypothesis. The argument goes like this: the first human, Adam, must have had a navel (as we inherited ours from him), despite the fact that he didn't need one as God created him. So God must have given him the feature to create the appearance of human ancestry. Thus, the seemingly ancient fossil record might also be evidence of God's creation, put there by Him to again create a sense

BELOW LEFT: *'Plan of the Brain' – one of several 'brain maps' of alternative science and mysticism from* The Book of Life: The Spiritual and Physical Constitution of Man *(1898) by 'Dr Alesha Sivartha', which appears to be the pseudonym of a Kansas physician named Arthur E. Merton.*

BELOW: *'Chart of the Hand', from the same work.*

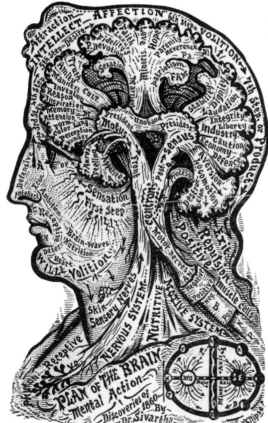

of endless history, and test our faith. The book sold poorly, the critical reception best represented by the reaction of the *Westminster Review*, which described Gosse's theory as 'too monstrous for belief'.

The theme of psychic abilities of the human mind is a particularly rich area in twentieth-century crackpot science, but there are two works that stand out for me. In Russia, a telepathy researcher named Bernard Bernardovich Kazhinskiy enlisted the help of Vladimir L. Durov, a celebrated circus artist and animal trainer who appeared to have the ability to control animals with 'mental suggestion'. 'Biological Radio Communications' is Kazhinskiy's term for this mind control, and also the title of the spectacularly strange book he published in 1963, which chronicles the 1278 experiments he conducted with Durov over a period of twenty months in which the former circus performer attempted to telepathically communicate with dogs by staring at them for hours on end.

What if this extrasensory perception (ESP) was an ability of plants, too? That was the question asked at around the same time by Grover Cleveland 'Cleve' Backster Jr, a specialist in hypno- and narco-interrogation for the American Central Intelligence Agency. While at a loose end in the early hours of 2 February 1966, Backster decided to hook up a *Dracaena fragrans* houseplant to a polygraph machine. He wondered if he could elicit a stress response by burning its leaves, and then he claimed that as he went to strike a match, the plant reacted. This proved to him that not only had the plant shown fear, but that it had read his mind.

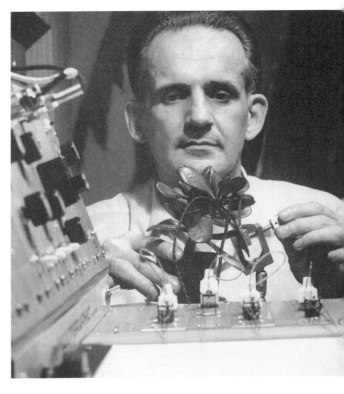

Cleve Backster attaching a houseplant to a lie detector.

The Secret Life of Plants (1973) by Peter Tompkins and Christopher Bird reported Backster's findings that plants had a previously undiscovered 'primary perception' that could pick up on human thought, and he became an instant celebrity. Invited onto the talk show circuit, he was interviewed by Johnny Carson, David Frost and others; and a popular documentary with the same title as the book was distributed by Paramount Pictures with a soundtrack by Stevie Wonder. All this, despite the fact that Backster's research, and the book as a whole, were derided as pseudoscientific nonsense by the scientific community.[3]

---

3 The Swedish writer August Strindberg (1849–1912) also conducted experiments based on his own scientific theories, despite a similar lack of scientific training. Prominent was his idea that plants had nervous systems. He was caught by a policeman injecting low-hanging apples with morphine, but after he explained his theory and it was decided he wasn't a fruit poisoner, he was released.

And finally we have the work of Pat Kelly, an American patent lawyer who in 1977 'started wondering whether it's possible to keep a severed head alive'. His 461-page book *If We Can Keep A Severed Head Alive ... Discorporation and U.S. Patent 4,666,425* appeared in 1988 written under the name 'Chet Fleming'. 'My background had nothing to do with medicine and only a small connection to biochemistry,' he wrote. 'I hadn't studied the subject of severed heads ... The idea just popped into my mind, unexpected and uninvited, followed by a difficult set of questions.'

If We Can Keep A Severed Head Alive ... is a manifesto of sorts for his 'prophetic patent' (i.e. not yet in existence) obsession. US Patent 4,666,425 was filed by Kelly on 19 May 1987, assigned to the 'Dis Corporation, St Louis, Missouri'). His invention, 'referred to herein as a 'cabinet'', provides physical and biochemical support for a head which has been 'discorporated' (i.e. severed from its body). Kelly breaks down his chapters into sections titled Science and History; Legal Issues; What If ... ?; Religious Issues; and Technology and Ethics.

Kelly wrote 'I'm not trying to promote or encourage it, instead, I'm trying to slow it down so Congress and the public can control it. I will greatly appreciate any help in getting that message across.' In a review for the *British Medical Journal*, the

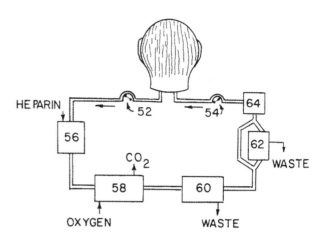

Chet Fleming/Pat Kelly's design for a 'cabinet' in which to keep a severed head alive.

immunohaematologist Terence Hamblin saw value in this, writing 'Mr. Fleming has done us a service in drawing our attention to this issue, and his ingenious method of stalling further development at present is rather fun'.

I've been fascinated by this book ever since acquiring copy number 1/88, the first he gave away to launch his severed head campaign, signed and dedicated to Monte C. Throdahl, a former chemical company executive and 'the finest scientist/manager I've ever known'. Sure, it's not a book one takes down from the shelf for a bedtime read too often. But if there's a title more effective in prompting horrified double-takes and the opportunity to tell a wonderfully odd story, then I've yet to come across it.

BOOKS OF SPECTACULAR SIZE

Let's start small. Surely the most impressive achievement in written succinctness is the following: 'm'. The world's shortest published poem is this four legged m, written by the Armenian-American poet Aram Saroyan in the 1960s. What exactly it means is unclear. As the m and the n appear to be in the process of dividing like a cell, the late mathematical poet and critic Bob Grumman called it 'a close-up of an alphabet being born'. Saroyan has form in this area, having knocked out the one-word poem 'Lighght' in 1965, which went on to be known as 'the most expensive word in history'. 'Lighght' earned Saroyan a $500 cash award from the *National Endowment for the Arts*, and kicked off a national debate in the United States over the waste of public money. 'If my kid came home from school spelling like that,' one congressman said, 'I would have stood him in the corner with a dunce cap.' Ronald Reagan was still making sarcastic allusions to 'lighght' twenty-five years later. 'I got intrigued by the look of individual words,' shrugged Saroyan. 'The word "guarantee," for instance, looks to me a bit like a South American insect.'

Whether he knew it or not, Saroyan was following in the footsteps of the Dutch poet and playwright Joost van den Vondel (1587–1679), whose work is said to have inspired John Milton, among others. In 1620, van den Vondel won a contest by writing a palindrome considered for some time the shortest poem in history. It is, in its entirety: 'U nu!', which translates as 'Now you!' Four centuries later the American poet Strickland Gillilan composed *Lines on the Antiquity of Microbes*, a couplet also known as *Fleas*. The poem reads: 'Adam / Had 'em.' On 4 June 1975, the boxer Muhammad Ali gave a speech at Harvard University, and afterwards discussed poetry on stage with George Plimpton, who recited *Fleas*. Ali responded, 'I've got one too: Me? Whee!'[1]

In terms of theatrical brevity, one of the shortest plays ever produced is *The Exile* by the French playwright Tristan Bernard (1866–1947). The curtain is raised to reveal the setting: a mountain cabin near the frontier, in which The Mountaineer sits beside a fire. There is a knock on the door, and The Exile enters the room. The entire play is the following exchange:

EXILE: *Whoever you are, have pity on a hunted man. There is a price on my head.*
MOUNTAINEER: *How much?*
CURTAIN.

But on to the books of remarkable scale themselves. Like Gulliver on his voyages, the collector of curiosities of scale must navigate two landscapes of opposing size: libraries of

---

1 According to James Boswell, Samuel Johnson was also fond of using such concision to witty end, boasting of an intellect so capacious that he could recite an entire chapter of Niels Horrebow's *The Natural History of Iceland* (1758). This chapter goes as follows: 'Chap. LXXII. Concerning Snakes. There are no snakes to be met with throughout the whole island.' (Chapter XLII is even shorter, commenting similarly on the lack of owls.)

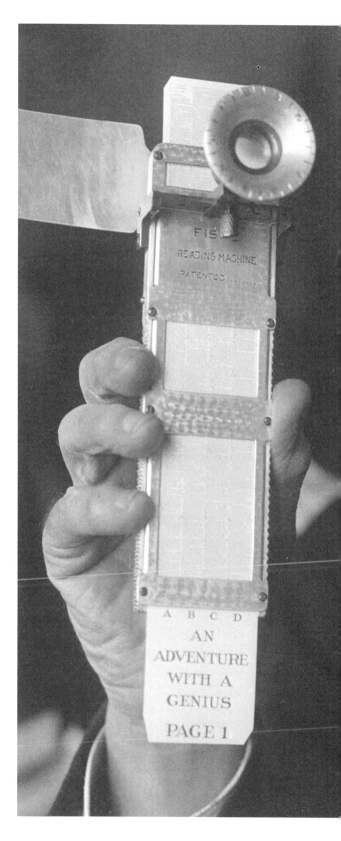

'Lilliputiana', as miniature books are sometimes affectionately called; and 'Brobdingnagiana', books fit for giants. Before browsing the skyscraping bookcases of the latter, it's advisable to first polish the eyeglasses and have a pair of tweezers at the ready as we squeeze into the world of the microbibliophile.

ABOVE AND RIGHT: *Before Kindles and e-readers, in 1922 there was Bradley Fiske's handheld Reading Machine. The metal device featured a magnifying lens to read whole books compressed into text too small for the human eye to read, printed on cards 15.24cm (6in) high. To demonstrate, Fiske showed journalists the first volume of Mark Twain's* Innocents Abroad *(around 93,000 words) condensed to thirteen cards.*

LILLIPUTIANA

During an otherwise unremarkable banquet thrown by the Duke of Buckingham in 1626 for Queen Henrietta Maria, wife of Charles I, out of a cold venison pie burst the 45-cm (18-in)-tall Jeffrey Hudson (1619–*c*.82), wearing a miniature suit of armour and waving a sword. The queen consort was so taken with the miniature seven-year-old child that Hudson soon moved into Denmark House as 'Lord Minimus, Queen's Dwarf', joining a menagerie of 'pets' that included a monkey called Pug and a Welsh giant named William Evans, who liked to pull a loaf from his pockets and make Hudson into a sandwich. Later in life, Hudson refused to humour any jokes about his modest dimensions. When Charles Crofts, brother of the Queen's Master of Horse, made such a wisecrack, Hudson challenged him to a duel. Crofts arrived chuckling, carrying a 'squirt' (a large syringe full of water that used to serve as a fire extinguisher) for his weapon, to the amusement of the crowd. The 1.06-m (3-ft-6-in) Lord Minimus drew his pistol and shot him through the head. Hudson lived to the age of sixty-three – you can find his tiny blue satin waistcoat, breeches and stockings preserved at the Ashmolean Museum in Oxford.

The adventures of Lord Minimus can be found in the diminutive work *The New Yeres Gift presented at Court from the Lady Parvula to the Lord Minimus commonly called Little Jefferie* (1636), a miniature volume of just a few inches' height, written by the anonymous 'Microphilus'.[2] The book was created specifically to defend 'Little Jefferie' from the ridicule of Sir William Davenant and his poem *Jeffreidos*,

Anthony van Dyck's portrait of Queen Henrietta Maria with Sir Jeffrey Hudson and pet monkey Pug.

which detailed a supposed duel Hudson had fought against a spurred turkey cock – but from the earliest days of writing, tiny volumes were a popular form of bookmaking.

People have always been fascinated with miniaturized objects, and craftsmen have always enjoyed showing off their skill with miniature work. The appeal of tiny books in particular is universal: the book collection of the American president Franklin D. Roosevelt, for example, numbered some 750 miniature volumes. And the world's largest museum devoted to the subject is not

---

2 Between 1740 and 1743, the publisher Thomas Boreman went the opposite way in subject matter for his tiny books printed for children, with giant themes like London monuments. *The Gigantick Histories* measure 2½ inches in height and came in two volumes for a child to fit into each pocket, so 'there would be no fear of growing lopsided, from the weight of such a gigantick work'.

where one might expect it to be: the Baku Museum of Miniature Books, Azerbaijan, holds more than 6500 examples collected from sixty-four different countries. In Japan, *mamehon* or 'bean-size books' flourished from the 1670s through to the late nineteenth century, and continue to be popular with the public. (It's worth keeping an eye out in Tokyo for *Mamehon-Gachapon*, vending machines that dispense miniature books in plastic eggs for 100 yen – about 75 pence.) A miniature book has even left Earth: on the first manned mission to the Moon in 1969, Buzz Aldrin took with him the miniature volume *The Autobiography of Robert Hutchings Goddard, Father of the Space Age: Early Years to 1927* (1966), to commemorate the fortieth anniversary of Goddard's invention of the first liquid-propellant rocket.

So exactly how small is 'miniature'? In the microbook world, the commonly agreed rule is that it shouldn't exceed 76mm (3in). This is the 'Bondy guideline', named after the dealer and miniature collector Louis Bondy. Officially, miniature books are usually referred to as '64mo' – a single leaf of paper printed with sixty-four pages on both sides and folded to result in the correct order of pages. 'I think there is some neuron in the human brain that is fired by objects of unexpected scale,' said Matthew Haley, Head of Books and Manuscripts at Bonhams, London, when I asked him about the continuing appeal of miniature books. He pointed to the miniature set of penitential psalms shown here, only 58 × 40mm. 'Truly a jewel.' It went on to sell at auction for £25,200.

Indeed, while later miniatures contained every subject of books of standard size, initially the earliest of these miniature incunabula (the term for works printed pre-1501) were religious works like these psalms.

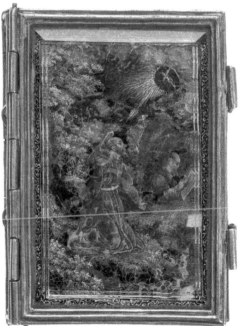

A miniature edition of penitential psalms of 1598 with a stunning binding of silver and hand-painted rock crystal showing St Francis receiving the stigmata.

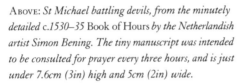

Above: *St Michael battling devils, from the minutely detailed c.1530–35* Book of Hours *by the Netherlandish artist Simon Bening. The tiny manuscript was intended to be consulted for prayer every three hours, and is just under 7.6cm (3in) high and 5cm (2in) wide.*

Above: *Many cuneiform tablets of ancient Mesopotamia are just a few centimetres in height and width and yet are inscribed with important information, from trader's inventories to couriered messages.*

Left: *Centuries before block printing was introduced in Europe, the Islamic world used the technique to produce miniature works like this talismanic scroll, consisting of prayers, incantations and Qur'anic verses, and kept in amulet boxes. Egypt, eleventh century.*

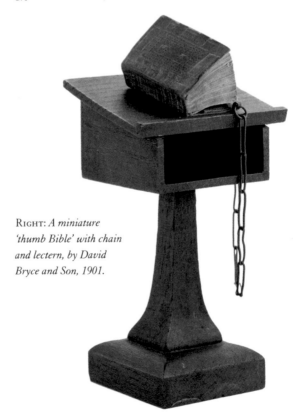

Right: *A miniature 'thumb Bible' with chain and lectern, by David Bryce and Son, 1901.*

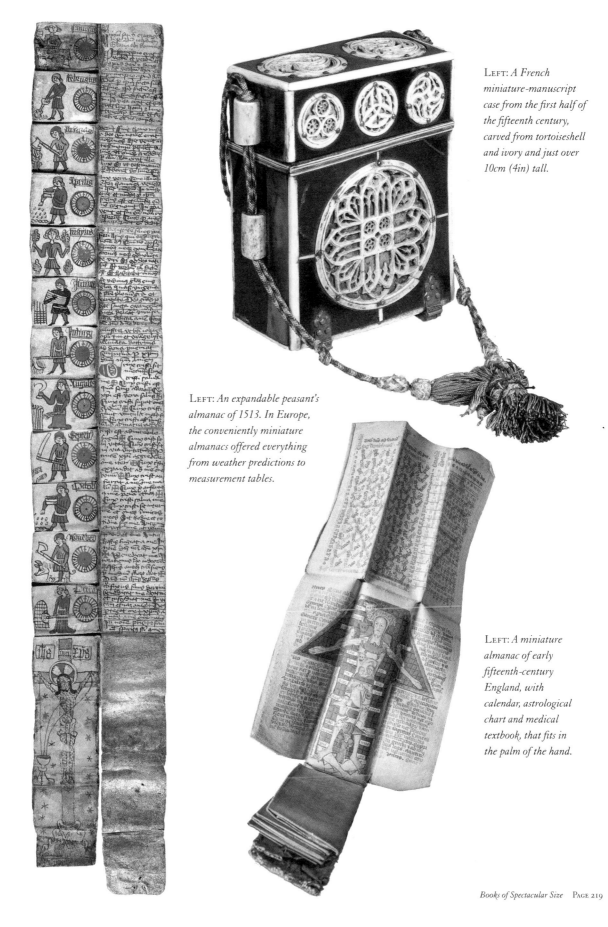

LEFT: *A French miniature-manuscript case from the first half of the fifteenth century, carved from tortoiseshell and ivory and just over 10cm (4in) tall.*

LEFT: *An expandable peasant's almanac of 1513. In Europe, the conveniently miniature almanacs offered everything from weather predictions to measurement tables.*

LEFT: *A miniature almanac of early fifteenth-century England, with calendar, astrological chart and medical textbook, that fits in the palm of the hand.*

LEFT: *A 7-cm (2¾-in)-tall collection of the Psalms of David from 1659, luxuriously bound in tortoiseshell.*

RIGHT: *A tiny sixteenth-century Italian prayer book manuscript written for and worn by a lady as a pendant hanging from a girdle or rosary.*

They mimicked the manuscript treasures created by the last great master illuminators like the Master of Claude de France, whose works the curators of the Morgan Library in New York have collected obsessively over the years. The most treasured is the *Prayer Book of Claude de France*, one of two tiny, precious manuscripts painted for Queen Claude of France, first wife of King François I, in 1517, the year of her coronation. The manuscript is just 7 × 5cm (2¾ × 2in) in size but, astonishingly, contains 132 miniature illustrations, with themes ranging from Biblical scenes to the queen's private worries, including her fear of being unable to produce healthy sons. Where once these intimate secrets were hidden for the Queen's eyes only, today visitors to the Morgan can browse them with an iPad.

A greater strain on the eye are 'thumb bibles', which emerged in the early seventeenth century. Over 300 editions of these Biblical abridgements survive, which were decorated with illustrations and usually made for children, and were the first miniature works to be produced in America. John Weever produced the earliest known example in verse form in 1601: an *Agnus Dei* carried six lines to each of the 128 pages. As only a couple of copies have survived, this is one of the most valuable miniature books in existence. Tiny Christian bibles were made in many unusual forms like this, and with the spread of missionaries could be found in increasingly unlikely places: as late as 1965, for example, in New Zealand a large number of miniature Gospels written in the Maori language were distributed for evangelical purposes.

Printed 'Thumbnail Qur'ans', on the other hand, first appeared in the late nineteenth century with the arrival of photolithography. The widest circulated edition of that time was produced by

RIGHT: *A thumb-sized Christian devotional with a binding of silver filigree, seventeenth century.*

A beautiful miniature Persian illuminated Qur'an, sixteenth century. 338 leaves at a size of 4 × 4cm (1½ × 1½in).

ABOVE: *The miniature 1878 edition of Dante's* La Divina Commedia, *with the minuscule typeface that destroyed the eyesight of those who made it.*

David Bryce of Glasgow in 1896, issued in his trademark metal locket with an inset magnifying glass, and worn by Muslim soldiers fighting for the British in World War I. But in fact miniature Qur'ans in manuscript form were worn this way, as talismans, centuries earlier. In the Ottoman era, miniature handwritten Qur'ans were known as *sancak*, after the standard-bearers, *sancakdār*, who fixed the books to their battle banners for protection as they charged into the fight, while some soldiers sealed them in gold and silver cases and wore them on their arms as amulets.

The main appeal of the miniature, to both maker and collector, was the artisanal challenge to produce the smallest book that contemporary technology allowed with such little room for error. As such,

the timeline of the miniature book becomes a sequence of record-setting efforts of such mind-boggling precision that just the thought of the work involved warrants an aspirin. The *Bloem-Hofje Door* ('Little Flower Garden'), for example, is a twenty-five-page poetry collection printed in 1673 in

BELOW: *A popular trend in the nineteenth century was to produce books inside a nutshell, like this miniature biography of Thomas Jefferson.*

LEFT: *The extremely rare* Das Kleinste Kochbuch Der Welt (*'The Smallest Cookbook in the World'), Vienna, c.1900. Approximately 23 × 21mm.*

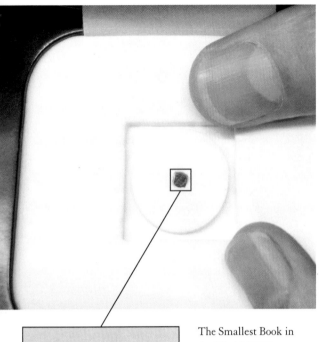

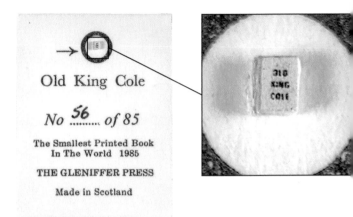

Old King Cole

No 56 of 85

The Smallest Printed Book
In The World 1985

THE GLENIFFER PRESS

Made in Scotland

The 12-page Old King Cole *(1985) issued by the Scottish Gleniffer Press. At a size of 1 × 1mm, its pages can only be browsed by using a needle.*

The Smallest Book in the World *(2002), created in Leipzig by the German typographer Joshua Reichert.*

Amsterdam by Benedikt Smidt at the age of only twenty-three to show off his abilities. With a text plate measuring just 7 × 13mm, for over 200 years this tiny work was the smallest book in the world, but that changed in 1819 when the French printer Henri Didot created the smallest typeface yet, a minuscule 2.5 point type (which looked like this); it was so small that to make it he had to invent an entirely new mould, the polyamatype.

Over fifty years later, to the delight of local optometrists, the Salmin Brothers of Padua, Italy, worked with a team of engineers to invent a now infamous microscopic typeface they called *carattere a occhio di mosca*, or 'fly's-eye'. The type was first used for the 'Dantino', a miniature 1878 edition of Dante's *La Divina Commedia*, but the project was overshadowed

by the fact that the 'fly's eye' was so achingly small that it physically damaged the eyesight of its compositor, Giuseppe Geche, and others involved in its printing. Each set of 32 pages required an entire month of meticulous work, and so the final count of 500 pages carrying 14,323 verses of the poem in a book that stands 4.5cm (1¾in) tall is a gigantic, yet somewhat dangerous, accomplishment. The use of a magnifying glass is recommended, but even so, reading it is rather an uncomfortable experience.

Throughout the twentieth century miniature books shrank impossibly, beginning with a bound edition of *Omar Khayyam* privately issued by Charles H. Meigs of Cleveland in 1900, at about a quarter of the size of a postage stamp in print so small as to be illegible to the naked eye. One copy was set in the bezel of a signet ring. And no modern microlibrary is complete without the smallest book in the world, helpfully titled *The Smallest Book in the World* (2002), printed in Leipzig, Germany, by the typographer

Joshua Reichert to commemorate the work of Johannes Gutenberg. Measuring 2.4 × 2.9mm, this is the world's smallest book in a published edition, with each page bearing a letter of the alphabet in a specially designed type; 300 copies were sold for around £100 – but be careful if you encounter one. Upon purchasing a copy from a German dealer at a book fair a few years ago, he told me a cautionary tale of his colleague who, while examining her own copy, had made the mistake of breathing. She then spent an entire afternoon on her hands and knees with a magnifying glass, searching the floorboards for a book the size of a peppercorn.

From here on, it just gets ridiculous. In 2007 at the Nano Imaging Laboratory at Simon Fraser University in Vancouver, British Columbia, Canada, the original story by Malcolm Douglas Chaplin of *Teeny Ted from Turnip Town* ('a fable about Teeny Ted's victory in the turnip contest at the annual county fair') was etched into thirty micro-tablets of crystalline silicon measuring 0.07 × 0.1mm using a focused gallium-ion beam, at a cost of $15,000 (around £10,000). The publisher Robert Chaplin created the 'nano book' in 2007 with the assistance of SFU scientists Li Yang and Karen Kavanagh. *Teeny Ted…* even has its own ISBN number, but you'll need a scanning electron microscope to read it. A later admirable effort was that of the Russian physicist Vladimir Aniskin in 2016. Using a lithographic stencil to spray metallic letters with a height of 15 micrometres, Aniskin wrote out three

character names from the 1881 story by Nikolai Leskov called *The Tale of Cross-eyed Lefty from Tula and the Steel Flea*. The story tells of three Russian master engravers who outperform their English rivals by creating tiny inscribed shoes for a clockwork flea. By inscribing the names of the three masters in a microbook smaller than the flea's shoe itself, Aniskin cleverly trumped them all.

RIGHT TOP: *Karen Kavanagh and Li Yang of Simon Fraser University stand beside a monitor showing the nano book* Teeny Ted from Turnip Town *in 2007.*

RIGHT BOTTOM: *Physicist Vladimir Aniskin's microbook* Levsha *('Left-Hander').*

BROBDINGNAGIANA

At the opposite end of the scale are Brobdingnagiana, or 'Goliaths of bookdom' as the book historian Walter Hart Blumenthal referred to them. To really do justice to the theme, I think it's worth gathering under this title both the phenomenally long works of the hypergraphic writer and the physically oversized books so elephantine as to threaten the structural safety of their libraries.

What motivates those attempting to write the longest book ever written? Between 1968 and 1974, Mrs Marva Drew, 51, of Waterloo, Iowa, cheerfully typed out in words every number from 1 to 1,000,000 on her manual typewriter. The project required 2473 sheets of paper. When she was asked why she did it, she replied, 'But I love to type'. According to Armen Shekoyan, an Armenian writer who is, at the time of writing, attempting to produce the world's longest novel: 'If you write a book according to the usual criteria, one person may like it, the other may dislike it; but when you write ten volumes, no one will say that the book is in eight.'

For the Yongle Emperor of China's Ming dynasty, commissioning the longest set of printed works in history was purely for his own convenience. The *Yongle Encyclopedia* or *Yongle Dadian* ('Great Canon of Yongle') is a mostly lost Chinese encyclopedia that incorporated all recorded knowledge, to provide a single reference work for its imperial reader. Work began in 1403. An initial team of 100 scholars grew to an army of 2169, who travelled across China to find written works to feed into the omnivorous book project. Some 8000 texts on every

subject from agriculture to religion to fiction were absorbed, and when the project was completed five years later in 1408 the encyclopedia comprised 22,937 manuscript rolls bearing some 370 million Chinese handwritten characters. All that was known of history, philosophy, the arts, the sciences and the Confucian canon was covered. The encyclopedia would have occupied roughly 40 cubic metres (1400 cu ft) of space – the same volume as a modern 11-metre (36-ft) truck trailer. No printed work has ever come close to rivalling the *Yongle Encyclopedia*;

A 1637 example of a dos-à-dos *('back-to-back') binding, in which a shared board serves as the back cover of two volumes – in this case a copy of the New Testament with a Book of Psalms ('Left-Hander').*

A c.1835 woodblock print by the great artist Utagawa Kuniyoshi of a scene from the epic Japanese novel series Hakkenden. *The character Inuta Kobungo Yasuyori subdues one opponent with his foot and fends off another, all while carrying the infant Inue Shinbei Masashi on his back.*

it was only on 9 September 2007, nearly six centuries later, that its textual size and scope was surpassed, and that online, by Wikipedia.

Theoretically, the record of the longest work could be claimed by printing the work *Googolplex Written Out*, published online in multiple PDF volumes by Wolfgang H. Nitsche in 2013, in which the number googolplex (1 followed by 10^{100} zeroes) is typed out in full. Before clicking 'Buy now' for a hard copy version, though, it's worth considering that in doing so you would be destroying all known existence. Printing all the zeros of a googolplex would require 10^{94} books. If each of these books had a mass of 100 grams, then the total mass of the set would be 10^{93} kilograms. For context, Earth's mass is a mere 5.972×10^{24} kilograms, and the mass of the Milky Way Galaxy has been estimated at 2.5×10^{42} kilograms, which still pales in comparison. Bottom line: do not print this book.

In Japan, the most commonly mentioned name in lengthy works is Kyokutei Bakin, who wrote his epic 106-volume novel *Nansō Satomi Hakkenden* ('The Eight Dog Chronicles') over twenty-eight years between 1814 and 1842, finishing at the age of seventy-five. Though he lost his sight toward the end of the process, Bakin still managed to finish the 38-million-word tale by dictating the last parts to his daughter-in-law, Michi. Inspired by *Shuǐhǔ Zhuàn* ('Water Margin'), one of the four great classical novels of Chinese literature, about a group of outlaws, the *Hakkenden* follows the adventures of eight samurai half-brothers, who through a rather complicated set of circumstances were

Opposite: Kuniyoshi's depiction of the character Yang Lin, 'the Multi-coloured Leopard', from Water Margin, *one of the four great classical novels of Chinese literature, which helped inspire* Hakkenden.

all fathered by a dog. The majority of the novel's 181 chapters relate the swashbuckling adventures of the dog-brothers during the riotous Sengoku period (350 years before Bakin's time).

In the West, the record for most published works by one author is at the time of writing held by none other than L. Ron Hubbard, founder of Scientology, who also wrote one of (this) world's longest novels. The ten-volume story *Mission Earth*, begun in 1985, runs to 1,200,000 words across 3992 pages, and bills itself as a 'satirical science fiction adventure set in the far future'. Critics were less favourable in their descriptions, and the book was even banned in places like Dalton, Georgia, where it was decried as 'anti-social, perverted, and anti-everything'.

Hubbard produced an astounding 1084 published works in his lifetime, and wrote under a variety of pseudonyms including Bernard Hubbel, Legionnaire 14830, René Lafayette, Joe Blitz and – a personal favourite – Winchester Remington Colt. His most curious work, though, is *Excalibur*, reportedly inspired by his reaction to nitrous oxide used in a dental procedure in 1938, and a book he was convinced was 'somewhat more important, and would have a greater impact upon people, than the Bible'. Though it was never published, Hubbard briefly advertised a very limited edition for $1500 per copy in 1957, with the warning that 'four of the first fifteen people who read it went insane'. He told his literary agent, Forrest J. Ackerman, that when he'd sent the manuscript to a New York publisher, the reader had jumped out of the skyscraper window. This book formed the basis for his later, infamous, work *Dianetics* (1950).

Henry Darger (1892–1973) was an equally eccentric though more reclusive American writer, who worked as a hospital janitor in

An illustration from Henry Darger's 15,145-page work The Story of the Vivian Girls …

Chicago, Illinois. After his death, amid the 'armpit-high' collections of string balls and medicine bottles at the cluttered studio apartment he'd rented for forty years, Darger's landlord discovered an enormous, thirteen-volume, 15,145-page manuscript of over 9 million words. The work was illustrated with over 300 drawings and watercolour paintings, the last few painted on sheets 3 metres (10ft) wide. *The Story of the Vivian Girls, in What Is Known as the Realms of the Unreal, of the Glandeco-Angelinian War Storm, Caused by the Child Slave Rebellion* recounts the adventures of seven innocent heroines, the Vivian Girls, who lead a rebellion against the evil, child-snatching,

adult Glandelinians. It's not known how long Darger worked on his book, but it was clearly several decades in the making. Today, his work has become known as one of the most famous examples of that of an 'outsider artist', and collections of his artwork can sell for millions.

Another prolific recluse was the chronically unsuccessful Boston poet Arthur Crew Inman, once described by *Time* magazine as a 'megalomaniacal bigot misogynist Peeping Tom hypochondriac' in a review of a published selection from his 17 million-word, 155-volume diary. Debilitated by hypochondria, Inman vented an unceasing stream of irritability in his journals while living in dark, soundproofed apartments. A typical excerpt: 'A Lithuanian came to read to me. I disliked her at once. She was common. Her voice sounded like an ungreased axle.' Inman's diary is one of the longest in the English language. 'I trust to do in nonfiction what Balzac did in fiction,' he once said. Begun in 1919, the diary tracks every moment of his life until 1963, when he found the construction noise of the nearby Prudential Tower so unbearable that he committed suicide with a revolver.

Meanwhile, in Washington: '7 a.m.: I cleaned out the tub and scraped my feet with my fingernails to remove layers of dead skin,' reads a typically riveting entry from the diary of Robert Shields (1918–2007), an American former minister and high-school English teacher of Dayton, Washington. From 1972 to 1997, for four hours every day, Shields kept a diary of entries made every five minutes,

with a special focus on his bowel movements. The diaries run to an astonishing 37.5 million words – words like: '6:30–6:35 p.m.: I put in the oven two Stouffer's macaroni and cheese at 350 degrees. 6:50–7:30 p.m.: I ate the Stouffer's macaroni and cheese and Cornelia ate the other one. Grace decided she didn't want one.' Shields compared the idea of ceasing writing the diaries to 'turning off my life', and considered his books useful for researchers in the future. 'Maybe by looking into someone's life at that depth every minute of every day, they will find out something about all people.' You can find the stacks of diaries in the collection of Washington State University, donated following Shield's death in 2007, along with a collection of his nose hair that he left behind in the hope it would be useful for 'further study'.

These lengthy works, however, sit in the shade of the book behemoths. This towering line-up is best introduced with the largest surviving medieval manuscript in Europe, which was supposedly created with the assistance of the Devil. According to legend, in the early thirteenth century in the Benedictine monastery of Podlažice in Bohemia, a scribe known as Herman the Recluse was condemned to be immured (walled up alive) for breaking his vows. After pleading for his life, Herman was spared by the abbot on the rather unfair condition that the monk write down all of humanity's knowledge in one night. Herman wrote frantically but at midnight he admitted defeat, and in desperation prayed for help

LEFT: *At the Kuthodaw Pagoda at Mandalay, Myanmar, completed in 1868 on the orders of King Mingdon, 730 tablets 1m (3ft 3in) wide and 1.5m (5ft) tall were inscribed in gold ink with the* Tripiṭ aka *and other Buddhist texts. Each stone 'page' is 12.7cm (5in) thick and is housed in its own* stupa, *a mound-like structure.*

ABOVE, RIGHT AND OPPOSITE: *The* Codex Gigas, *the largest existing medieval manuscript, said to have been written in one night by a monk charged with diabolic power, who included a portrait of the Devil in thanks.*

from the Devil. By morning, Lucifer had completed the beautifully illuminated work, and in thanks Herman included in the book a full-page portrait of the Prince of Darkness (shown here).

The author of the *Codex Gigas* certainly packed a lot into the enormous so-called *Devil's Bible*, which required 100 donkeys' hides to make the 309 parchment sheets for its yard-high pages. As well as a complete, copied-out *Vulgate Bible* (the principal Latin version), there is a range of other popular works including Isidore of Seville's entire encyclopedia, *Etymologiae*, assorted medical compilations and two books by Constantine the African. Its modern curators estimate that the hulking work is likely the product

The Codex Amiatinus, a 'Giant Bible' that is also the earliest complete Latin Bible. Created at Wearmouth-Jarrow, England, in the beginning of the eighth century, it features three detailed paintings.

of between twenty and thirty years' labour. It resides in the National Library of Sweden at Stockholm, having previously been kept at Stockholm Castle, where it was once thrown out of a fourth floor window to save it after a fire broke out. Luckily, the 74.8kg (165lb) book's fall was broken by it landing squarely on an oblivious passerby. The book survived, albeit with a few leaves knocked loose – the condition of its human crash-mat went unrecorded.[3]

The size of giant bibles represented the importance of the subject matter; their weight – requiring at least two people to carry – reflecting the gravitas of the Word of God. Practically, oversized proportions also allowed multiple readers to examine the book simultaneously. This was especially useful for another kind of text used in monastic services, the enormous antiphonaries, so cumbersome that they lived their lives largely unmolested on their robust lecterns. Their antiphons (short chants) are accompanied by heavily marked square- and diamond-shaped musical notation for the liturgical choir, widely used in both Ambrosian and Gregorian chanting. The singers grouped around the antiphonary, its size affording a shared use.

As impressive as an antiphonary is, an encounter with the Great Qur'an of Samarkand must have been truly awe-inspiring. The story goes that in 1399 Saray Mulk Khanum (1343–1406), Empress of Tamerlane and chief consort of Timur,

---

3 Lethal book defenestration has its own history – on the night of 3 February 1731, the Royal Palace of Brussels erupted in flames, and its librarians began frantically throwing books out of the window to save them. One onlooker was reported to have been killed by a particularly hefty flying folio.

Opening a giant antiphonary (medieval choral book) usually requires a floor to take the strain.

ordered the construction of the most beautiful mosque ever built while her husband was away at war. The greatest architects and artisans worked tirelessly on the project and in 1404 completed work on the Bibi-Khanym Mosque ('the Mosque of the Oldest Wife'). To this day you can find at the centre of its courtyard a formidable, empty stone lectern measuring 2.29 ×1.98 metres (7ft 6in × 6ft 6in), upon which sat one of the oldest Qur'ans in the world, bound in gold and weighing around 300kg (661lbs). The book had originally belonged to Osman (AD 579–656), son-in-law to Muhammad, who was murdered while reading it, his blood spilling onto the pages and transforming it

into a relic. A saint transported the ancient work to Samarkand where it rested for centuries on this lectern, worshipped by locals and pilgrims. Women wanting a son would circle the lectern three times in the hope of falling pregnant. When the Russians seized Samarkand in 1868 the Great Qur'an was brought to St Petersburg as booty, where it was held until 1924 when the Soviets returned it to the Uzbek people. Today the book's fragile deer skin is protected by a carefully regulated environment at the Mui Mubarack Museum in Tashkent.

Of course, some giant books were created for sheer spectacle. In this category there is really none more impressive than the American literary leviathan *The Story of the South*, which was made for the 1925 exposition at the Grand Central Palace, New York, where each industry of the South exhibited its most impressive work. (It would later be displayed at the City Hall of Baltimore, but then it disappears from records, quite possibly broken up due to its inconvenient size.)

ABOVE: *The giant stone lectern at the fifteenth-century Bibi-Khanym Mosque at Samarkand, one of the most magnificent mosques of the Islamic world.*

BELOW: *The towering Klencke Atlas, made for King Charles II of England by the Dutch scholar and merchant Johannes Klencke, presented in celebration of the Restoration. At 1.76 metres (almost 6ft) tall, and 2.3 metres (7ft 6in) wide when open, the book dwarfs its reader.*

The Story of the South was so floor-splinteringly large – at 2.08 metres (6ft 10in) in height, and 2.79 metres (9ft 2in) in width when open – that motors were required to turn its pages. It loomed over its audience on an enormous mechanized easel, which raised the total height to 3.7 metres (12ft 2in), as tall as an adult African elephant, and brought the total weight to over half a ton. The two 12-horsepower engines helped to turn the book's nineteen bed-sheet-sized pages, which detailed the contributions from the Southern states in the building of the republic. The main challenge for the book's creators, though, was the binding. What creature could be large enough to produce a leather hide capable of enveloping the boards? After searching around, an ox hide 3.66 metres (12ft) long was finally sourced in Texas. (Though this measurement seems unlikely, if there's any place that could produce a sufficiently monstrous bovine, it's Texas.)

Ninety years later, in Brazil in 2014, a tax lawyer named Vinicius Leôncio completed his own monster, created from an entirely different motivation: protest. The result of twenty-three years' work, *Pátria Amada* ('Beloved Country'), is a 7.5-ton testament to the ridiculous immensity and complexity of Brazilian tax laws. Leôncio was the first to bring together every Brazilian tax code in one volume (complete for only a brief moment, as thirty-five new tax laws are added to Brazilian legislation each day). Its 41,000 pages means that when laid on its back the book is 2.10 metres (6ft 11in) thick, towering over any prospective reader.

Leôncio spent R$1 million (about £205,000) of his own money to print the book in a shed in the city of Contagem, using an imported Chinese printer accustomed to cranking out billboard posters. Over twenty-three years Leôncio spent an average of five hours a day

The Brazilian lawyer Vinicius Leôncio perches atop his gigantic book, a protest printing of his country's excessive number of tax laws.

researching and collecting the laws, with a staff that grew to thirty-seven. Three heart attacks, a divorce and a new marriage failed to dissuade him from his task of highlighting 'the surreal, punishing experience' of dealing with a tax system gone haywire. 'I simply thought that something should be done about the humiliation we must endure to pay our taxes in this country,' he said.

Though he was delighted to hear the story of his book would be included here, and kindly provided me with the accompanying photograph, Sr Leôncio is very happy to have left the project behind. And in response to one final question: No, he says, he has no plans to publish a second edition.

Following Four Pages: The Birds of America *(1827–38) in enormous 'Double Elephant Folio' size (99cm/39½ in tall by 66cm/28½in wide) was the American naturalist John James Audubon's attempt to paint every bird in North America. Remarkably, the birds are painted life-size. In 2010, a complete copy of the first edition was sold in London at Sotheby's for £7,321,250, making it one of the most expensive books ever sold at auction.*

Drawn from Nature by J.J. Audubon, F.R.S. F.L.S.

Great White Heron, ARDEA

PLATE CCLXXXI.

ARDEA OCCIDENTALIS, *Male adult spring plumage. View Key-west.*

Engraved, Printed & Coloured by R. Havell. 1835.

Drawn from Nature by J. J. Audubon, F.R.S. F.L.S.

Engraved, Printed and Coloured by Rob.ᵗ Havell, 1838.

1.—Profile view of Bill at its greatest extension.

2.—Superior front view of upper Mandible.

3.—Interior front view of upper Mandible.

4.—Inferior front view of lower Mandible.

5.—Interior front view of lower Mandible with the Tongue in.

American Flamingo.

PHŒNICOPTERUS RUBER, Linn.

Old Male.

6.—Profile view of Tongue.

7.—Superior front view of Tongue.

8.—Inferior front view of Tongue.

9.—Perpendicular front view of the foot fully expanded.

PLATE CCCXI

American White Pelican
PELICANUS AMERICANUS, *Aud.*

STRANGE TITLES

'What's in a name?' mused Shakespeare in *Romeo and Juliet* (first published in print in 1597 as *An Excellent Conceited Tragedie of Romeo and Juliet*). Would he have said the same, one wonders, if he'd been around to hear that F. Scott Fitzgerald's *The Great Gatsby* was at one point titled *Trimalchio in West Egg*; or that for *Dracula*, Bram Stoker considered *The Dead Un-Dead*? There is certainly an art to the great title, as demonstrated by the late English humourist Alan Coren, who when choosing a name for a collection of essays in 1975 noticed that the most popular books in Britain at that time were about cats, golf and Nazis. So he called his book *Golfing for Cats* and slapped a swastika on the front cover.

We also learn that care should be taken to avoid tempting an ironic fate. Bill Hillman, the American author of the 2014 guide *Fiesta: How to Survive the Bulls of Pamplona*, was gored by the bulls of Pamplona that same year – and again the next year. And in the 2017 British national election, the Conservative politician Gavin Barwell, author of *How to Win a Marginal Seat*, lost his marginal seat.

The humorous literary award known as the Bookseller/Diagram Prize for Oddest Title of the Year has been running since 1978, with past winners including *Oral Sadism and the Vegetarian Personality* (1986) by Glenn C. Ellenbogen, *The Joy of Waterboiling* (2018) by Achse Verlag and *The Dirt Hole and its Variations* by Charles L. Dobbins (2019). But we can go back centuries earlier to find their ancestors. The following are some of the more curious lurking in the corners of library catalogues.

Ecloga de Calvis; or, In Praise of Bald Men (*c*.910) by the French monk Hucbald

The First Blast of The Trumpet Against the Monstrous Regiment of Women (1558) by John Knox

The Loathsomenesse of Long Haire … with the Concurrent Judgement of Divines both Old and New Against It. With an Appendix Against Painting, Spots, Naked Breasts, etc. (1654) by Rev. Thomas Hall

On the Conciliation of Spirits, or: How to Get Acquainted With Ghosts (1716) by H. A. Matcke and G. E. Hamberger

Arse Musica; or, The Lady's Back Report … (1722) by the Countess of Fizzle Rumpff (Jonathan Swift)

Satan's Harvest Home: or the Present State of Whorecraft, Adultery, Fornication, Procuring, Pimping, Sodomy, And the Game of Flatts, (Illustrated by an Authentick and Entertaining Story) And other Satanic Works, daily propagated in this good Protestant Kingdom (1749) by Anonymous

An Essay on the Art of Ingeniously Tormenting; with Proper Rules for the Exercise of that Pleasant Art (1753) by Jane Collier

The Egg, Or The Memoirs Of Gregory Giddy, Esq: With The Lucubrations Of Messrs. Francis Flimsy, Frederick Florid, And Ben Bombast. To Which Are Added, The Private Opinions Of Patty Pout, Lucy Luscious, And Priscilla Positive. Also The Memoirs Of A Right Honourable Puppy. Conceived By A Celebrated Hen, And Laid Before The Public By A Famous Cock-Feeder (1772) by Anonymous

The Adventures Of An Irish Smock, Interspersed With Whimsical Anecdotes Of A Nankeen Pair Of Breeches (1783) published by George Lister

An Essay upon Wind, with Curious Anecdotes of Eminent Peteurs (1787) by Charles James Fox

The Adventures of a Pin, Supposed to be Related by Himself, Herself, or Itself (1790) by J. Lee

Sun-beams May Be Extracted From Cucumbers, But the Process is Tedious (1799) by David Daggett

The Adventures of an Ostrich Feather of Quality (1812) by Sherwood, Neely and Jones

Memoirs of an Old Wig (1815) by Richard Fenton

Holidays with Hobgoblins (1861) by Dudley Costello

How to Ride a Velocipede: Straddle a Saddle, Then Paddle and Skedaddle (1869) by Joseph Firth Bottomley

Heaven: Where It Is, Its Inhabitants, And How To Get There (1881) by Dwight L. Moody

Ducks; and How to Make Them Pay (1890) by William Cook

Ghosts I Have Met, and Some Others (1890) by John Kendrick Bangs

How to Cook Husbands (1898) by Elizabeth Strong Worthington

A Treatise on the Use of Flogging in Medicine and Venery (1898) by Johann Heinrich Meibom

Fishes I Have Known (1905) by Arthur A. Henry Bevan

The Absent Treatment of Disease, With Particular Reference to Telepathy (1906) by Sheldon Leavitt, MD

Moles and their Meaning ... Being a Modernised and Easy Guide to the Ancient Science of Divination by the Moles of the Human Body (1907) by Harry De Windt

An Irishman's Difficulties with the Dutch Language (1912) by Cuey-Na-Gael

Old Age, Its Cause and Prevention (1912) by Sanford Bennett

Pigs: How to Make Them Pay (1918) by C. Arthur Pearson, Limited

Does the Earth Rotate? No! (1919) by William Westfield

The Radiation Cookery Book (1927) published by Radiation Ltd, Birmingham

A Handbook on Hanging (1928) by Charles Duff

What Would Christ Do About Syphilis? (c.1930) by Dr Ira D. Cardiff

Psychic Self-Defense: Practical Instructions for the Detection of Psychic Attacks, & Defence Against Them (1930) by Dion Fortune

Thought Transference (Or What?) in Birds (1931) by Edmund Selous

Your Answer to Invasion – Ju-Jitsu (1941) by James Hipkiss

Who's Who in Cocker Spaniels (1944) by Marion Frances Robinson

Cabbages and Crime (1945) by Anne Nash

The History and Romance of Elastic Webbing
(1946) by Clifford A. Richmond

Mrs. Rasmussen's Book of One-Arm Cookery
(1946) by Mary Laswells

Harnessing the Earthworm (1949)
by Thomas J. Barrett

Shag the Caribou (1949) by C. Bernard Rutley

Frog Raising for Pleasure and Profit (1950)
by Dr Albert Broel

Practical Kinks for Coal Mining Men (1950)
by Anonymous

Your Feet Are Killing You (1953) by Dr Simon
J. Wikler (see also *Your Feet Are Literally
Killing You* (1979) by T. O. 'Tip' Berg)

*The Boring Sponges Which Attack
South Carolina Oysters* (1956)
by Bears Bluff Laboratories

A Weasel in My Meatsafe (1957)
by Phil Drabble

Atomic Gardening for the Layman (1960)
by Muriel Howorth

The Inheritance of Hairy Ear Rims (1961)
by Reginald Ruggles Gates and P. N. Bhaduri

Onions and Their Allies (1963)
by Henry Albert Jones, Louis Kimball Mann

Brainwashing is a Cinch! (1966)
by James Maratta

*Barbs, Prongs, Points, Prickers and Stickers:
A Complete Catalogue of Antique Barbed Wire*
(1970) by Robert T. Clifton

Be Bold with Bananas (1972)
by Crescent Books (Editor)

*The Jewish-Japanese Sex and Cook Book and
How to Raise Wolves* (1972) by Jack Douglas

Gleeful Guide to Occult Cookery (1974)
by Will Eisner

*Proceedings of the Second International
Workshop on Nude Mice* (1977) edited
by Tatsuji Nomura et al.

*The Madam as Entrepreneur: Career
Management in House Prostitution* (1978)
by Barbara Sherman Heyl

Highlights in the History of Concrete (1979)
by C. C. Stanley

That Amazing Ingredient, Mayonnaise! (1979)
by Pat Morrison

Gravity is a Push (1979) by Walter C. Wright

The Joy of Chickens (1981) by Dennis Nolan

The Theory of Lengthwise Rolling (1981) by G. S.
Nikitin, Alexander Tselikov, S. E. Rokotyan

*The Trombone in the Middle Ages and the
Renaissance* (1982) by George B. Lane

Nuclear War: What's in it for You? (1982)
by Ground Zero Fund, Inc. (Editor)

*A Basic Guide to the Occult for Law Enforcement
Agencies* (1986) by Mary Jane Herold

*Manifold Destiny: The One! The Only! Guide to
Cooking on Your Car Engine!* (1989)
by Chris Maynard, Bill Scheller

How to Avoid Huge Ships (1993)
by John W. Trimmer

Dating for Under a Dollar: 301 Ideas (1999)
by Blaire Tolman

*How to Good-bye Depression: If You Constrict
Anus 100 Times Everyday. Malarkey? or
Effective Way?* (2000) by Hiroyuki Nishigaki

The Bible Cure for Irritable Bowel Syndrome
(2002) by Don Colbert, MD

Everything I Know about Women I Learned from My Tractor (2002) by Robert Welsch

People Who Don't Know They're Dead: How They Attach Themselves to Unsuspecting Bystanders and What to Do About It (2005) by Gary Leon Hill

Does God Ever Speak through Cats? (2006) by David Evans

Ghosts: Minnesota's Other Natural Resource (2007) by Brian Leffler

Collectible Spoons of the Third Reich (2009) by James A. Yannes

After You Shoot: Your Gun's Hot. The Perp's Not. Now What? (2010) by Alan Korwin

The Origin of Feces (2013) by David Waltner-Toews

How to Date Buildings: An Easy Reference Guide (2017) by Trevor Yorke

Open Wide for the Handsome Sabertooth Dentist Who Is Also a Ghost (2017) by Chuck Tingle

A sheet of punctuation marks from A Pickle for
the Knowing Ones or Plain Truth in a
Homespun Dress (1802), a book as eccentric as
its author, Timothy Dexter, a Massachusetts
businessman with little sense who nevertheless
found success with phenomenal luck. When he
sent a load of bed-warming pans to the tropical
West Indies, Dexter's enterprising captain
managed to sell them as ladles to the local
molasses industry. The wool mittens Dexter sent
on another voyage were bought by Asian
merchants to export to Siberia. His bibles for the
East Indies were bought by missionaries, and the
stray cats he sent to the Caribbean islands were
welcomed as a solution to their rat problems. At
one point Dexter was tricked by rivals into
sending a shipload of coal to Newcastle (which
would be like exporting crude oil to Saudi
Arabia), but his vessel happened to arrive during
a local miners' strike and he made a fortune. At
the age of fifty he self-published A Pickle ..., an
8847-word rant against politicians, the clergy and
his wife, with seemingly random capitalization
and an absence of punctuation for no apparent
reason. In response to criticism, to the back of the
second edition he added this sheet of punctuation
marks, for readers to distribute among the text
themselves. I hope he would enjoy this tribute.

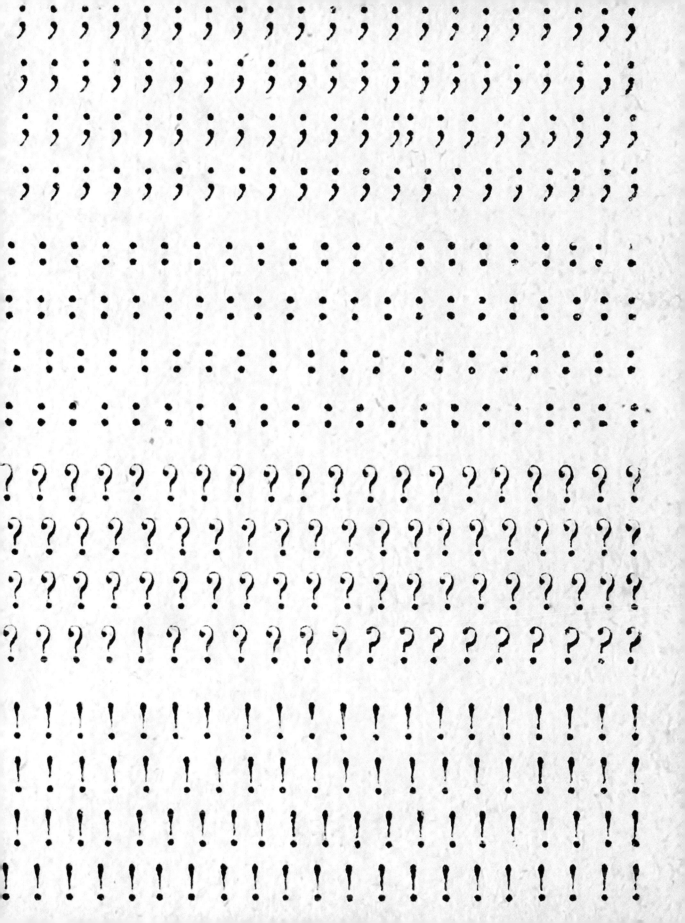

SELECT BIBLIOGRAPHY

Ash, R. & Lake, B. (1998) *Bizarre Books*, London: Pavilion Books

Basbanes, N. A. (1995) *A Gentle Madness: Bibliophiles, Bibliomanes and the Eternal Passion for Books*, New York: Henry Holt & Co.

Basbanes, N. A. (2001) *Patience & Fortitude*, New York: HarperCollins Publishers

Bauer, M.S. (2009) *A Mind Apart: Poems of Melancholy, Madness, and Addiction*, Oxford: Oxford University Press

Bishop, T. (2017) *Ink: Culture, Wonder, and Our Relationship with the Written Word*, Toronto: Penguin Canada

Bloch, I. (1909) *The Sexual Life of Our Time in its Relations to Modern Civilization*, London: Rebman Ltd

Bondeson, J. (1997) *A Cabinet of Medical Curiosities*, London: I. B. Tauris Publishers

Bondy, L. (1981) *Miniature Books*, London: Sheppard Press

Bromer, A. C. & Edison, J. I. (2007) *Miniature Books: 4000 Years of Tiny Treasures*, New York: Abrams Books

Copp, P. (2014) *The Body Incantatory: Spells and the Ritual Imagination in Medieval Chinese Buddhism*, New York: Columbia University Press

Darnton, R. (2009) *The Case for Books: Past, Present and Future*, New York: Public Affairs Books

Davenport, C. (1929) *Beautiful Books*, London: Methuen & Co. Ltd

Davenport, C. (1927) *Byways Among English Books*, London: Methuen & Co. Ltd

Davenport, C. (1907) *The Book: Its History and Development*, London: Archibald Constable & Co. Ltd

Davies, O. (2009) *Grimoires: A History of Magic Books*, Oxford: Oxford University Press

Dibdin, T.F. (1809) *The Bibliomania; or Book Madness*, London: W. Savage

Disraeli, I. (1791) *Curiosities of Literature*, London: J. Murray

Ditchfield, P. H. (1895) *Books Fatal to their Authors*, London: Elliot Stock

Duncan, D. & Smyth, A. (eds.) (2019) *Book Parts*, Oxford: Oxford University Press

Eisen, E. X. (2018) https://www.theparisreview.org/blog/2018/10/31/writing-in-blood/

Eliot, S. & Rose, J. (eds.) (2009) *A Companion to the History of the Book*, Oxford: Blackwell Publishing

Febvre, L. & Martin, H-J. (1976) *The Coming of the Book: The Impact of Printing, 1450–1800*, London: New Left Book Club

Finkelstein, D. & McCleery, A. (2005) *An Introduction to Book History*, New York/London: Routledge

Fishburn, M. (2008) *Burning Books*, Basingstoke: Palgrave Macmillan

Ford, B.J. (1992) *Images of Science: A History of Scientific Illustration*, London: British Library

Fowler, C. (2012) *Invisible Ink*, London: Strange Attractor

Garfield, S. (2018) *In Miniature: How Small Things Illuminate the World*, Edinburgh: Canongate Books

Gekowski, R. (2013) *Lost, Stolen or Shredded: Stories of Missing Works of Art and Literature*, London: Profile

Gilbar, S. (1981) *The Book Book*, New York: Bell Publishing Company

Gillett, C. R. (1932) *Burned Books*, Norwood: Plimpton Press

Gordon, Stuart (1995) *The Book of Hoaxes*, London: Headline Book Publishing

Grafton, A. (1997) *The Footnote: A Curious History*, London: Faber and Faber

Haggard, H. W. (1913) *Devils, Drugs and Doctors*, London: Harper & Brothers

Haight, A. (1978) *Banned Books*, New York: R. R. Bowker LLC

Houston, K. (2016) *The Book: A Cover-to-Cover Exploration of the Most Powerful Object of our Time*, New York: W. W. Norton

Jackson, H.J. (2001) *Marginalia: Readers Writing in Books*, London: Yale University Press

Jackson, Holbrook (1930) *Anatomy of Bibliomania*, London: Soncino

Jackson, K. (1999) *Invisible Forms*, London: Picador

Johns, A. (1998) *The Nature of the Book: Print and Knowledge in the Making*, Chicago: Chicago University Press

Kahn, D. (1974) *The Codebreakers*, London: Weidenfeld and Nicolson

Katsoulis, M. (2009) *Literary Hoaxes*, New York: Skyhorse Publishing

Kells, S. (2017) *The Library: A Catalogue of Wonders*, Melbourne: The Text Publishing Company

Kelly, S. (2005) *The Book of Lost Books*, New York: Viking

Kelly, T. F. (2019) *The Role of the Scroll*, New York: W. W. Norton & Company

Kwakkel, E. (2018) *Books Before Print*, Leeds: Arc Humanities Press

Láng, B. (2008) *Unlocked Books*, University Park, PA: Pennsylvania State University

Lyons, M. (2011) *Books: A Living History*, Los Angeles: Getty Publications

Maggs Bros. (1932) *Curiouser and Curiouser: A Catalogue of Strange Books and Curious Titles*, London

Olmert, M. (1992) *The Smithsonian Book of Books*, Washington D.C.: Smithsonian Books

Page, N. (2001) *Lord Minimus: The Extraordinary Life of Britain's Smallest Man*, London: HarperCollins Publishers

Pearson, D. (2008) *Books as History: The Importance of Books Beyond Their Texts*, London: British Library

Petroski, H. (1999) *The Book on the Bookshelf*, New York: Alfred A. Knopf

Pietsch, T. W. (ed.) (1995) *Fishes, Crayfishes, and Crabs: Louis Renard's Natural History of the Rarest Curiosities of the Seas of the Indies*, Baltimore/London: John Hopkins University Press

Robinson, A. (2009) *Lost Languages*, New York: Thames & Hudson Inc.

Rubenhold, H. (2005) *Harris's List of Covent-Garden Ladies*, Stroud: Tempus Publishing

Singh, S. (1999) *The Code Book*, London: 4th Estate

Sutherland, J. (2009) *Curiosities of Literature*, London: Arrow

Tucker, S. D. (2016) *Forgotten Science*, Stroud: Amberley Publishing

Van Straten, G. (2017) *In Search of Lost Books: The Forgotten Stories of Eight Mythical Volumes*, London: Pushkin Press

Welsh, D. V. (1987) *The History of Miniature Books*, Albany: Fort Orange Press

Witkowski, G-J. (1898) *Tetoniana: Curiosités Médicales, Littéraires et Artistiques sur les Seins Et L'allaitement*, Paris: Imprimerie Lemale et Cie, Havre

Wootton, D. (2006) *Bad Medicine: Doctors Doing Harm Since Hippocrates*, Oxford: Oxford University Press

Yu, J. (2012) *Sanctity and Self-Inflicted Violence in Chinese Religions, 1500–1700*, Oxford: Oxford University Press

INDEX

'The man who publishes a book without an index ought to be damned 10 miles beyond Hell, where the Devil himself cannot get for stinging nettles.'

John Baynes (1758–87)

ACKNOWLEDGEMENTS

I would like to express my deep appreciation to all who provided such indispensable help in the creation of this book: to Charlie Campbell at Kingsford Campbell, to Ian Marshall at Simon & Schuster, and Laura Nickoll and Keith Williams for their tireless work in creating such a beautiful book. Thank you to Franklin Brooke-Hitching for enduring years of questions, and to my entire family for their support. Thanks also to Alex and Alexi Anstey, Daisy Laramy-Binks, Megan Rosenbloom, Lindsey Fitzharris, Matt, Gemma and Charlie Troughton, Georgie Hallett and Thea Lees, and to my friends at QI: John, Sarah and Coco Lloyd, Piers Fletcher, James Harkin, Alex Bell, Alice Campbell Davies, Jack Chambers, Anne Miller, Andrew Hunter Murray, Anna Ptaszynski, James Rawson, Dan Schreiber, Mike Turner and Sandi Toksvig.

I am especially grateful to those who have been so generous in giving interviews, lending expertise and allowing the reproduction of the magnificent images collected here, in particular: Daniel Crouch and Nick Trimming at Daniel Crouch Rare Books and Maps, Richard Fattorini, Philip Errington and Chiara De Nicolais at Sotheby's, Matthew Haley at Bonhams, Joe Jameson at Peter Harrington, Tobias Schrödel, Dr Neil Wilson, David Nathan-Maister, Vladimir Aniskin, Vinicius Leôncio and Philipe Martins. Thanks also to the wonderful staff of the British Library, the Metropolitan Museum of Art, the Library of Congress, the New York Public Library, the National Library of Medicine and the Wellcome Collection, the Prinzhorn Collection, the Beinecke Rare Book and Manuscript Library, Yale University, the Rijksmuseum, The Morgan Library and Museum, Bayerische Staatsbibliothek, the John Carter Brown Library, Bibliothèque Royale de Belgique and the Richard Lane Collection at the Honolulu Museum of Art.

PICTURE CREDITS

The Arnamagnæan Institute, University of Copenhagen Pg 28; The Arnamagnæan Institute, University of Copenhagen, Copenhagen, Denmark. AM 377 fol., 455v-456r. Photograph: Suzanne Reitz Pg 117; Auction Team Breker Cologne Germany © 2019 Pg 137 (bottom); BabelStone, Wikipedia Pg 143 (top); Bayerische Staatsbibliothek München, Cgm 48, fol. 37r Pg 181; Beinecke Library, Yale University Pg 4–5, 19 (top), 40, 70–73, 144, 166; Ben Denzer Pg 41; BiblioArchives / LibraryArchives Pg 89; Biblioteca Civica Hortis, Trieste Pg 201 (bottom three images); Bibliothèque Royale de Belgique Pg 195; Bonhams Pg 190–191, 217 (both images), 224; Boston Public Library Pg 85 (all images); Bristol Archives Pg 51; British Library Pg 23 (top left), 29 (bottom), 47 (top), 58, 60–61, 74 (top), 110 (top), 112 (both images), 114, 116, 128, 147, 153 (top), 167, 174–175 (both images), 177, 197, 199 (top), 201 (top left, top middle); The British Library Board/Bridgeman Images Pg 234 (bottom); California Digital Library Pg 211 (both images); Center for the History of Medicine, Countway Library Pg 210; CEphoto, Uwe Aranas Pg 136 (bottom); Cristian Chirita Pg 90 (top); Daderot Pg 23 (right); Courtesy of Dr Neil Wilson Pg 38; Daniel Crouch Rare Books and Maps Pg 33 (bottom right); David Nathan-Maister Pg 44 (both images); Dorotheum, Wikipedia Pg 97 (top); dpa picture alliance / Alamy Pg 107; Etan J. Tal Pg 176; Francis A. Countway Library of Medicine, Medical Heritage Library Pg 132–133; Getty Research Institute Pg 79, 205; Haeferl/Wikimedia Pg 35 (bottom); Ghent University Library Pg 118–119; Heidelberg University Pg 142; Henry Groskinsky / The LIFE Picture Collection via Getty Images Pg 212; Houghton Library, Harvard University Pg 54; Houston Museum of Natural Science Pg 35 (top); Institute of Slavonic Studies Pg 141; INTERFOTO / Alamy Pg 33 (bottom left); The J. Paul Getty Museum, Los Angeles Pg 112 (both images); The J. Paul Getty Museum, Villa Collection, Malibu, California, gift of Lenore Barozzi Pg 26; John Carter Brown Library Pg 178–179; Kevin Knight, Beáta Megyesi, Christiane Schaefer Pg 78; Keystone Press / Alamy Pg 84; Lawrence J. Schoenberg Collection of Manuscripts, Kislak Center for Special Collections, Rare Books and Manuscripts, University of Pennsylvania Pg 75; Leofstan Pg 221 (bottom right); Library of Congress Pg 16, 32 (top left), 99, 106, 161 (bottom), 162, 185, 209 (top), 215 (both images), 222 (top right), 226; Mac Armstrong, Wikipedia Pg 82; Mamma Haidara Library, Timbuktu Pg 43 (top); Marcin Wichary Pg 137 (top); Marie-Lan Nguyen Pg 24, 33 (top); McGill University Pg 46; Metropolitan Museum of Art Pg 27 (right), 65 (bottom), 140, 169, 218 (top left and bottom left), 219 (top right); Nicholas Herman Pg 32 (bottom); Museums Victoria Pg 136 (top left and second from bottom); Music Library, University of California, Berkeley Pg 183; Nara National Museum Pg 180 (both images); National Archives of the Netherlands Pg 42, 120–121; National Gallery of Art Pg 216; National Library of Medicine, Maryland Pg 64 (left), 134–135, 198 (both images), 204 (bottom two images); National Library of New Zealand Pg 218 (bottom right); Division of Cultural and Community Life, National Museum of American History, Smithsonian Institution Pg 36; National Museum of Warsaw Pg 27 (bottom); NATT-at-NKM/Flickr Pg 37; N P Holmes Pg 111 (right); Per B. Adolphson, National Library of Sweden Pg 230–231; Peter Harrington Rare Books Pg 127; Petrus Agricola/Flickr.com Pg 172; Philipe Martins Pg 235; Princeton University Library Pg 43 (bottom); Newberry Library Pg 45; Prinzhorn Collection, University Hospital Heidelberg, Inv. Nr. 743 Pg 20–21; Punishar, Wikipedia Pg 136 (second from top); Rare Book and Manuscript Library, Pennsylvania University Pg 146; Richard Lane Collection, Honolulu Museum of Art Pg 204 (top); Rijksmuseum Pg 153 (bottom), 202; Royal Danish Library Pg 30, 110 (bottom); Royal Library, Copenhagen Pg 219 (left); Scott Peterson via Getty Images Pg 63; Simon Fraser University Pg 223 (top); Skokloster Castle / Erik Lernestål / CC BY-SA Pg 220 (top left, bottom right); Smithsonian Libraries Pg 11 (bottom), 29 (top), 56 (both images), 94–95; Sotheby's Pg 171, 220 (bottom-left); Staatsbibliothek Bamberg Pg 47 (bottom); Stadtbibliothek im Bildungscampus Nürnberg, Amb. 317.2°, f. 34r Pg 50; Reproduced with the Kind Permission of the Surgeons' Hall Museums, The Royal College of Surgeons of Edinburgh Pg 53; Swarthmore College Pg 143 (bottom); Courtesy of Tobias Schrödel Pg 86–87; Trey Jones Pg 65 (top); University of California Libraries Pg 163; Uploadalt, Wikipedia Pg 74 (bottom); Vladimir Aniskin Pg 223 (bottom); Wagaung, Wikipedia Pg 229; Walters Art Museum Pg 220 (top right); Waseda University Library Pg 12–13; University of Pittsburgh Pg 236–239; Wellcome Collection Pg 1, 8, 11 (top), 23 (bottom left), 48, 49, 52, 57, 139, 152 (top right and bottom), 154–158 (all images), 159, 160, 182, 184, 194, 199 (bottom left and right), 200, 201 (top right), 203 (both images), 206 (both images), 207, 219 (bottom right); Wellspring/Courtesy Everett Collection/ Alamy Pg 228; Yorck Project Pg 66, 170, 196, 232; Ziegler175, Wikipedia Pg 234 (top); ウィキ太郎 (Wiki Taro) Pg 189.

Front cover: Wellcome Collection
Pg 6–7: Cincinnati public library, 1954

All other images are the author's own or public domain.

First Published in the United States in 2021 by Chronicle Books LLC.

Originally published in Great Britain by Simon & Schuster UK Ltd, 2020 A CBS company.

Copyright © 2020 by Edward Brooke-Hitching

No part of this book may be reproduced in any form without written permission from the publisher.

Library of Congress Cataloging-in-Publication Data is available.

Manufactured in Italy.

ISBN 978-1-7972-0730-8

Editorial Director: Ian Marshall.
Design: Keith Williams, sprout.uk.com.
Project Editor: Laura Nickoll.

The author and publishers have made all reasonable efforts to contact copyright-holders for permission, and apologise for any omissions or errors in the form of credits given. Corrections may be made to future printings.

Chronicle books and gifts are available at special quantity discounts to corporations, professional associations, literacy programs, and other organizations. For details and discount information, please contact our premiums department at corporatesales@chroniclebooks.com or at 1-800-759-0190.

Chronicle Books LLC
680 Second Street
San Francisco, California 94107

www.chroniclebooks.com